Teacher Burnout in the Public Schools

SUNY Series in Educational Leadership
Daniel Duke, Editor

Teacher Burnout in the Public Schools

*Structural Causes and
Consequences for Children*

ANTHONY GARY DWORKIN

State University of New York Press

Published by
State University of New York Press, Albany

©1987 State University of New York

For information, address State University of New York
Press, State University Plaza, Albany, N.Y., 12246

Library of Congress Cataloging-in-Publication Data

Dworkin, Anthony Gary.
    Teacher burnout in public schools.

    (SUNY series in educational leadership)
    Bibliography: p. 211
    Includes index.
    1. Teachers—Texas—Houston—Job stress.   2. Burn
out (Psychology)   3. Teacher turnover—Texas—Houston
4. Faculty integration—Texas—Houston.   I. Title.
II. Series.
LB2840.2.D96   1986   371,1'001'9   86-5713
ISBN 0-88706-348-9
ISBN 0-88706-349-7 (pbk.)

10 9 8 7 6 5 4 3 2 1

To my parents, Harry and Dorothy Dworkin, with love and appreciation for a lifetime of encouragement

Contents

viii

Figure

Tables

Appendix:

Acknowledgments

This book began as a 1977 report to the Houston Independent School District on the impact of a faculty desegregation ratio upon staff morale and student achievement. It grew to be a compilation of three complete research projects, including a longitudinal study of teachers. The support and encouragement of numerous individuals enabled this large study to reach its conclusion. I wish to thank those individuals associated with the Hogg Foundation for Mental Health in Austin, Texas, for the funding which made it possible to aggregate the data sets. Two people from the foundation have been especially encouraging and helpful. To Adrian Fowler, my project officer at the Hogg Foundation, and to Marian Coleman go my most sincere gratitude.

My colleagues at the Center for Public Policy and the College of Social Science at the University of Houston—Dean Tom Mayor and Professor Ed Williams, as well as Mary Alice Mayor—provided financial assistance in the final stages of the project. Four graduate students at the University of Houston were instrumental in the early collection and processing of the data. Dr. Jimy M. Sanders was my research assistant on the original study for the school district in 1977. Dr. Dorothy F. Caram worked with me on an analysis of the factors which lead to teacher burnout: under my direction, she completed her doctoral dissertation in education using the teacher data. She was also instrumental in obtaining the 1978–1982 exit data on teachers in the study in chapter 2. Ruth L. Telschow worked with me on the study of teachers who stayed in the public schools (chapter 3). Her M.A. thesis was based upon those data. Finally, Terry M. Trauth served as my research assistant, coder, and programmer on the entire project. With the assistance of Greg Reimer of the Social Science Data Lab, Terry completed the computer links between the student and teacher data sets (chapter 4).

Others who were helpful in the early stages of this work were Professors James Mcnamara of Texas A. and M. University, Frank Black of Murray State University, and Waymond Webster of Prairie View A. and M. University, all of whom served with me on the original Singleton Faculty Desegregation Ratio consulting team for the Houston Independent School District. It was that team that collected the student and the first teacher data sets. I would also like to thank several present and former members of the school district, including Dr. Billy Reagan, general superintendent of the district; Joseph Angle, superintendent; Dr. Michael Say, formerly an associate superintendent with the district; and Ronnie Veselka, director of the district's research office. I am also indebted to Richard C. Shaw and John P. O'Sullivan, former presidents of the Houston Federation of Teachers, for providing Ruth Telschow and myself access to the data which were analyzed in the third chapter of this book.

I wish to thank my colleagues in the Department of Sociology at the University of Houston with whom I discussed several theoretical and methodological issues associated with teacher burnout. Of particularly valuable assistance were Professors Jon Lorence, Janet Saltzman Chafetz, Helen Rose Ebaugh, Joseph Kotarba, Zena Blau, and Allen Haney.

Two colleagues played major roles in the conversion of the Hogg Foundation report into the present book. Professor Mark Ginsburg of the College of Education at the University of Houston carefully read the report and raised several critical questions, at the same time providing me with a generous supply of reprints from which to glean possible answers. Dr. Margaret LeCompte, formerly of the Houston Independent School District and now of the University of Cincinnati, read and reread the manuscript and provided valuable suggestions regarding both writing style and substantive content. It was she who often suggested new and fruitful directions for rewriting troublesome passages. Without the aid of these two people I am sure that the final product would be of lesser value.

Very special thanks are due to those associated with the State University of New York Press, whose encouragement has been greatly appreciated. To Bill Eastman, the press director, and to former and present editors Kay Richardson and Lois Patton I extend my warm appreciation. The insights and suggestions of Daniel Duke, general editor of the SUNY Series in Educational Leadership, have played a significant role in making this book possible. Dan was also responsible for reminding me to write my own book after some fourteen colleagues told me how I should revise it.

Finally, to my best colleague, my wife, Dr. Rosalind J. Dworkin of Baylor College of Medicine, I want to offer a grateful thank you for assistance, proofreading, and conceptual suggestions throughout the analysis, preparation, and production of the original report and its conversion into the present book.

1

Introduction

In the past quarter-century, much has appeared in the social sciences and in education on the impact of desegregation upon the public schools. Considerable attention has been paid to the consequences of desegration for student self-esteem, academic achievement, attendance, flight, dropout behavior, and interracial cooperation and conflict. Somewhat less work has been dedicated to understanding the impact of desegregation on teacher morale, coping behavior, and career commitment.

This study is concerned with an overlooked but crucial link between teacher burnout occasioned by faculty desegregation and the learning outcomes and attendance behavior of students. Little evidence is currently available to school decisionmakers to help them assess whether teachers who are burned out and uncommitted to teaching adversely affect the education and attendance of their pupils, although there is much speculation that such teachers hinder student gains. The issue is of major importance. American public schools currently spend millions of dollars on plans to reduce teacher turnover and to rekindle enthusiasm in teachers who have lost their motivation to teach. In times of diminished resources for public education, it may well be that these monies could better be spent on educational programs for children. In examining the educational consequences of teacher burnout and turnover, this book seeks to help school districts and educators make more enlightened judgements in their allocation of diminishing financial resources.

The Nature of Teacher Turnover

Teaching is a vulnerable occupation that is characterized by much-higher-than-average rates of turnover. These rates are slightly lower than

1

those for other semiprofessions such as nursing and social work (Etzioni, 1969; Price, 1977) but higher than those for many clerical occupations in which women are concentrated (Price, 1977). Those who enter teaching can expect to be underpaid, undervalued, and overworked. As Lortie notes, teaching is a "special but shadowed" occupation (1975:10).

> Teaching seems to have more than its share of status anomalies. It is honored and disdained, praised as "dedicated service" and lampooned as "easy work." It is permeated with the rhetoric of professionalism, yet features incomes below those earned by workers with considerably less education. It is middle-class work in which more and more participants use collective bargaining strategies developed by wage-earners in factories. (1975:10)

There are many reasons for the anomalies associated with the status of teacher, not the least of which is the fact that in this century it has become a female occupation. Furthermore, in the large urban centers of this country, teaching has increasingly become a minority female occupation. As the percentage of majority students in big city schools has diminished, the percentage of majority group teachers has likewise diminished.

Even in the era when few career opportunities were open to college-educated women, the turnover rate among public school teachers exceeded that of other professionals, including professional women. Using nationwide data, Mason and Bain (1959) reported an annual turnover rate for public school teachers of 17 percent. Over half a century ago, Waller (1932) also noted that teachers were more likely to become discouraged and to quit than workers in many other occupations. Similar reports of high levels of turnover among teachers have been given by Mason (1961), Davis (1965), and Pavalko (1965, 1970).

While teacher turnover is often seen as a problem faced by school districts, it is also viewed as a benefit. Urban schools are frequently faced with monetary squeezes. When teachers quit, school districts usually replace them with neophytes, thereby maintaining a reduced annual budget. If enough teachers quit, the necessary pay raises associated with seniority can be minimized. Moreover, as was the case in the 1970s, teacher turnover rates have permitted school districts to maintain an equilibrium between declining enrollments and staff size through attrition rather than through wholesale terminations.

But teacher turnover can also present a severe organzational problem for public schools. When teachers quit, school districts lose the investments they have made in workshops, in-services, and teacher socializaiton activities. Since teachers who quit are usually replaced by more plentiful neophyte teachers, school districts must reinvest in training the new personnel to meet district expectations. Although a single teacher dropout may not adversely affect student achievement and staff that disrupts the teaching of the remaining staff and contributes to low morale. High levels of turnover, combined with the frequent necessity to fill vacancies with beginning teachers, lowers the overall quality of teaching. Numerous investigations, including studies by McNamara et al. (1977) and Murnane (1975), have shown that inexperienced teachers produce lower student achievement scores on standardized tests than do their more experienced counterparts. High levels of turnover may also produce a snowball effect in which the remaining teaching staff comes to define the campus or the district as an undesirable workplace. This situation may accelerate additional turnover. Repeated high turnover rates due to low morale, combined with the normal attrition through retirement, leaves a school without a leadership core among the staff, since the experienced teachers who share some of the management duties with the principal are absent. Finally, since teachers vary in their specializations and expertise, the loss of key teachers with crucial substantive skills may limit course offerings, or at least the quality of such offerings, at the school.

Throughout the 1960s and early 1970s, teacher turnover rates produced critical teacher shortages. The burgeoning school-aged population, combined with the growing turnover rates during the difficult years of court-ordered desegregation, greatly taxed the ability of colleges of education to produce enough new teachers. Most of the 1970s and early 1980s saw a substantial change. With fewer children entering school, the demand for teachers diminished. Even in the 1970s and early 1980s, however, not all districts experienced diminishing enrollments or diminishing demands for teachers. Some districts also had to keep a balance of teachers of different races on their payrolls to satisfy federal school desegregation mandates. One such district provided the data for this study. For such school districts, teacher turnover continued to be a severe problem. As we shall see shortly, the remainder of the decade of the 1980s and much of the 1990s will create demands for teachers which will again tax the supply.

While the report of a 17 percent annual turnover rate during the 1950s appears to be high, it is much lower than the rates reported during the 1960s and 1970s. Charters (1970) studied the turnover of a cohort of new teachers in the Oregon public schools from 1962 through 1966. By the end of the first year, more than one-third of the women and one-fifth of the men had left teaching. By the end of the final year of the study, just 40 percent of the men and 28 percent of the women were still teaching. Two general observations grew out of the Charters study: men are more likely to survive in teaching than are women, and the rate of attrition declines progressively after the first year.

Anderson and Mark (1977) and Mark and Anderson (1978) replicated the original Charters study and found some support for the earlier work. Their data base involved eight cohorts, tracked over an eight-year period from 1968 through 1975 in the St. Louis schools. The rate of attrition in the newer study decreased at an increasing rate, just as Charters had shown, although male and female turnover rates approached parity. Most striking, however, was the finding that attrition rates for each year decreased from older to newer cohorts. Thus, while over one-third of the new teachers in 1968 quit in their first year, less than one-fifth of the new teachers in the 1975 cohort quit in their first year. In the St. Louis schools, teachers in each successive cohort are decreasingly likely to quit, and of course are decreasingly likely to quit with each successive year of experience. Mark and Anderson (1978) suggest that such a finding bodes ill for school districts which rely upon attrition to overcome declining enrollments or tightened fiscal policies.

That turnover rates were higher in the 1950s and 1960s than in the 1970s can be explained by many social factors. Since most new teachers were young women, either unmarried or married but without children, teaching at that time served as a temporary occupation prior to a career as wife and mother—especially during the era of the feminine mystique. Brookover and Erickson (1975), Pavalko (1965, 1970), Lortie (1969, 1975), and Geer (1966) reported that half of all the beginning teachers in the 1950s and 1960s expected to be out of teaching within five years. Likewise, more than a quarter of those completing teachers' training did not intend to begin teaching after graduation. Nonetheless, nearly 60 percent of those who planned to leave teaching or not enter it after graduation hoped to enter teaching after their children were grown. By contrast, women entering careers of any kind in the 1970s and 1980s could expect to be in the labor force even if they had young children. The present state of the economy, combined with greater opportunities for a career and a family created by the feminist movement, mandates and encourages the presence of two-earner families.

Faculty desegregation ratios, which increased the percentages of minority faculty members assigned to schools in urban areas and necessitated the hiring of more minority faculty, provide another explanation for the decline in turnover rates among the younger teachers in the Anderson and Mark (1977) and Mark and Anderson (1978) studies. The National Institute of Education (1976) chronicled the increase in minority teacher hirings during the 1970s. In addition, Gottlieb (1964) and Dworkin (1980) each presented evidence that the turnover rate among minority teachers is much lower than that of majority teachers. Gottlieb contended that black teachers in the Chicago area were several times more likely to be satisfied with their jobs than were white teachers. Dworkin studied teachers in Houston and noted that white teachers were three times more likely to want to quit teaching and actually to quit teaching than their minority counterparts. Dworkin explained these differences in terms of three factors: minorities have fewer career alternatives other than teaching than do majorities; minorities (as well as teachers from low-income backgrounds) have invested a greater share of their own and their families' resources in the quest for a teaching certificate than have majorities; and minorities and the poor are more likely to experience upward mobility by entering teaching, thereby gaining additional social and emotional rewards.

The actural increase in the percentage of minority teachers is however, not large enough to be solely responsible for the drop in the turnover rate in the 1970s. Most responsible for the national decline in turnover rates are the economic factors which necessitate continued female participation in the labor force, adjustments in desegregation, and alternative academic and career opportunities for women. More teachers today may be aware of the racial makeup of the schools to which they will be assigned than they were when schools were undergoing student desegregation. Furthermore, with alternative academic majors open to women and alternative careers perceived as viable options, fewer women may be entering teaching because they have nothing better to do. Finally, the wholesale displacement or firing of minority teachers during the early stages of desegregation (see National Education Association, 1965, and United States Commission on Civil Rights, 1979) has generally been stemmed by federal faculty desegregation ratios and the enforcement of desegregation mandates.

Although turnover rates in the 1970s and early 1980s compared favorably with those during the 1950s and 1960s, there has remained a shortfall in the difference between the demand for teachers and the available supply. In the early 1970s, however, this shortfall was calculated in terms of actual needs by school districts compared with an adjusted figure for a current teaching staff and the number of people graduating with a teaching degree. By contrast, recent calculations estimate the shortfall in terms of the number of teachers needed to provide "minimum quality education" (compare National Education Association, 1974 and 1983). A concept such as 'quality education' incorporates practices and considerations like the temporary replacement of teachers with substandard qualifications while those teachers retrain; the reduction of overcrowded classes; the increased need for teachers with special education training; demands created by nursery schools, kindergartens, and extended day programs; the reduction of the number of teachers misassigned vis-à-vis; their specializations; and increases in the number of subjects offered by schools (see National Education Association, 1983:33–34).

The actual demand for teachers, not controlling for quality factors, declined in the later 1970s and early 1980s principally because the "baby boom" generation had completed its public education (see Landon Y. Jones, 1980). With this large cohort either in college or in the labor force, the supply of public school teachers exceeded the demand by 88.7 percent. However, with the quality factor considered, the supply falls short of demand by 38.5 percent (National Education Association, 1983:35).

Several national surveys have demonstrated that the problems of teacher turnover and teacher shortages are resurfacing. Studies by the National Commission on Excellence in Education (1983), the National Center for Educational Statistics (1982), and the Rand Corportation (Darling-Hammond, 1984) observe that within the next five to ten years there will be intensely critical shortages in teaching areas such as science, mathematics, special education, computer science, English, and bilingual education. During the fiscal year 1985, the National Science Foundation allocated $7 million to address science and mathematics education in American schools and the critical shortage of science and math teachers (National Science Foundation, 1984).

Several factors account for this growing shortage. The supply of available teachers has diminished because college-educated women, the principal population from which teachers are recruited, are experiencing an explosion in career alternatives which provide more financial, social, and psychological rewards than teaching. A continued decline in the earning capacity of the current teaching population and a continuation in the "de-professionalization" of teaching (Duke, 1984) discourages those who are already teaching. The present pool of public school teachers is aging, with little assurance that the supply will be replenished (Darling-Hammond, 1984). At the same time, the demand for teaching is beginning to escalate. The massive "baby boom" generation (Jones, 1980), born between 1946 and 1964 and representing one-third of all Americans alive today, is finally having their children after deferring parenthood for careers. Although their family size remains small, the sheer numbers in that generation insure an increasing need for school teachers. However, because the "baby boom" generation and the one immediately prior to it deferred having children until their careers were established and kept their family size small, they created a "baby bust" generation. It is this small group, born between 1965 and 1976, which must provide the pool of future teachers in the next ten to fifteen years.

Exacerbating the shortfall calculated on the basis of the needs for quality education is the growing rate of teacher dissatisfaction and burnout. At the same time that this dissatisfaction increases the likelihood of teacher turnover, it also increases the probability that students will encounter teachers who would prefer to do something other than teach. In a recent national poll of public school teachers conducted by the National Education Association (NEA), only 21.8 percent of the teachers indicated that "if they had the chance to go back to college and start over again, they would certainly become a teacher" (1982:74,116). Combining the "certainly would" and "probably would" responses, the NEA found that 46.4 percent would again choose teaching. By contrast, 76.8 percent in 1961 and 78.0 percent in 1966 checked the "certainly would" and "probably would" categories. In those years, the "certainly would" response accounted for between 49.9 percent and 52.6 percent of the teachers (NEA, 1982:74). Clearly, then, teachers today are less satisfied with their career choices than they were in the 1960s. The myriad articles on teacher dissatisfaction, teacher turnover, and teacher burnout published in the past several years and cited in this and ensuing chapters adds credence to the NEA findings.

The turnover rates reported earlier reflect national figures from urban, suburban, and rural schools combined. In most urban districts, the turnover rates exceed those reported nationally for all school districts. Some inner-city school districts lose up to one-half of their teachers each year. Generally speaking, teacher quitting behavior is selective. In the early 1960s, Charters (1970) found that age, sex, years teaching, and size of the school district affected turnover rates. Older teachers, males, teachers with more experience on the job, and teachers in larger school districts tended to be less likely to quit than those without such characteristics.

Chapman and Hutcheson (1982) have emphasized the social and psychological factors that differentiate teachers who quit from those who do not. In their study of 690 alumni from several Indiana universities, the authors found that those who stayed were more likely to have high levels of confidence in their teaching ability, less likely to stress job autonomy, and less likely to emphisize salary considerations as important in a career than those who quit. Those who remained in teaching, according to Chapman and Hutcheson, "were characterized as having greater organizational skills (organizing time, developing new approaches, planning and organizing activities)," while those who left teaching "were characterized as having greater analytical skills (analyzing and evaluating, interpreting numerical data)" (1982:103). Dworkin (1980) found that both social-psychological and demographic variables differentiated teachers who quit from those who did not. Younger, white teachers of middle-class origins assigned to schools whose racial makeup differed significantly from that desired by the teachers were several times more likely to quit than any other category of teacher. In addition, Dworkin, Joiner, and Bruno (1980) observed that teachers whose general expectancy or locus of control was external (those who believed that their destinies were out of their own hands) were even more likely to want to quit and actually to quit teaching if assigned to schools whose student bodies' racial composition they considered undesirable.

Despite the optimism of Chapman and Hutcheson (1982) that teachers who stayed in education had better organizational skills than those who left, there is a growing awareness that the level of competence of public school teachers has declined. Armed with an abundance of data, Darling-Hammond (1984) reported that the Scholastic Aptitude Test (SAT) scores of students planning to become teachers were significantly lower than the scores obtained from students in training for other careers. A seven-year follow-up study of teachers in North Carolina (Schlechty and Vance, 1981) reported that teacher turnover is competence specific, with those who scored within the highest decile on the National Teacher Examination (NTE) were much more likely to quit teaching than those in the lowest decile. In fact, by the end of the seven-year study, two-thirds of the lowest scorers remained in teaching, but only about one-third of the highest scorers were still teachers.

Responding to criticism that their seven-year, North Carolina study was not generalizable to the national pool of teachers, Vance and Schlechty (1982) analyzed the National Longitudinal Survey (NLS) panel data set of the high school class of 1972. The NLS data set explores the work attitudes and experiences of over 22,000 individuals who graduated from high school in 1972. Through successive waves of interviews, the careers of this sample have been followed. Vance and Schlechty analyzed the data on more than 4,400 individuals who by 1979 had attained at least a baccalaureate degree. They found that SAT scores were highest for those who were not recruited into colleges of education and lowest for those who not only enrolled in colleges of education and became teachers but who planned to stay in teaching past age 30. Between these extremes ranked from high to low SAT scores were education majors who never entered teaching, followed by education majors who entered but quit teaching, and finally, education majors who were teaching but planned to quit before age 30. The investigators contended that "teaching not only fails to attract the most able, but it also attracts a disproportionate share of the least able'' (1982:25). In fact, concentrating only upon individuals who entered teaching, Vance and Schlechty found that less than 20 percent of the higher scorers on the SAT (above the 60th percentile on the exam), less than 20 percent of the middle scorers, and about one-third of the lowest scorers intended to remain in the teaching beyond age 30. They also noted that college students are aware that education majors are the choice of the less capable and that this awareness increases the likelihood that enrollments in education courses will be lower than they might otherwise be. In short, there is a self-fulfilling prophecy that education courses are for ''dummies'' which insures that many capable students will neither become education majors nor enroll in such courses.

In order to reduce high turnover rates and problems of teacher burnout, several urban school districts, including the one in Texas studied in this investigation, have adopted a variety of staff stabilization plans. Targeting vulnerable population of new teachers, districts have tried using incentive pay, increased fringe benefits, and team teaching strategies using master teachers. Although these strategies have encountered some short-term success in slowing down turnover rates in the pilot schools where they have been attempted, the realities of tight fiscal management and the loss of federal funding to many educational programs have meant that these programs have limited futures. Moreover, economic incentives alone are unlikely to compensate teachers for the absence of supportive interpersonal relations or any of the other social-psychological factors which attract people to teaching (see, for example, Chapman and Hutcheson, 1982:104).

To a considerable extent, the social forces of the urban scene and the demographic and legal aspects of desegregation have accelerated the turnover rate in the urban school districts. Among the causes of teacher burnout and turnover frequently cited are relatively low pay, problematic security on some school campuses, oversized classes, culture shock, the growing bureaucratization of urban education, and the belief by teachers that students, parents, school administrators, and the general public are unconcerned about teachers and schools (see the presentations by Moeller, 1964; National Institute of Education, 1976; Lortie, 1975; Orfield, 1975; Collins and Noblit, 1976; Dworkin, 1980; and National Education Association, 1982). I shall briefly discuss some of these factors.

Teachers' Salaries

A perennial problem faced by public school teachers is the inadequacy of their salaries. Even considering that the teaching contract is for ten months rather than for twelve, teachers earn considerably less than other college-educated workers. Moreover, they can expect that their salaries are unlikely to keep pace with inflation. In fact, as Lortie notes, "the typical salary schedule projects an ultimate income which is no more than twice that received in the first year" (1975:7). According to the survey of public school teachers conducted by the National Education Association in 1983, one out of every nine teachers holds a second job outside of education during the school year, and an additional one in four assumes extra paid duties (including coaching and driving school buses) within the school district to compensate for the level of salaries offered to them by the schools (1981:83).

Between the 1969–70 and 1979–80 academic years, nationwide teachers' salaries nearly doubled—from $8,635 to $16,001. However, the salaries actualy declined in purchasing power by $1,468, once one controls for inflation (Ornstein, 1980). Nevertheless, in a poll conducted for *Phi Delta Kappan*, a national education journal, only 8.7 percent of the school teachers thought that salaries were the most pressing problem faced by American schools, while 62.2 percent thought that the general issue of school financing (including facilities and teaching materials) and student discipline were more pressing issues (Elam and Gough, 1980). The American public, as revealed by a Gallup poll conducted for *Phi Delta Kappan*, felt in 1982 that the issue of teacher salaries was most responsible for driving teachers out of education (Gallup, 1982:46). Certainly, a substantial increase in teacher salaries would be welcome and might forestall turnover: however, there are other severe structural and organizational problems in American education which contribute significantly to turnover.

Public Confidence in Public Education

A 1969 Gallup poll conducted for *Phi Delta Kappan* revealed that 75 percent of the general public felt that teaching was a desirable career for their children. By 1980, the percentage of respondents who felt that teaching was a desirable career for their children had dropped to 48 percent. Among parents whose children were enrolled in public school, 80 percent would have liked their children to become teachers in 1969, compared with 56 percent in 1980. In the 1980 sampling, younger respondents (under age 30), college-educated respondents, and whites were less likely to want their children to become teachers. The percentages for these categories were 43 percent, 45 percent, and 47 percent, respectively (Gallup, *Phi Delta Kappan*, 1980:38).

Several investigators have noted that the occupational prestige of public school teachers, already generally lower than that of other "professional" occupations, has been declining (see especially Lortie, 1975: and Dworkin et al., 1978). Declines in student tests scores, accompanied by increases in the cost of education, changes in the ethnic composition of American public schools (especially in urban areas), and changes in the ethnic composition of the teaching staff, have sparked a public distrust of public education and a demand for accountability and competency testing of teachers.

Since 1974, Gallup has asked the public to assign grades to American public education. In that year, 48 percent gave their local public schools a grade of "A" or "B." By contrast, the 1982 sample was less generous. Only 37 percent felt that local schools deserved such high marks. Furthermore, only 22 percent assigned grades of "A" or "B" to the nation's public schools as an aggregate. (See Gallup, 1982:39.)

The decline in the public's confidence in public education and in the public's desire to see its children become teachers puts an additional strain on existing teachers, who are less likely to be respected and more likely to be challenged by parents. Because of this lack of respect, they can rely less upon their authority (command) over children and parents to gain compliance and must rely more upon influence (persuasion). Such action, as Chafetz (1980) observes in her study of family power, means that the probability of success in proportion to the personal effort and resources that must be expended to get one's way is considerably depressed. Teachers who can gain compliance through authority are less likely to fail and less likely to become exhausted than teachers who must resort to influence to gain compliance.

Student Discipline and School Violence

The school problem most often cited in the Gallup polls conducted for *Phi Delta Kappan* was student discipline. In 1982, a total of 27 percent of the national sample thought that lack of discipline was the biggest problem faced by American schools, with another 20 percent indicating that drug-related issues were the biggest problem (Gallup, 1982:38). In Elam and Gough's *Phi Delta Kappan* sample of teachers, discipline was considered to be the biggest problem by 33.2 percent. Discipline was ranked first by the public and second by the teachers in the two samplings.

Between 1976 and 1977, the National Institute of Education designed and funded a three-phase "Safe School Study." In the first phase, questionnaires were sent out to 4,000 school principals in a representative national survey; in the second phase, 642 junior and senior high schools were targeted for on-site interviewing; and in the third phase, an intensive qualitative study was done of 10 schools with serious crime and violence problems. The study revealed that 40 percent of the robberies and 36 percent of the assaults which are experienced by teenagers occurred on school grounds. Of these, 42 percent of the attacks resulted in in injury. The risk of attack and robbery was greatest in urban schools. The report also indicated that "the proportions of public secondary school teachers victimized by theft, attack, and robbery are roughly similar to those of students." In addition, "an estimated 12 percent of the nation's teachers have something stolen from them each month . . . and one-half of 1 percent of the teachers are physically attacked at school in a month's time" (1978:3). This figure translates to approximately 130,000 teachers victimized by robbery or theft each month and 5,200 teachers attacked each month across the nation.

Desegregation and "Culture Shock"

Teacher colleges rarely prepare their white, middle-class education majors for work in inner-city schools. Gottlieb (1964) noted that the white teachers in his Chicago public school study were dismayed that parents, children, and other school personnel seemed unconcerned about the education of the children. Concern over lack of interest in education was a particularly discouraging aspect of teaching for these teachers and a major source of job dissatisfaction. Haskins (1969) and Clark (1965) found that inner-city school teachers rarely interacted with one another, thereby exacerbating their overall sense of isolation. Rist (1973) commented that it was normative in such schools for teachers to do their work and then leave soon after the children, never staying after school or discussing new ideas. Rist compared inner-city teachers to alienated assembly line workers.

Orfield (1975) has commented that the desegregation of urban schools is especially traumatic for middle-class white teachers because it forces them to confront their own stereotypes about minorities and taxes their ability to teach. As Orfield observes,

> I met many white teachers who said that they didn't realize that they didn't know how to teach because they were teaching in a very pleasant middle-class professional neighborhood. All the kids came in and all the kids went out and went to college, and they all got C's. Then when they had children who came from a more troubled background who needed to be taught, they found they didn't know how (1975:129).

Ogbu (1974) adds that when middle-class, white teachers made extra efforts to help minority children, they were shown no appreciation by either the children or their parents. In fact, the parents were prone to comment that the teachers were being paid well enough for their work, given the differences between the earnings and fringe benefits received by the teachers and the incomes of the inner-city parents. These parents felt that the teachers should expect nothing else.

The early years of desegregation were particularly stressful on all teachers. In fact, according to Collins and Noblit (1976), it was not uncommon for a receiving school (one which was to have students of another race bused to it) to be provided with only an hour or two of instruction on handling problems which might occur because of desegregation. Faculty desegregation was also done without much forewarning or preparation. In the Houston experience, where teachers were transferred under the aegis of the court-ordered Singleton Ratio, teachers were notified over a weekend that they had been reassigned to schools which were often across town from where they had been teaching the previous week (see Dworkin et al., 1977).

In the early 1950s, neophyte teachers in northern cities were frequently sent first to ghetto schools, assignments which were defined as undesirable. If the teachers did not quit and received favorable evaluations, they would then be transferred to middle-class or suburban schools (Becker, 1952). Dworkin (1968) has compared such on-the-job training for teachers with basic training in the Prussian Army of the 18th and 19th centuries. In both, there was actually no basic training. Rather, the incumbents were sent to the front lines, and if they survived, they were eventually promoted up through the ranks and into a more comfortable job.

Faculty desegregation has tended to be more successful and complete than has student desegregation (Center for National Policy Review, 1977a, 1977b). Therefore, schools are likely to have a balance of majority and minority faculty but heavy concentrations of students of one race. Furthermore, because busing of minority students to majority schools is more common than the reverse, minority schools tend to be overwhelmingly one-race schools (with minority enrollments representing 90 percent or more of the student body), while majority schools tend to have only a slight plurality of majority students. New teachers who are white are much more likely to experience racial isolation than are new teachers who are black or brown. Such isolation is likely to exacerbate turnover and helps to account for Dworkin's (1980) finding that majority teachers are twice as likely to quit teaching than are minority teachers.

Teaching has often been thought of as a route toward upward mobility for individuals from working class and farm backgrounds

(Carlson, 1951; Havighurst, 1964). However, Betz and Garland (1974) and Dworkin (1980) have noted that teaching has actually not been such a route, at least since the 1930s. Dworkin (1980) computed intergenerational mobility ratios by dividing the percentage of teachers of each of three races, separated into age cohorts, whose fathers were employed in a given occupational category by the percentage of males of each race in that category reported by the census at the time when the teachers were in high school and contemplating a career in education. The data indicated that white teachers have been disproportionately drawn from professional, technical, managerial, proprietary, and official backgrounds since the 1930s, and black teachers increasingly so since the 1940s. Only Mexican Americans, who represent about 5 percent of the teaching population, have been increasingly drawn from lower-status occupational backgrounds over the past thirty years. With continued or increasing percentages of the teaching population coming from middle-class origins, but with white and middle-class flight of students heightening the class homogeneity of urban schools (Armor, 1980), the likelihood that teachers and students will not share common backgrounds, values, and expectations increases. The likelihood that middle-class teachers will experience culture shock also increases, as does the probability that teachers will exit to other careers because of this culture shock. The improvement in organization since the early desegregation efforts is thus offset by the increasing class disparity between teachers and students, and so does not appreciably mitigate teacher turnover. (See LeCompte, forthcoming, for a proposed strategy, taken from the training of anthropologists for field research, to reduce the effects of "culture shock.")

Other Causes

Other factors can be enumerated to account for the turnover rate of public school teachers. Some pertain to the social-psychological characteristics of the teachers, while others involve the demography of the school or the school's organizational climate, including the administrative style of the principal. Sarason, Davidson, and Blatt (1962), Sarason (1977 and 1978–79), Stinnett and Henson (1982), and most recently Duke (1984) have noted that during their training professionals expect much more autonomy than they actually encounter, that much of teacher training has little relevance to what is experienced in actual teaching, and that the teaching role is increasingly characterized by anxiety and ambiguity. Duke (1984: 26–37) cites four sources of teacher ambiquity and anxiety: "job reduction," in which noninstructional duties, including student discipline, are sometimes turned over to paraprofessionals but which may diminish teacher control over the classroom; "job simplification," in which curricula are made "teacher-proof" through the use of teaching packages which require the teacher only to serve as "guides"; "job expansion," caused by personnel cutbacks which consolidate and enlarge class sizes or cause teachers to assume the duties of displaced colleagues; and "job enrichment," in which teachers assume a variety of new responsibilities, often legally mandated, including mainstreaming the handicapped, combatting sexism and racism, and completing endless reports to satisfy watchdog agencies which assess the accountability of all involved in education. Duke cogently observes that

> teachers, like others, derive satisfaction from feeling indespensible. This source of satisfaction has been steadily diminished—the victim of job reduction and job simplification, prescriptive laws, the growing spectre of legal liability and malpractice suits, and seniority rules. Innovations aimed at reducing or simplifying the tasks of teaching tell teachers that they are not perceived to be intelligent enough to manage complex operations. Prescriptive laws tell them that they are not trusted by the public and its representatives. The threat of lawsuit and its financial burden tell them that conformity is a safer, if not more satisfying, course of action. Seniority rules tell them that factors other than talent and training are valued as a basis for determining who will keep his or her job (1984: 132).

In the course of this book I shall explore numerous factors which affect the attitudes and actions of public school teachers, relating each to consequences for students. In accordance with the observations of the researchers just cited, it is the contention of this investigation that central among the forces behind teacher alienation, burnout, and turnover is a basic contradiction between the training of public school teachers in colleges of education and the experience of teaching in urban public schools. Out of this contradiction emerge the necessary conditions for teacher alienation. Colleges of education provide their students with an ideology which defines as essential the shaping and moulding of young minds, and a methodology (pedagogy) by which that shaping can be attained. A plethora of factors, which I shall explore in chapters 2 and 3, separate the teacher from the realization of both the ideology and the methodology, thereby heightening the teacher's sense of meaninglessness and powerlessness.

As I noted early in this introductory chapter, my goal is to explore the impact of teacher burnout and turnover on students. To accomplish that goal, I shall analyze data collected in the Houston Independent School District on students and their teachers.

The Context of Faculty Desegregation

Although the desegregation of faculties was incorporated in the Brown decisions of 1954 and 1955 (Brown Brothers v. Board of Education of Topeka 347 U.S. 483, at 494, and 349 U.S. 249), the displacement of black teachers during the desegregation process continued into the 1960s. In 1969, the U.S. Fifth Circuit Court established what has been known as the "Singleton Ratio" by mandating that every campus in a school district must reflect the same proportion of black and white teaching staff as the district manifests as a whole. There could be no significant variations in the racial distributions of teaching personnel in schools whose student bodies were predominantly black or predominantly white. The ruling, initially handed down to the Jackson, Mississippi, school districts (Singleton v. Jackson Municipal Separate School Districts et al. 419 F.2d 1211 [1970]), was subsequently applied to over two hundred school districts nationwide, including some twenty-two in Texas.

In Houston, the Singleton Ratio was applied as a result of the Fifth Circuit Court case Ross v. Eckels (Civil Action No. 10444). Specifically, the court held that

> effective no later than August 24, 1970, the principals, teachers, teacher aides, and other staff who work directly with children at a school shall be assigned so that the ratio of Negro to white teachers in each school, and the ratio of other staff in each, are substantially the same as each such ratio is to the teachers and other staff, respectively, in the elementary schools, or in the junior high schools, or in the senior high schools, or in the technical and vocational schools (if the ratio varies with respect to such levels of school), with no more than a 5% variance, above and below, in each school (September 18, 1970:2).

The order was mandated retroactively to the beginning of the school year. Thus, teachers assigned to one school in August were reassigned in September. With so little time to implement the order, the school district was forced to act without considering the disorganization that would result. Since white schools had almost no black faculty and black schools almost no white faculty, teachers were shuffled around with some devastating consequences. Because white teachers outnumbered blacks two to one, each black school had to surrender nearly two-thirds of its faculty. Teachers were transferred on the basis of seniority. Even before faculty desegregation, black teachers were less likely to quit than were white teachers: turnover was therefore lower in black schools, and the median years of teaching experience in black schools was higher than in white schools. Consequently, black schools tended to have to surrender not only more teachers, but more experienced teachers than did white schools. Many black teachers with excellent teaching reputations were sent to white schools, while the white schools were able to satisfy the ratio by transferring more inexperienced teachers and many teachers recently hired for the fall semester. In addition, before the Cisneros v. Corpus Christi Independent School District (467 F. 2d 848 [1972]), Mexican Americans were considered to be white and were calculated into the white percentage for the computation of the ratio. Mexican American teachers were sometimes sent to black schools as whites.

In 1973, the school district returned to the court to have the 5 percent variance modified to 10 percent, citing that it was impossible to satisfy the ratio and also insure that teachers were assigned to teach the topics for which they were trained and certified. In the next year (1974), the district returned to the court again to request that the variances be changed to 10 percent at the elementary level and 15 percent at the junior and senior high levels. The court granted the changes in variances. In 1970, the court had appointed a community-staffed, biracial (and after Cisneros, triracial) commission to oversee the implementation of the ratio, which have to be recomputed before each academic year. Since white, middle-class teachers are most likely to quit, districts under the Singleton Ratio continue to be forced to concentrate their recruiting efforts on finding white teachers. The teachers who quit are thus most likely to be replaced by teachers who are equally likely to quit, thereby converting schools into revolving doors for new faculty (Dworkin,1980).

Numerous black leaders in Houston, speaking of the initial implementation of the Singleton Ratio, recounted to me that the mandate "gutted the black schools." The school board voted in 1977 to petition the court to modify or abandon the ratio. However, before such action could be taken, the board instructed the general superintendent to hire an outside research and consulting team to assess the impact of the Singleton Ratio on student achievement and faculty morale in the district. I served as chairperson of that consulting team, and some of the data presented in the ensuing chapters of this work originated from the studies conducted by the consulting team (see Dworkin et al., 1977, and McNamara et al., 1977). Other team members included James F. McNamara of Texas A. and M. University, Frank Black, then of Texas

Southern University, and Waymond Webster of Prairie View A. and M. University.

Present Investigation

Four data sets are used in this research project. The first consists of 3,444 usable questionnaires collected from the teachers of the Houston Independent School District in 1977 under the aegis of the Singleton Ratio study. The second data set involves the exit records of every teacher sampled in 1977 who subsequently quit teaching between 1977 and 1982. The third data set is from a sample of 291 teachers who were members of a local teachers' union, 91 of whom were in the original 1977 sample. These last data, collected in 1981–82 by Ruth Telschow, a former graduate student in sociology, and by myself, provide an opportunity for me to follow up on teachers who have remained in teaching. The final data set consists of two years of academic records and attendance data on students in the school district's grades 4, 5, and 6 at the time of the 1977 teacher survey. A computer match linked 2,287 of the children with the teacher data in the original sample.

This book reports on three separate studies, and consequently has three self-contained research chapters (chapters 2, 3, and 4). I have already provided a cursory examination of the nature of teacher turnover and the link between that turnover and desegregation. In the next chapter, I shall develop a model of teacher burnout and test it on the data sets for the 1977 teacher survey and the subsequent exit records collected between 1977 and 1982. The emphasis will be on demonstrating the connection between burnout and role-specific alienation, and also on exploring the impact of burnout on plans to quit teaching and actual quitting behavior. Policy recommendations regarding the relative importance of burnout and turnover will also be addressed.

The third chapter relies upon the data collected from the teachers' union in 1981–82. It explores a group of teachers who have stayed in the school district and places particular emphasis upon teacher stress and the administrative and organizational actions which a school district can take to mitigate the links between stress, burnout, and a teacher's plans to quit teaching. Theories of social buttressing and support are advanced and tested.

The fourth chapter takes the models of teacher burnout, plans to quit teaching, and quitting behavior and applies them to an investigation of the impact of such teacher career attitudes and actions on student achievement and attendance. This study explores the impact of the burnout of social service professionals upon their clients. The data come from the computer matches of the teacher data presented in chapter 2 with data on their own students. The chapter addresses the impact of teacher burnout on children, asking whether or not a sufficient amount of variance in student outcomes is explained by teacher burnout to merit the proportion of school resources currently being allocated to improving teacher morale. Two models are advanced and tested: one emphasizes the centrality of teacher and school effects on students, and the other points to the power of home and student characteristics in accounting for student performances.

The final chapter combines the findings of the three studies, summarizes the supported hypotheses in each, and the attempts to articulate those emphases into a coherent policy for urban public education.

2

Burnout, Plans To Quit, and Quitting Behavior

In the previous chapter I observed that the combined social forces of federally mandated faculty desegregation, diminished public support for teachers, and stressors within urban schools are responsible for the high rates of teacher turnover. Teachers, according to Shinn (1982) and Katzell, Korman, and Levine (1971), are three times more likely to quit their jobs and even more likely to want to quit their jobs than are similarly trained professionals. My assumption is that stresses associated with the teaching role reduce enthusiasm and heighten the desire to quit. The desire to quit in turn heightens the likelihood that the teacher will quit. Teacher burnout becomes the conceptual mechanism which translates work experiences into behavioral intentions and actual behavior. In addition, burnout becomes the social-psychological element linking job experience with job commitment, given that the desire to quit and actual quitting behavior represent dimensions of occupational commitment.

Before developing a set of models to explain burnout, plans to quit teaching, and actual quitting behavior, it is necessary to explore some of the interconnections between burnout and commitment, as well as the conceptual similarities between burnout and a more sociological construct, alienation. It is the contention of this investigation that burnout is in fact sufficiently similar to a form of role-specific alienation that the terms might well be used interchangeably. Unfortunately, however, the concepts of burnout, commitment, and alienation tend to be confounded by multiple interpretations and usages. None of the constructs approaches what Blumer (1956) had once termed a "generic variable"—one about which there is sufficient agreement over conceptual and operational definitions that replication and consistent

21

hypothesis testing is plausible. However, there is a research tradition in the study of alienation and commitment upon which I may rely in developing my view of these two concepts. The picture is considerably obscured when we approach burnout. In the initial sections of this chapter I will first focus on the explication of the construct *alienation*, then attempt to develop a conceptual definition of *burnout*, and finally elaborate on the concept of *commitment* in order to provide a theoretical grounding for measuring intentions to quit teaching and actual quitting behavior.

Alienation

The concept of alienation has received considerable currency in the social sciences since the time of Marx and Hegel. There have been numerous excellent summaries of the concept and its implications. Among the better works are those by Seeman (1959, 1975), Lystad (1972), Israel (1971), and Shepard (1977). Essential to each of the conceptualizations of alienation is what Seeman (1975) has described as a "discrepancy"; that is, there is a nearly universal view that alienation involves a gap, measureable either objectively or subjectively, between what an actor attains and what an actor could or ought to be able to attain within the social order. In the more social-psychological conceptualizations of alienation, the discrepancy is a felt loss; in more structural models, the loss may not be easily recognized by the actor. A defining distinction between the structural and phenomenological views of alienation can be characterized by Touraine's (1973) observation, translated from the French by Seeman (1975:93) as to whether alienation is "the deprivation of sensation or the sensation of deprivation."

For some investigators, the core discrepancy centers around the expropriation of surplus value occasioned by the separation of labor from the means of production (see, for example, Marx, 1906, 1959; Wright, 1976, 1978; Wright and Perrone, 1977; and Poulantzas, 1975). Others, including Carchedi (1977), expand the core in analyses of the global functions of capital and worker militancy in modern industrial societies. Still others expand the concept of alienation to include the gap between ideal and actual fulfillment of human needs and wants, or to the phenomenological perception that one's activities ultimately are not meaningful or worthwhile. For such investigators, alienation is primarily an issue of self-estrangement, or as Blauner (1964) and Mottaz (1981) have argued, the conjoined effects of the recognition that what one is doing is meaningless and that one is unable to effect changes in the condition to make the activities more meaningful.

The present research posits a view of alienation which best articulates the phenomenological perspective. It is an alienation born of consciousness, in which the actor comes to recognize that there is a discrepancy between his or her expectations about a work career and the career outcomes.

Alienation has been viewed in relation to several settings, ranging from society as a whole to specific workplaces. Whether those settings are interchangeable has not been resolved (Shepard, 1977). Some, such as Srole (1956), Dean (1961), Merton (1964a, 1964b), and Rotter (1966), have addressed global alienation from society. My focus here is considerably more restricted. The present study is concerned with role-specific alienation—in particular, with alienation from the teaching role—regardless of whether or not the teacher also senses an alienation from the greater society. The present research also posits a view of alienation which articulates a social-psychological perspective: it is alienation in which the teacher comes to recognize that there is a descrepancy between career ideals and career realities.

Much fruitful research has adopted the assessment of alienation posited by Seeman (1959, 1975). Taking a variety of conceptualizations of alienation, Seeman, in a succession of articles published between 1959 and 1975, derived five, and later six, dimensions of the concept. Beginning with Marx's view of alienation and fortified by the work of Rotter and his students, Seeman sees one aspect of alienation as a sense of "powerlessness," or the relative lack of control over the events in one's life or work. A second dimension is "meaninglessness," or a sense that one's actions and the social world in which one operates are either absurd (in the existential fashion by which Camus's (1946) stranger came to see his world) or incomprehensible. The third dimension of alienation depicted by Seeman is "normlessness," a Durkheimian view in which the rules are either inoperative, conflicting, or absent; thus obendience to the rules will not provide one with socially desired ends. The next view of alienation is that of "isolation," or the sense that one is alone, perhaps unwelcome, but at least estranged from others. Seeman adds two other dimensions: "cultural estrangement" and "self-estrangement." The former reflects the "rejection of commonly held values in the society (or subsector)," while the latter is the "engagement in activities which are not intrisically rewarding" (1975:93–94).

While self-estrangement may seem to most closely approximate the kind of alienation which leads professionals to abandon their careers, it has been demonstrated by Blauner (1964) and more recently by Mottaz (1981) that a measure of self-estrangement is empirically indistinct from the combination of measures of meaninglessness and powerlessness. Furthermore, Mottaz has (1981) observed that the conjoined effects of meaninglessness and powerlessness best predict job commitment among blue collar, white collar, and professional workers.

When workers find their jobs to be meaningless and when they come to believe that they can do nothing to inject meaning into them, their attention turns more forcefully toward pecuniary demands (Blauner, 1964). The workers do not seek "fulfillment" through work or the creation of a product, but rather work for a paycheck. In another view, when opportunities are blocked and work is seen as unfulfilling, the search for sociability becomes the focus of the worker's attention (Kanter 1977). Unfortunately, in urban public schools, neither pecuniary issues nor sociability are available options to teachers. Teachers are poorly paid, and salaries are tied to formulae unrelated to effort or commitment. In inner-city schools, where teachers of diverse ethnic background are employed, there may be no interaction among faculty. Citing the work of Clark (1970), the National Institute of Education reported, "In schools where teachers do talk to each other the conversations are usually limited to passing on of derogatory information about students" (1976:90). Furthermore, especially in such schools, teachers may come to see their students as objects, or at least persons not to be trusted or to become familiar with as individuals (Clark, 1970; Noblit, 1979; Fox and Wince, 1976). In addition, as Jackson (1968) observes, the average teacher in a large school interacts with no less than one thousand students, colleagues, administrators, and parents each day. Such a sensory overload increases the need for quiet free time, away from even the most casual aspects of sociability. Thus, another outlet for the stresses which come from a sense of meaninglessness is diminished.

Burnout

Since Freudenberger (1974) first coined the term to describe persons in the helping professions who "wear out," *burnout* has received much attention in the social-psychological and social-organizational literature, and especially in the popular press. Maslach (1982) has recently decried the proliferation of uses of the concept. In fact, a few years ago, *Time* magazine proclaimed in an editorial that there now exists the "burnout of almost everybody" (Morrow, 1981:84). The concept is applied so boardly that it seems to be used to account for any deviation from satisfaction, enthusiasm, idealism, and ebullience. There is an irony that burnout now represents one side of a dual pathology. If people lose the initial enthusiasm they once had in a role, they are said to be "burned out." However, if they retain the same level of enthusiasm for that role year after year, then they are said not to have "grown and expanded" in that role. This nebulous character of the term has made for its popularity but also prevents it from having much heuristic or scientific value.

One of the unfortunate realities of much of the research on burnout is that investigators have relied upon what may be termed a "trait definition" of burnout. Trait definitions are enumerations of the characteristics of individuals identified as having the phenomenon to be conceptualized. Although the use of trait definitions approaches a valid technique of analytic induction, those definitions too often tend to be little more than a compilation of the symptoms of members of a particular sample, along with a listing of some of the effects of the phenomenon to be studied and some of its causes. With trait definitions so constituted, generalizability as well as theory construction and testing is nearly impossible.

Constructs cannot be generated for one study, then redefined for another, and then totally modified for a third with any hope of comparability of findings. Recently Maslach (1982) and Maslach and Pines (1979) have catalogued no less than fifteen distinct and unrelated definitions of burnout used in the social-psychological literature alone. Freudenburger (1974) has identified burnout as cynicism, negativism, inflexibility, rigidity of thinking, unhappiness, boredom, psychosomatic symptoms, and a condition in which helping professionals wear out in their pursuit of impossible goals. Burnout has also been seen as exhaustion, depersonalization, a sense of reduced personal accomplishment, chronic fatigue, depression, and a desire to withdraw. Spaniol and Caputo (1979) see burnout as the inability to cope with the stress of work and personal life. Calamidos (as reported by Cedoline, 1982) identifies burnout as comprising a set of five stages, including physical burnout, intellectual burnout, social burnout, psycho-emotional burnout, and finally, spiritual burnout. No less than twenty-eight symptoms are incorporated in the five stages, which are used interchangeably with the definition of the construct. In turn, each stage also has numerous other lists of symptoms (most of which are indicative of stress), so that burnout becomes equated with sexual impotency, bruxism (excessive teeth grinding, especially at night), sweating, accident proneness, excessive worry about work, malicious humor, alcoholism, impaired decision making, dehumanization, paranoia, absenteeism, and depression.

While many—including Maslach (1976, 1987a, 1978b, 1982) Cherniss (1980), Iwanicki and Schwab (1981), Schwab and Iwanicki (1982), Cherniss, Egnatios, and Wacker (1976), and Paine (1982b)—have identified stress as a significant causal element in burnout, some—including Heath (1981) and Cedoline (1982)—have suggested that burnout and stress are interchangeable. By contrast, Pines, Aronson, and Kafry (1981) see burnout and tedium as isomorphic. Finally, Schwab and Iwanicki (1982) and Kahn et al. (1964) identify role conflict and role ambiguity as the cause of stress and burnout. Schwab and Iwanicki also use conflict and ambiguity, or the perception thereof, as equivalent to burnout. Some investigators use the symptoms of burnout as surrogates for a definition of the construct; others use the variable which are said to cause burnout as if they were identical to the construct burnout itself; still others define burnout in terms of its end products.

Recent writers—including Shinn (1982), Maslach (1976), Pines, Aronson, and Kafry (1981), Jones (1980), and Maslach and Jackson (1979)—have reported that burnout is implicated in behavioral intentions to exit a role and in actual role exits. Some have used the terms *burnout* and *role exit* interchangeably. However, Cherniss (1980) warns that the terms ought not to be confused, since some people exit roles without being burned out and many remain in a role long after they have lost their enthusiasm for it. To confuse burnout with a role exit is to negate the concept of role entrapment—which I have suggested elsewhere is more pervasive among teachers than is turnover (Dworkin, 1982). Surely, some agreement is in order. While the creation of the construct *burnout* as a generic variable—that is, one upon which there is universal agreement (Blumer, 1956)—is too presumptious for this book, an attempt will be made to develop a definition of burnout which is in agreement with an established body of sociological literature: the literature on alienation, especially role-specific alienation.

Burnout and Alienation: Toward a Synthesis

If burnout is not to be conceptualized on the basis of trait definitions, and if causes as well as effects of burnout cannot be included in a definition of the construct, what can we draw from existing literature to develop a sociological definition of burnout? One recourse is to return to the numerous definitions that emphasize not symptoms but theoretical constructs which have logically been shown to typify burnout. However, the constructs chosen must not describe more transitory phenomena, since burnout is to be seen as a relatively nontransitory attitude toward a role. Thus, burnout ought not to be thought of as fatigue or job dissatisfaction—a point that Cherniss (1980) and Maslach (1982) both make. If burnout represents a serious, changed attitude toward a role, then it should be more global than attitudes about specific aspects of a role.

The work of several recent investigators provides us with a means to develop a definition of burnout which will articulate with much sociological research. On the basis of her prior work and her development of a burnout scale, Maslach (1982) has come to view burnout as a loss of idealism and enthusiasm about work (or about a role) characterized by exhaustion, depersonalization, depression and low morale, and withdrawal. Of course, some of these elements approach another trait definition. However, there is a difference: faced with a growing discrepancy between reality and ideal expectations, Maslach's respondents come to externalize the blame for their failures on their patients or clients. They further come to redefine their efforts as futile and divorced from their ambitions, goals, and "nature." In short, they acquire a sense of meaninglessness about their work. Cherniss describes burnout as "a process in which the professional's attitudes and behavior change in negative ways in response to job strain" (1980:5).

Maslach (1978a, 1978b), Cherniss, Egnatios, and Wacker (1976), and Cherniss (1980) observe that burnout issues from stress and is particularly likely to be found among the new professionals who work for bureaucracies. Without the ability to negotiate a role bargain within the social service bureaucracies, these professionals soon acquire a strong sense of powerlessness. Thus, meaninglessness and powerlessness become essential elements in burnout. The strong sense of inefficacy among many burned-out professionals has also been documented by Shin (1982). Numerous investigators have also reported that burnout is accompanied by withdrawal as well as feeling of rejection by clients (some of whom are blamed by the burned-out professional for refusing to get better, to learn, or to improve in order to spite the professional). Schwab and Iwanicki (1982) factor-analyzed the Maslach Burnout Scale (Maslach and Jackson, 1979) and observed that the items which had the highest factor loadings were those which conveyed a sense of meaninglessness and powerlessness on the part of the respondents. Cherniss (1980) reported that burnout appears to be an alienation from work which sometimes serves to protect the workers from further disillusionment. Like the ritualist in Merton's paradigm of alienation (1964b), the professional who is burned out no longer embraces the goals and ideals which attracted him or her to the profession, but now mechanically "goes through the motions," mindlessly pursuing the means to those goals.

Burnout also involves a sense of normlessness. Several investigators—including Schwab and Iwanicki (1982), Cherniss, Egnatios and Wacker (1976), Maslach (1978a, 1978b), and Paine (1982b)—speak of the individual's sense of conflict between rival expectations on the job and ambiguities regarding the appropriate rules of behavior. Some, such as Schwab and Iwanicki (1982), have reported that an important element of burnout is the sense of role conflict and role ambiguity. In a study of child care workers, Mattingly (1977) noted that burned-out professionals reported a sense of a conflict between the need to give help and the inability to help enough. In the absence of appropriate norms for actions, these workers experienced both role conflicts and role overloads. In addition, Sparks and Hammond (1981) reported that central to the concept of burnout among teachers is a sense that the norms are unenforceable. These researchers further argued that teachers also sense a feeling of powerlessness and inefficacy, isolation, and meaninglessness.

It is clear, then, that underlying many of the psychologistic definitions of burnout, and devoid of idiosyncratic trait definitions, is a construct which is strikingly similar to a definition of perceived alienation. In fact, before the recent fascination with trait definitions, some early researchers working on burnout thought of it in terms of alienation. The Berkeley Planning Associates measured burnout as job-related alienation in their study of 1977.

In light of the strong similarity between alienation and burnout, the following conceptual definition is offered and used in the present research: *Burnout is an extreme form of role-specific alienation characterized by a sense that one's work is meaningless and that one is powerless to effect changes which could make the work more meaningful. This sense of meaninglessness and powerlessness is heightened by a belief that the norms associated with the role and the setting are absent, conflicting, or inoperative, and that one is alone and isolated among one's colleagues and clients.*

Consistent with the caveat offered by Cherniss (1980), intentions toward quitting and actual role exits will not be incorporated into my definition of burnout; neither shall I assume that burnout uniformly leads to such an attitude and behavior. To do such would dismiss a priori a potential alternative problem of urban public schools: teacher entrapment, or the condition in urban public schools in which a substantial number of teachers possess all of the attitudinal components of burnout, or role-specific alienation, but remain in disliked jobs for entire careers. People who have invested much in a career and who must rely upon their work to purchase a sense of meaning through leisure and activities away from work cannot be expected to abandon that work. It is ultimately true that we rarely abandon roles without embracing new ones. Role exits are simultaneously role entrances. With no other economic resources, it is unlikely that experienced employees run from careers; they mainly run to new careers. In the absence of options, one remains on the job.

Commitment

Burnout and alienation represent the negative outcomes of role performances. As we have seen, these concepts may often be advanced to explain intentions to quit and role exits. By contrast, the concept of commitment is evoked to describe idealism, enthusiasm, and the continuance of a role performance. Commitment is a positive aspect of a role performance. Neither commitment nor burnout ought to be viewed as synonymous with job satisfaction or dissatisfaction, which are more transitory, task-specific orientations and evaluations of roles (Mobley et al., 1979). Thus, a worker may be dissatisfied with some aspect of a job but may still be willing to continue in that role because it is seen as a stepping-stone to some more meaningful and more rewarding one within the organization (Kanter, 1977; Ritzer and Trice, 1969; Blau and Scott, 1962) or because, on balance, the role is not displeasing. Satisfaction and dissatisfaction are more likely to be affected by temporary stresses and strains and are likely to change when a particularly troublesome or particularly enjoyable event passes. Burnout (or alienation) and commitment, on the other hand, reflect the continued buildup of stressors or satisfying elements which affect the whole role. They include a perception on the part of the role incumbent that such conditions are unlikely to change in the foreseeable future.

Theories of commitment therefore represent a body of explanations for the absence of burnout and role-specific alienation as well as for the continuity of performances. From an analysis of those theories can be drawn the blocks of conceptual variables designed to explain burnout and the intentions and behaviors which might logically issue from burnout. In other words, theories of commitment obviously can be advanced to explain noncommitment, and therefore burnout, intentions to quit, and role exits.

The concept of work commitment has received considerable attention in the social, behavioral and management sciences; yet its definition and measurement have remained elusive. As Price (1977), Andrisani (1978), and Mobley et al. (1979) have each observed, work commitment, while related to alienation and satisfaction, has often mistakenly been used interchangeably with those two terms. The result has been a vast number of studies displaying widely divergent correlations between varying indicators of commitment, alienation, and satisfaction and a host of structural and social-psychological predictors. (See for example, the surveys of Mobley et al., 1979; Price, 1977; Porter and Lawler, 1965; and the dialogue in the literature between those who view commitment from a structural and exchange perspective and those who emphasize intrinsic social and economic factors.) As such, commitment has been examined with respect to a sense of alienation among industrial workers (Blauner, 1964; Shepard, 1970, 1977; and Form, 1973); among semiprofessionals (Etzioni, 1969; Simpson and Simpson, 1969; Alutto, Hrebiniak, and Alonzo, 1973; and Cherniss, 1980); among managers and corporate executives (Ritzer and Trice, 1969; Stevens, Beyer, and Trice, 1978; and Kanter, 1977); among members of religious orders (Ebaugh, 1977); and even among members of utopian communities (Kanter, 1968). The concept has gained considerable currency in the social-psychological analysis of decision making, especially when cognitive consistency models are advanced (Lewin, 1948; Festinger, 1964; Janis and Mann, 1977).

Generally speaking, commitment may be thought of as an affective attachment that an actor has to a person, object, role, or setting such that the probability of perseverence and continuance of a relationship to that person, object, role, or setting is enhanced. When co-workers and superiors, a job or career, and a workplace are involved, we may speak of job or organizational commitment. Commitment is, as Becker observes, that concept which is advanced to account for "consistent lines of activity" (1960:33). For Price (1977), work commitment is a "motivation," a "willingness to work," and a "dedication," and is indicated by a lack of absenteeism and turnover behavior. A similar viewpoint has been expressed by Mobley et al. (1979). Kanter (1968) provides a tripartite model of commitment that involves conformity to norms (control commitment), solidarity with co-workers (cohesion commitment), and preseverence of affiliation (continuance commitment). Kanter has cogently argued that commitment conjoins individual wants, needs, and experiences with the demands of an organizational structure. (See also Porter et al., 1974).

A central difficulty with the concept of commitment is that, as Becker has noted, it is an observed motivational element

> whose occurrence is inferred from the fact that people act as though they were committed. Used in this way, the concept has the same flaws as those psychological theories which explain behavior by referring to some unobserved state of the actor's psyche, this state deduced from the occurrence of the event it is supposed to explain. (1960:35)

Within the past two decades, models of career and organizational commitment within a work setting have been viewed from two distinct sociological perspectives. The first, advanced by Becker (1960) and based upon the ideas of Schelling (1956, 1960), views commitment as the structural additon of "side-bets," that is, factors external to the career or work activity, which make increasingly more painful the abandonment of a career or line of activity. The Becker model represents a theory of motivation in which the actor, in justifying past or present actions to self and to others, evokes explanations which are external to actual career considerations. Side-bets are usually measured in terms of such structural factors as age, race, years on the job, educational attainment (especially within a career speciality), marital status, and number of children. They have been shown by Becker (1960), Becker and Strauss (1956), and Alutto, Hrebiniak, and Alonzo (1973) to account for commitment as indicated by attitudes toward quitting.

In the second perspective, Ritzer and Trice (1969), Shoemaker, Snizek, and Bryant (1977), and Stevens, Beyer, and Trice (1978) have found greater support for a social-psychological model which emphasizes satisfaction and solidarity as forces behind work commitment. For these investigators, factors intrinsic to the work, including a sense of satisfaction that one's work is meaningful and a feeling of collegiality with co-workers, better account for the continuance of career behavior than do accumulated side-bets.

It is apparent that the dichotomy between Ritzer and Trice's conceptualization of commitment satisfaction and solidarity and the side-bet perspective of Becker is very similar to the exogenous-endogenous dichotomy of determinants of interaction advanced by Thibaut and Kelley (1959) and the intrinsic-extrinsic split which Herzberg (1966) uses in his two-factor theory of job satisfaction. In the above-mentioned approaches, the combination, rather than the mutually exclusive use of intrinsic or extrinsic factors, heightens the predictability of action. Andrisani (1978) finds such a combination of approaches most helpful in explaining job satisfaction in his analysis of the National Longitudinal Data sets. Shoemaker, Snizek, and Bryant (1977) suggest that side-bet variables may have greater explanatory power in terms of organizational commitment, while the strength of satisfaction and solidarity variables is greater in explaining career or occupational commitment (however, these authors contend that satisfaction and solidarity variables also do an acceptable job in explaining organizational commitment). Moreover, there is much evidence garnered from studies of cognitive dissonance (Festinger, 1964; Janis and Mann, 1977) to illustrate that actors who invest many resources in a career (such as side-bets) are likely to convince themselves that they also gain intrinsic satisfaction from their work and their colleagues (satisfaction and solidarity). Evidence presented by Stevens, Beyer, and Trice (1978) has pointed to the possibility that different commitment variables play differing roles throughout a worker's lifecycle. Satisfaction and solidarity may be of greater importance in attracting an actor to a career, but side-bets, as they accrue, become more influential later in the actor's life.

It is generally agreed that commitment involves more than continuing in a specific line of activity—that is, the absence of voluntary turnover. Identification with group goals and willingness to expend extra efforts for the organization or group are also essential aspects of commitment. However, the central concern for the sociological tradition established in the ongoing debate between those supporting the Becker position on side-bets and the Ritzer and Trice position on satisfaction and solidarity has been with the issue of voluntary turnover as a manifestation of commitment or the lack thereof. Commitment scales which ask the respondent to "assume that you were offered a job not in (e.g., teaching). Would you leave (e.g., teaching) under any of the following conditions?" clearly focus upon continuation commitment and issues of voluntary turnover. The current research likewise focuses on this narrower definition of commitment. The reason for such a tack is obvious. If school districts remain concerned about teacher burnout (role alienation) and its impact upon role exits, then a conceptualization of commitment as an explanation for perseverance of a line of activity and as the mechanism which retards voluntary turnover is most appropriate.

In her study of men and women in an industrial organization, Kanter (1977) proposes that, where blocked career mobility exists, workers tend to emphasize social relations over other factors (Ritzer and Trice's solidarity variable) as a basis for continued role relationships. In contrast, Dworkin and Chafetz (1983) maintain that in organizations characterized by very low levels of vertical mobility (not the relative immobility of Kanter's respondents), idealism, such as seeing one's work as a calling, may be a significant factor in accounting for continuation behavior. In this instance, immobility may heighten the significance of Ritzer and Trice's satisfaction and solidarity variable. It is apparent, then, that the two approaches are not mutually exclusive, and there is no necessity to choose between a side-bet or a satisfaction and solidarity approach to commitment. Rather, these two perspectives may be joined to provide better insight into the mechanisms of work commitment, thereby providing us with a more general theory of commitment.

Dworkin (1982) has reexamined the samples from which the side-bet and the satisfaction and solidarity models gain support and suggests an additional reason why the two models may be part of a larger whole. The studies which support a side-bet hypothesis sampled individuals in semi-professions, including nurses and classroom teachers, while data which gave credibility to the satisfaction and solidarity thesis were gathered from personnel managers and park rangers. The former group has specialized training which is not readily translatable into other occupations or industries; the latter group has greater translatability. Outside a hospital setting or a school, nurses and teachers have few marketable skills, whereas the skills of the personnel manager are generalizable to other industries or other fields where decision making on personnel matters is involved. Likewise, the manifold skills required of a forest ranger, including forestry, agriculture, public relations, fire fighting, conservation, and some police work, suggest that this is an occupation that does not limit career alternatives. Thus what distinguishes the two classes of occupations, and therefore the relative influence of side-bet and solidarity and satisfaction variables, is the extent to which individuals in each occupation can translate their skills into other fields without substantial retraining. A high degree of overspecialization limits one's choice of career. The reader may recognize that the distinction between high and low translatability corresponds closely to the distinction made by Gary Becker (1964: chapter 2) between specific and general training as investments in human capital.

In his study, Dworkin (1982) used coders to sort the various occupational roles within the school district into those which were thought to have analogues in other economic sectors and those which did not. Occupations were thus catagorized as either translatable or nontranslatable, with the former facilitating easy career change while the latter mitigated career change. Teachers in the sciences, mathematics, business, industrial arts, and bilingual programs were coded as translatables, while those in elementary classes and in the humanities and social sciences were coded as nontranslatables.

Two separate analyses were conducted to discern the role of translatability on commitment attitudes and behaviors. In the first, a series of regressions was run comparing the relative power of side-bet versus satisfaction and solidarity variables in explaining the desire to stay or to quit teaching. Among teachers who were not translatable, the side-bet variables better explained the desire to stay or quit, while among teachers who were translatable, the satisfaction and solidarity variables better accounted for quitting or staying. Only slightly more than 8 percent of the nontranslatable teachers who were dissatisfied with their job and wanted to quit actually did quit teaching. By contrast, three-quarters of those with translatable skills who were dissatisifed with their jobs and wanted to quit teaching actually did quit. Dworkin concluded that both models of commitment played a role in accounting for the desire to remain in a line of activity, and that both were moderated by the employee's degree of translatability. Further more, although dissatisfaction and the desire to quit are driving forces behind actual quitting behavior, quitting is more problematic for individuals who have no other career alternatives.

If the rates of burnout and low commitment among public school teachers exceed the turnover rates, then the problems which school districts face are misstated as being solely problems of turnover, as indicated by the various supply and demand reports published by the Texas Educational Association. Rather, the problems facing school districts also include teacher entrapment, in which teachers dislike their jobs and dislike their students but have made too many investments in the career and too few saleable skills to permit them to change careers.

Theoretical Constructs

On the basis of the prior research on teacher turnover and the foregoing discussion of the concepts of burnout (or role-specific alienation) and commitment, four sets of independent theoretical constructs and two sets of dependent theoretical constructs can be advanced. Associated with each construct are sets of independent or dependent variables. The exogenous constructs include actor traits, building characteristics, and two commitment-relevant constructs (side-bets and satisfaction and solidarity). The two endogenous constructs are attitudinal and behavioral role exits (operationalized as the intention to quit teaching and actual quitting behavior). The constructs are linked in a regression model to explain first the intention to quit teaching and then actual quitting behavior. An overall ordinary least squares (OLS) regression solution is first presented, and is then followed by a commonality analysis which partitions the variance in the dependent variables into unique and shared or confounded parts within the framework of a factorial pattern. See appendices A and B for the measurement of the variables in each construct.

Actor Traits

Actor traits are an aggregation of the social-psychological and social-structural aspects of an actor which serve to predispose him or her to one response rather than another. They represent factors which an actor generally brings to a job setting, rather than elements which emerge from interactions in the setting. These traits tend to place perceptual or real limits on the available options to an actor when he or she is confronted with desirable or undesirable situations. The social-psychological components of the construct represent generalized beliefs and attitudes an actor has about himself or herself and others which make more predictable his or her situationally based attitudes and actions. For example, the probability that a racially prejudiced actor will want to quit and actually quit is likely to be heighteded if he or she is assigned to schools where he or she is racially isolated. Likewise, an individual who feels little personal efficacy is not likely to define an undesirable teaching assignment as a challenge and is likely to want to escape. In fact, Dworkin, Joiner, and Bruno (1980) have found that externals (those who feel their destinies are not controlled by their own actions) are more likely to want to quit teaching if they are assigned to a school whose racial composition they define as undesirable than are internals (those who feel they can control their destinies).

It is, of course recognized that the extent to which situationally based attitudes and actions are predictable is in part dependent upon many other variables, including reference group factors, many of which are specified in other parts of this model. (For a discussion of situational factors in the link between attitudes and behaviors, see Deutscher, 1973: and Dworkin and Dworkin, 1982.) The structural predispositions represent demographic aspects of the actor which may serve to limit or enhance options available to such individuals in situations defined as desirable or undesirable. Such structural variables, while not uniform in their ability to influence attitudes and actions, are significantly correlated with modes of action.

In their original conceptualization, Schelling (1960) and Becker (1960) identified side-bets as those structural variables extrinsic to the actual tasks associated with a line of activity which make it increasingly more difficult to abandon that line of activity. Beginning with the work of Ritzer and Trice (1969), and preceeding through the research of Alutto, Hrebiniak, and Alonzo (1973), Shoemaker, Snizek, and Bryant (1977), and Stevens, Beyer, and Trice (1978), it has been a frequent practice in the commitment literature to characterize as side-bets many of the structural variables we might identify as actor traits. The present research deviates from that practice. Here actor traits are thought of as more global aspects, while side-bets are thought of as somewhat more career-specific structural factors. Side-bets, it is felt, should be structural factors which are sufficiently related to the work role that they are likely to be consistent in their influence on commitment. Thus, race, sex, age, and marital status, while they may have an impact on job options, may be inconsistent in the direction of their impact, given a particular job context. As Dworkin (1982) observes, it may be that being married, rather than making career changes more costly, may actually make career changes more plausible. Perhaps the encouragement of a spouse to change jobs, accept an offer elsewhere, or even the nagging of a spouse to improve an income level is the factor that leads to the selection of a better-paying job. Similarly, with the advent of Affirmative Action, race and sex may open up new opportunities rather than retard career options. In light of these considerations, a distinction is made in this research between side-bets and actor traits. The former refer to investments made in a particular career which make career changes more difficult, while the latter are more general demographic aspects of the actor which affect career options and decisions to leave careers with somewhat less predictability.

The variables which characterize actor traits are divided into two classes: purely demographic aspects of the actor which tend to predispose him or her to certain patterns of response, and the actor's social-psychological propensities. The former consist of age, sex, race, father's social class (class origin), and education. The latter consist of two variables, a measure of stereotyping racial groups other than one's own, and a modified version of the Rotter I-E (locus of control) measure of general expectancies.

Prior research on the data sets revealed that the class measure used by Wright and Perrone (1977) was preferable to the social status measure (Duncan's Socioeconomic Index, or SEI) presented in Reiss, et al. (1961) in predicting attitudes towards one's job (see Dworkin, et al., 1978; and Caram, 1982). Likewise, marital status and number of children—even number of children enrolled in the school district—were unassociated with role alienation or intentions to quit teaching (see Dworkin, Sanders, and Black, 1978; and Caram, 1982).

Side-Bets: Commitment Measure 1

The revised conception of side-bets, defined as investments one makes in a job or career which are independent of the tasks of the job—and hence independent of feelings of job satisfaction or collegiality—involves eight variables. These include total years teaching; tenure or contract status; major duty code, or the specific job title within the hierarchy of the school district; additional educational training beyond the bachelor's degree in one's specialization; experiences of mobility within job titles, again within the hiearchy of the school district; salary paid by the school district; income independence, or the difference between a total family income and one's salary; and translatability, or the extent to which one could move to another career without undergoing substantial retraining or abandoning one's skills.

Satisfaction and Solidarity: Commitment Measure 2

The satisfaction and solidarity measures involve social-psychological factors which are intrinsic to the role performance. Six separate measures comprise the construct. The first is an assignment attitude scale, which is a measure of the teacher's attitudes toward the racial composition of the school to which he or she is assigned. This measure compares perferred and disliked campus racial distributions with the actual racial distribution at the assigned school. The result is an effect-coded dummy variable (see Dworkin, 1980).[1] A second measure is transfer experience, or the extent to which the teacher has been transferred from a desired school to one not desired or vise versa. Again, desirability is assessed vis-à-vis the racial composition of the student body.[2] The remaining measures include an attitude scale reflecting attitudes toward the Singleton Ratio and administrative policies regarding faculty desegration; a measure of interracial norms and interracial solidarity among colleagues; a measure of the discrepancy between the teacher's view of the optimum administrative style of principals versus the view of that teacher's own principal;[3] and an index of the perceived racial discrimination experienced by one's own group on the campus.

Finally, the satisfaction and solidarity block of variables includes an eight-item, role-specific alienation scale designed to assess burnout. The items are drawn from a modified version of the Coughlan (1970) teacher alienation measure and from the work of Dworkin, Frankiewicz, and Copitka (1975). The measure taps feelings of meaninglessness, powerlessness, normlessness, and isolation from colleagues and students. In response to the cogent arguments by Blauner (1964) and Mottaz (1981), no separate assessment of self-estrangement is attempted, since those authors have shown that self-estrangement is the merger of meaninglessness and powerlessness.

Building Characteristics

Building characteristics represent aspects of the work setting which may selectively attract or repel employees. They are demographic in nature and depict the setting to which an actor characterized by a set of actor traits arrives. Building characteristics are the context in which attitudes and beliefs are grounded. The literature associated with educational attainment and with work commitment stresses the importance of environmental factors. Much of the work on school desegregation and teacher commitment—including McNamara et al. (1977) and Murnane (1975), as well as St. John (1975)—has pointed to the importance of variables such as grade level, school size, percentage of minorities in the student body, and the previous year's turnover rate as significant factors. Junior high schools tend to be more stressful for teachers, as do larger schools, minority schools, and schools with established histories of higher-than-average rates of teacher turnover. The attitudes of the school administrator toward his or her role and relations with teachers has been found by Stapleton, Croft, and Frankiewicz (1979), Fulcher (1970), Hearn (1971, 1974), and Conklyn (1976) to lead to greater levels of teacher stress, dissatisfaction, and turnover.

Six variables are contained in the building characteristics block. Among them are school size, expressed as the number of students enrolled in the school; grade level taught, divided into elementary school, junior high and middle school, and senior high school; and the turnover rate of teaachers at the school for the previous year. In the case of itinerant teachers assigned to several campuses, the grade level, school size, and turnover rate are computed for the school to which the teacher is officially assigned and in which most of his or her teaching is done. The racial composition of the school is assessed in three separate ways. The first, termed RAISOST, is intended to indicate the racial isolation of the teachers from the student body of the school, and is computed by subtracting the percentage of the teacher's own race in the student body from 100 percent. The second form of racial isolation computed is RAISOTE, or the racial isolation of the teachers from other certified staff. It is computed by subtracting the percentage of certified school employees at the campus who are members of the identified teacher's own race from 100 percent. The last measure reflects the conjoined effects of the two other indices of racial isolation. This variable, identified as PERMINGR represents the percentage of minority-group individuals in the school, regardless of whether the others are students, teachers, or other staff. Not included in the current analysis are the race of school, magnet school, and busing variables (presented in Appendix B). These are used in the student data analysis presented in Chapter 4.

Burnout

I have argued that burnout is an extreme form of role-specific alienation in which meaninglessness and powerlessness are central but which is heightened by a sense of isolation and normlessness. The construct *burnout* is assessed by the use of eight Likert-type items, two of which tap meaninglessness, powerlessness, isolation, and normlessness. The items used in the analysis were originally derived from a variant of a student alienation scale developed by Holian (1972) and a study by Coughlan (1970) of teacher alienation. They were modified by Dworkin

(1974) and by Dworkin, Frankiewicz, and Copitka (1975) for a study of teachers commissioned by the Houston Teacher's Association (see also Dworkin and Dworkin, 1976). The specific items were as follows:

Meaninglessness:

> "I see my job as contributing very little to the betterment of the world."

> "My experiences in school have proven that public school teaching is a rewarding career."

Powerlessness:

> "The longer I am in shcool, the more I realize how little control I have over things that happen here."

> "Those who make the ultimate decisions in the school system really pay attention to my ideas and suggestions as a teacher."

Normlessness:

> "Many of the school rules are so rigid and/or absurd that a good teacher must defy regulations."

> "Teachers can get what they want without breaking the rules."

Isolation:

> "Sometimes I think that a teacher could drop dead or quit and nobody would know or care."

> "The people I work with and my students make me feel that I am of vital importance to the school."

Factor analysis of the alienation/burnout items revealed that the measure was unidimensional (see appendix C, table C.1). In addition, the scale had an acceptably high coefficient of reliablity (Cronbach's alpha = .862).

The factor analysis suggests, however, that I modify slightly my view of burnout as operationalized in this study. Several investigators, including Schwab and Iwanicki (1982), Cherniss (1980), Maslach (1982), and Cedoline (1982), have pointed to role conflicts and role ambiguities, as well as feelings of being alone, in characterizing burnout among professionals. The factor analysis likewise reveals a significant role for isolation and a somewhat less central role for normlessness. Therefore, I shall not restrict my conception of burnout to meaningless and powerless, but will also include the other two aspects of alienation.

Intentions To Quit Teaching

Two additional Likert-type items are used to construct the measure of intentions to quit teaching. The items are: "I am seriously planning to leave the field of education," and, "I cannot imagine myself choosing any other career than teaching." The Pearson product-moment correlation between the items is .80 once direction of working has been controlled. The Cronbach's alpha for the two-item measure is .64, which, while somewhat low for many scales, is quite adequate for a two-item scale (see Robinson and Shaver, 1973).

Actual Quitting Behavior

It has generally been the case that studies of commitment and burnout involve either large cross-sectional data sets or case studies based on a few individuals. In some studies—such as those conducted by Ritzer and Trice (1969), Alutto, Hrebiniak, and Alonzo (1973), Shoemaker, Snizek, and Bryant (1977), and Stevens, Beyer, and Trice (1978)—respondents are presented with hypothetical situations and asked if they would leave their jobs under prescribed conditions. In these studies the actual likelihood of job-exiting behavior is not assessed and remains problematic. In other studies, employees are asked during exit interviews why they elected to quit (see Mobley et al., 1979; and Price, 1977). These studies rely upon retrospective histories which are colored by the decision to leave, in other words, by a fait accompli. Thus, once one has resigned from a position, it is unlikely that prior attitudes and preparatory conditions leading up to that decision to leave can be accurately enumerated and freed from the biasing effects of having publicly announced the decision to leave.

By contrast, many of the studies of burnout—including those by Maslach (1978a, 1978b), Cherniss (1980), Cedoline (1982), and the contributors to the edited work on burnout by Paine (1982)—do have longitudinal data and thus can assess the link between job attitudes and exit behavior. However, these studies are based upon very small samples, making generalization about the causal variables, especially between burnout and quitting behavior, somewhat problematic. In fact, Cherniss's major study is based on twenty-eight cases—seven each in four occupations.

In the current study, the enumeration of job attitudes and burnout was conducted on a large sample of teachers prior to any exit behavior.

Actual role exits were then monitored for the sample of teachers over a five-year period. By using actual data collected at exit interviews by the school district, one avoids the weaknesses of previous studies. There is no doubt that the teachers quit, nor is there any confounding of their job attitudes with their quitting behavior. The exit interview data provided by the school district was gathered from every teacher who quit between 1978 and 1982. Through a computer match with the social security numbers of the teachers in the Singleton Ratio sample, every teacher who completed a questionnaire in the 1977 study and subsequently quit teaching was captured in the exit sample. The reader should be aware that none of the teachers who quit, as best as we could ascertain, returned to teaching with the five years of the study's data collection. However, it is not the contention of this study that burnout or turnover are permanent. It is possible that some of the teachers who quit will someday return to teaching, especially if they find their new careers dissatisfying. The intent of this book is to explain burnout and turnover, not to forcast future actions of individual teachers.

Theoretical Models

Combining the constructs provides us with three theoretical models with which to explain burnout, intention to quit teaching, and actual quitting behavior. Earlier I noted that the concept of satisfaction and solidarity depicts the intrinsic aspects of work which lead to commitment. The concept expresses a view that what holds actors to a job is a sense of making a significant contribution, a sense of being able to make one's work more meaningful, and a sense that one is respected and respects one's co-workers. Unfortunately, the construct of satisfaction and solidarity comes strikingly close to describing the opposite of burnout and role alienation. Satisfaction and solidarity describe the presence of meaningfulness, powerfulnesss, and the absence of isolation; burnout describes the exact opposite. To exclude burnout from the satisfaction and solidarity block of variables significantly diminishes the block's conceptual relevance and contradicts commitment theory. On the other hand, to include variables which assess meaningfulness, powerfulness, and the absence of isolation in the satisfaction and solidarity block and then have that block predict burnout is dangerously close to committing a tautology. A compromise seems in order. In testing the model which predicts plans to quit and actual quitting behavior, burnout will be entered as part of the satisfaction and solidarity block. However, when I attempt to explain burnout, it will be deleted from the block and moved over as an endogenous variable, with the remainder of the satisfaction and solidarity block entered as exogenous predictors. As such, three regression models can be constructed to explain burnout, intentions to quit teaching, and actual quitting behavior. The models, taking an OLS format, are as follows:

Model 1: The regression of burnout on the predictors

$$Y_{BO} = a + bX_{AT} + bX_{BLDG} + bX_{SB} + bX_{SS} + e$$

Model 2: The regression of plans to quit teaching on the predictors

$$Y_{PTQ} = a + bX_{AT} + bX_{BLDG} + bX_{SB} + bX_{SS} + e$$

Model 3: The regression of quitting behavior on the predictors

$$Y_{Q} = a + bX_{AT} + bX_{BLDG} + bX_{SB} + bX_{SS} + e$$

In each instance, AT represents actor traits; BLDG represents building characteristics; SB represents side-bets; SS represents satisfaction and solidarity; and e represents measurement error. Of course, Y_{BO}, Y_{PTQ}, and Y_Q represents burnout, plans to quit, and actual quitting behavior, respectively.

The three theoretical models offer explanations for the link between three dependent variables and twenty-seven independent variables. The dependent variables are the burnout or role-alienation scale, a scale measuring intention to quit teaching, and a measure of actual quitting behavior. In both the burnout or role-alienation scale and the intention-to-quit scale, high scores indicate high alienation or strong intentions to quit, while low scores represent the reverse. The quitting measure is a dummy variable coded such that one means actually quitting and zero represents staying. (For a presentation of the percentages, means, and standard deviations associated with each of the variables, see appendix B).

Predicted Associations

Actor Traits

In an earlier analysis, Dworkin (1980) explained the lower desire to quit teaching among older teachers, teachers from lower-class origins, and minority teachers by three factors. Teachers from these groups tended to have fewer alternative career networks upon which to rely for other jobs; they had invested a larger share of their own resources and the resources of their parents in obtaining a teaching credential, and thus foregoing their investments would be costly; and for many of them teaching represented actual intergenerational upward mobility. In addition, since older women had been socialized in an era when few other career opportunities were open to them, teaching was a route towards economic independence. I hypothesize that there will be a negative association between the dependent variables and age, minority status, and social class origins (when recoded so that high scores indicate low social class).

Since female public school teachers tend to be somewhat more traditional in their sex role orientations than other college-educated women (Lortie, 1969, 1975; Hurn, 1978; Frazier and Sadker, 1973), one may expect that, if given the opportunity to exit the labor force, they would be more prone to do so. A Houston Independent School District survey conducted in 1978 revealed that up to 40 percent of the white female teachers who quit teaching exited the labor force to stay home and raise their families. Since female teachers do have the alternative of becoming full-time housewives, it is hypothesized that females are more likely to quit than males. Charters (1970) found that, among cohorts of teachers in his Oregon sample, women were more likely to quit than men. Mark and Anderson (1977, 1978) were unable to confirm that finding in their sample of Missouri teachers. However, as Dworkin and Chafetz (1983) have found, males are more likely to feel burnout and want to quit but are also provided with an escape route into administration not available to females.

Dworkin, Joiner, and Bruno (1980) found that under some conditions, such as assignment to undesirable teaching settings, externals are more likely to quit teaching than are internals. Likewise, Lefcourt (1976) observed that externals tend to flee unpleasant situations, while internals define such situations as a challenge and therefore remain. I therefore hypothesize a positive association between externality and burnout, plans to quit, and quitting behavior.

Teachers who hold negative stereotypes about racial groups other than their own are likely to find the racial mix of students and colleagues in their schools somewhat disquieting. Caram (1982) noted that prejudiced teachers tend to be less satisfied with teaching in urban public schools even if they have been assigned to a school in which their own race is in the majority. It is therefore hypothesized that there will be a positive association between stereotyping and burnout, plans to quit teaching, and actual quitting. A plausible rival hypothesis, however, would hold that teachers who stereotype may be less well educated and of a lower class origin than their nonstereotyping peers. As such, they would have fewer career alternatives and thus might be less likely actually to leave teaching.

Side-bets

The work of Ritzer and Trice (1969), Alutto, Hrebiniak, and Alonzo (1973), Shoemaker, Snizek, and Bryant (1977), and Stevens, Beyer, and Trice (1978) all demonstrate that any investment which must be foregone in a job change is likely to retard actual quitting behavior and intentions to quit to some degree. Investments identified by the researchers who have examined commitment include many of those I have included in this construct. It is hypothesized that additional years of teaching,[4] a permanent contract (tenure), additional educational degrees in one's educational specialty, higher salary, a higher-status major duty code, and upward mobility within the school district will be negatively associated with burnout, plans to quit teaching, and actual quitting. On the other hand, income independence, which makes abandoning the teaching job less costly, and translatability, which offers career alternatives (Dworkin, 1982), should be positively associated with burnout, plans to quit teaching, and quitting.

Satisfaction and Solidarity

The same researchers who examined side-bets also examined the satisfaction and solidarity construct. Any attitude which heightens a feeling of colleagiality or a sense of contribution ought to retard burnout, plans to quit, and quitting. By contrast, feelings of rejection, conflicts, and negative experiences ought to heighten the attitudes associated with role exits. I hypothesize that the greater the perception of descrimination against a member of one's own racial group at a school, the greater the burnout, plans to quit teaching, and actual quitting. Dworkin (1980) found that assignment to a disliked school was a significant factor in a teacher's desire to exit the teaching role. Likewise, the greater the difference between a teacher's perception of an ideal administrative style for his or her principal and the style endorsed by that principal, the greater the burnout, plans to quit, and actual quitting by the teacher (see Caram, Dworkin, and Croft, 1983). I hypothesize that a favorable attitude toward the Singleton Ratio, which assigned the teachers to their teaching. Exit interview data were gathered for the years 1978 through 1982 for the study. A total of 644 teachers in the original sample quit the district between the sampling period and the termination date for the collection of the data. Of these, 510 of the teachers were determined to exit the teaching role, and 134 were coded as retirements, deaths, reassignments, nonvoluntary exits (terminations), or transfers to other districts. The interviews were conducted by district personnel as a normal job exit procedure. During 1978 through 1982 a total of 5,239 such interviews were conducted on all certified personnel, regardless of whether they were in the 1977 study.

Between 1977 and 1982, the Houston Independent School District reported a teacher turnover rate of approximately 24 percent per year, with a rate of 17 percent for the year 1981–1982. By contrast, 18.6 percent of the sample quit between 1977 and 1978, and another 19.1 percent quit in the following years. Two reasons may be advanced to explain the difference between the district's reported turnover rate and that found in the current investigation. First, the district represents an open-system model in which teachers who quit are replaced by new, inexperienced teachers. The sample is a closed system. Teachers entered the sample in 1977 and none were added after that date. Since beginning teachers are most likely to quit, turnover rates in a system which adds replacements from the more turnover-prone populations will report higher rates of turnover for its total teaching population. Second, when the district reports turnover rates to the media, it does not distinguish between voluntary and involutary turnover. Deaths, retirements, and firings are incorporated into the district's percentages. In the sample under investigation, such cases were not defined as quitting.

Preliminary Concerns

Before testing the regression models of teacher burnout, plans to quit teaching, and actual quitting, two issues ought to be addressed. First, one should assess the feasibility of using a measure of burnout conceptualized as role-specific alienation to address issues of teacher commitment. Then one should attempt to assess the magnitude of the burnout problem in the public schools. Both of these assessments rely upon an examination of the components of burnout, and in particular, of the measurement of meaninglessness.

Burnout and Commitment

Previously I argued that the focal issue in alienation and in burnout is a sense that one's efforts and activities are meaningless and even absurd and that one is powerless to effect any change in one's role or setting to make the role more meaningful. Building upon the arguments of

Blauner (1964) and Mottaz (1981), I contend that the major share of the variance in a teacher's intention to quit teaching could be explained by those aspects of burnout which tap meaninglessness and powerlessness. Cherniss (1980) and Paine (1982b) have also suggested that normlessness and isolation are crucial elements in burnout. To assess this connection, I have regressed the measure of intention to quit teaching on each of the components of burnout (alienation), as follows.

Regression of Intentions to Quit on Burnout

Element of burnout	r	b	s.e.	F	beta
Meaninglessness	.527	.590	.028	436.32	.383
Powerlessness	.353	.144	.024	22.74	.087
Normlessness	.294	.077	.024	10.75	.057
Isolation	.447	.204	.027	57.50	.153

Intercept = .187   R = .564 R^2 = .318

The items assessing burnout, or role-specific alienation, exert a substantial effect upon intentions to quit teaching, and meaninglessness exerts the greatest effect of all. The beta for meaninglessness is more than twice the magnitude of any other component. In fact, the R^2 for meaninglessness alone is .278, which is nearly half the total variance accounted for in plans to quit. Powerlessness, however, is not the second best predictor, but a weaker third. Isolation is much stronger. Thus, the teacher who sees his or her work as meaningless is likely to want to quit. When that sense of meaninglessness is combined with a feeling that one is alone and unwanted, the desire to quit is somewhat heightened, and heightened again when one also senses powerlessness. It is likely that the combination of being a social service professional concerned about people and the absence of mobility opportunities—which Kanter (1977) suggests propels employees toward social relations on the job—makes isolation a more powerful independent variable than powerlessness in plans to quit. Nonetheless, powerlessness is still a significant element in burnout's impact on the desire to quit. That meaninglessness is the prime element in affecting such a desire provides support for the views of Blauner (1964) and Mottaz (1981). However, that isolation is also a component of considerable strength leads me to use more of the elements of alienation in my view of burnout. Providing teachers with evidence that their efforts are appreciated and valued, as well as creating a school climate in which teachers do not feel isolated from other teachers and from students, ought to be a significant policy concern for school administrators. In current school, a favorable attitude toward their assignment to the school (assignment attitude), and a favorable transfer experience will all be negatively associated with burnout, plans to quit teaching, and actual quitting.

Building Characteristics

Among the building variables, it is hypothesized that any form of racial isolation regarding either the student body or the faculty will be positively associated with burnout, plans to quit, and quitting behavior. Likewise, as the percentage of members of racial groups other than one's own—regardless of whether they are students, faculty, or noncertified staff—increases, the level of burnout and plans to quit will increase. Quitting behavior will also be more likely (see Collins, 1979).

Peer turnover rates are hypothesized to be positively associated with burnout, plans to quit teaching, and actual quitting behavior. Schools which have had a higher-than-average level of turnover in preceding years are more likely to be places of low morale, school disorganization, and high levels of present and future turnover. Past turnover rates are assumed to have a snowball effect upon present turnover rates and thus individual quitting behavior. Teachers who quit act as members of a symbolic reference group for other teachers still in the public schools—reminders of the viability of the role exit option. It is highly likely that even though present teachers may not interact with those who quit, reports of new careers and new successes are likely to filter back to an ex-teacher's former colleagues.

There are several countervailing pressures which come into play in ascertaining the effect of school size and grade level on burnout, plans to quit, and quitting behavior. Small schools increase the opportunity for administrative surveillance over the activities of the teachers and thus heighten job stress. But small schools also offer teachers a greater sense of solidarity, esprit de corps, and a *gemeinschaft* than do large schools, thereby mitigating burnout. Large schools are more likely to be impersonal (Noblit, 1979; National Institute of Education, 1976), thus increasing a sense of alienation.

However, because so many of the large schools are also high schools, the faculty are more likely to have advanced degrees in their specializations and a heightened sense of professional identification, both of which retard plans to quit and quitting behavior. Elementary schools have a larger percentage of young, female teachers with fewer side-bets than do junior and senior high schools (Pavalko, 1965, 1970; Lortie, 1975). Nonetheless, the likelihood of victimization by students is lower in elementary schools than in other schools (National Institute of Education Report, 1978). In the light of the absence of clear recommendations from previous research, I offer no hypotheses regarding the direction of the effects of grade level and school size on burnout, plans to quit and quitting.

Sampling Methodology

The population from which the sample was drawn came from the master personnel data tape of the Houston Independent School District. Questionnaires were mailed directly to the home addresses of the teachers. Instructions accompanying the questionnaires provided the standard human subjects information and assurances of confidentiality and anonymity. To facilitate a higher return rate and to insure that district administrators would not have access to individual reponses, the respondents were instructed to return the questionnaires in a pre-addressed, stamped envelope to the principal investigator at the Unviersity of Houston. The raw data never were made available to Houston Independent School District personnel.

At the direction of the school district administration, administrative staff above the level of principal and noncertified employees (without a teaching certificate) were not sent questionnaires. After employees who were not certified, higher-level administrators, and employees no longer associated with the district were excluded, a total of 7,000 usable names and addresses were sent questionnaires. Of these, 3,559 returned their questionnaires. Meetings with teachers' groups, unions, and notices in newsletters to teachers were used to enhance the return rate. Questionnaires were mailed out in June 1977, and the last questionnaire was returned to the principal investigator in September of that year. Of the 3,559 questionnaires returned, 115 were unusable. The returned questionnaires represented a return rate of 50.8 percent, and the usable questionnaires lowered that rate to 49.2 percent.

It is important to note that on each of twelve demographic and organization variables, the sample matched the district's population characteristics within a percentage point or less. These variables include age, race, gender, occupational categories in the district, individual campus assignment, total years of exierence, years in the particular school district, grade level of teaching, racial composition of student body, salary, contract status (tenure status), and academic degrees earned. Thus, no measurable structural bias separated the returned from the unreturned questionnaires, thereby permitting generalizations to be made to the total population (see Bridge, 1974).

Beginning in 1978, the Houston Independent School District has provided my colleague, Dorothy Caram, and me with exit interview information on all the teachers in the 1977 sample who subsequently quit fact, Mottaz (1985) has recently noted that worker satisfaction is firmly linked to such "intrinsic factors," rather than solely to issues of pay and work reduction.

The Magnitude of the Problem

Whenever a social problem is investigated, some attempt is made to estimate the prevalence of the problem within a population. Much of the work on burnout, since it has relied upon small samples and case studies, has been unable to determine the percentage of the professional social service population affected, although estimates have ranged from less than 10 percent to over 80 percent (Cedoline, 1982). On the basis of prior work, therefore, I cannot determine whether burnout among public school teachers is only of minor proportions or is a rampant malady.

The difficulty in determining the burnout rate in the teaching population has two causes. First, previous work has relied upon case studies that include clinical evidence and in which individuals seek help. With these small and often self-selected samples, rates of a phenomenon are impossible to gauge. A second source of difficulty comes from the conceptual looseness of which I spoke earlier, including the overreliance upon trait definitions. Thus, sampling and conceptual problems have prevented previous investigations from assessing the magnitude of the problem. While the definition used in the present study—role-specific alienation—may not be universally accepted, I offer a suggestion for estimating the problem among urban public school teachers. Using a large sample and a consistent definition not reliant upon symptoms, traits, or factors which may vary with the psyches of the teachers, I can approach an estimate of the magnitude of teacher burnout in urban public schools.

As in the work by Caroll and White (1982), burnout in this research is viewed as a continuous variable ranging from low to high, rather than as a discrete variable (burned out or not burned out). I have also measured burnout in terms of a role-specific alienation scale, relying upon a factor score coefficient from that scale to indicate a teacher's level of burnout. My variable burnout is thus standardized in z-score format, with a mean of approximately zero and a standard deviation of one.

By definition, two-thirds of my cases will fall between one standard deviation above and one standard deviation below the mean. Thus, if I were to define high levels of burnout (critical levels of burnout) as above one standard deviation above the mean, then something slightly over 16 percent of the teaching population could be thought of as being significantly affected by burnout. There remains an artificiality to such a statistical cutting point.

There is another solution for those who seek to estimate the magnitude of the burnout problem in the schools. Since meaninglessness is theoretically the most powerful aspect of burnout and empirically had the highest consistent factor loadings, and since this dimension of burnout or alienation best accounted for the variance in intentions to quit teaching, we may use the percentage of teachers who agreed or strongly agreed with the meaninglessness items to estimate the magnitude of burnout. The percentage of teachers who agreed or strongly agreed with both meaninglessness items was 17.9 percent, while the percentage who agreed or strongly agreed with either of the two items was 22.8 percent. If I also argue that any response other than a disagreement or a strong disagreement reflects some degree of burnout (include the neutral response), then the percentages escalate to 28.1 percent for the two items and 37.3 percent for either item. Thus, at the most I could contend that as many as one out of every three teachers in the urban school district under study is at some level of burnout from the teaching role. More conservatively, however, I could establish a burnout rate of one in every five teachers.

Testing the Models

As indicated earlier in this chapter, a test of the models advanced to explain the impact of actor traits, building characteristics, side-bets, and satisfaction and solidarity upon burnout, plans to quit teaching, and quitting necessitates a multistage process of analysis. Initially, the dependent variables are regressed upon the aggregate of predictors (using an OLS modeling format) with the intention of filtering out nonsignificant predictors. The models are then rerun using an abridged set of independent variables. The result is a test of my hypotheses and an indication of the effect of each of the independent variables upon the dependent variables. The final stage of the analysis involves a technique known as "variance partitioning," or "commonality analysis." This last stage, although not intended to test hypotheses (Pedhazur, 1982), permits me to avoid overestimating the amount of variance within a dependent variable that any conceptual block of independent variables can explain. (For a discussion of the criteria for statistical significance in testing the OLS models, along with the logic of commonality analysis and its algebraic equations, see appendix D.)

Testing Model 1

The use of all the predictors of burnout previously hypothesized presents a ponderous model with many insignificant F values and numerous b values that are less than twice their standard errors.[5] The 27 predictors yielded a multiple R of .575 and an R^2 of .331. The F value for the entire model was 40.967. After all insignificant variables are removed, the revised model, presented in table 2.1, provides an R of .566 and an R^2 of .320. The accompanying F value associated with the model climbed to 68.91.

Table 2.1
Revised Model of Teacher Burnout

Variable	Total covar. r	b	s.e.	F	Beta
Age	-.218	-.008	.002	11.43	-.097
External locus	.317	.094	.008	146.55	.219
Black teacher	-.138	-.218	.040	30.25	-.103
RAISOST	.194	.002	.001	7.74	.072
Experience	-.181	-.008	.004	3.31	-.067
Tenure	-.049	-.071	.026	7.79	-.055
Salary	-.040	-.000	.000	2.54	-.000
Income independence	.051	.001	.000	4.51	.038
Administrative style differences	.263	.262	.019	72.67	.153
Discrimination	.274	.289	.040	52.55	.133
Racial norms	-.243	-.047	.011	18.84	-.081
Attitude toward Singleton Ratio	-.342	-.246	.019	159.31	-.241
Assignment attitude	-.113	-.058	.023	6.12	-.047
Intercept = .114		R = .566	R^2 = .320	F = 68.91	

An examination of the individual predictors drawn from the actor traits block reveals that burnout diminishes with age but that the effect is very slight. Teachers who have an external locus of control (that is, use explanations of luck and fate to account for their life events and do not tend to believe that they control their own destinies) are associated with higher burnout responses, and the effect is striking. The implication is that externals generally burn out while internals are much less likely to do so. Race also exerts an effect. A black teacher is associated with a lower burnout response than either a brown or white teacher.

Only one building characteristic variable is significantly implicated in burnout. Racial isolation from the student body (RAISOST) heightens burnout: however, the effect is small.

The side-bet variables associated with burnout include experience, tenure, salary, and income independence. For each additional year of experience in the classroom after the fifth year, there is a slight drop in burnout. Tenure is also weakly associated with a decreased level of burnout. Among economic variables, salary increases as burnout decreases, but as income independence increases, burnout increases. The influence that a single unit of each of these two variables has upon burnout is very small, even when one considers that the units of salary and income independence are expressed in one-dollar increments. Thus, if salary alone were used to encourage enthusiasm on the part of teachers, it would take a salary increase of $303,030 dollars to convert one unit of burnout into one unit of enthusiasm (the b between salary and burnout is -.0000033). An income independence level increase of $33,333 is necessary to heighten burnout by one unit (the b between income independence and burnout is .000030). A substantially smaller amount of outside income is needed to translate the experiences in teaching into burnout than is the amount of money needed to buy enthusiasm. A school district that wishes to buy off its teachers and reduce their sense of meaninglessness and powerlessness through pecuniary efforts must therefore be prepared to spend monumental sums of money. In the next chapter I shall explore an alternate strategy.

Among the satisfaction and solidarity variables, administrative style differences, perception of discrimination, racial norms, attitude regarding the Singleton Ratio, and assignment attitude all have significant effects on burnout. For each unit of disagreement in administrative style between a teacher and his or her principal, there is a corresponding increase of 16 percent of a unit of burnout. Teachers who perceive that they are the targets of discrimination in a school are associated with an increase of nearly 30 percent of a unit of burnout. By contrast, teachers who believe that there are racial norms of cooperation at their school are associated with nearly 5 percent of a unit decrease in burnout. The effect of a disagreement with one's principal over his or her administrative style is small but still evident. Teachers who perceive that they are targets of

discrimination are also likely to report more burnout than are those who
do not perceive such discriminition, but again, the effect is a small one.
By contrast, teachers who believe that there are norms for racial cooperation at their school are less likely to report burnout. This variable, too,
has a small effect on burnout. A substantially larger effect is present for
attitudes toward the Singleton Ratio. Teachers who feel that the racial
assignment of faculty has had a positive effect on morale are much less
likely to experience burnout than those who feel that the ratio hurts
morale. Finally, teachers who like the schools to which they are assigned
(positive assignment attitude) report lower burnout levels than those
assigned to schools about which they are neutral, and still lower levels
than those assigned to schools they define as undesirable.

In sum, then, the portrait of the burned-out teacher is that of a
young, white person who has an external locus of control and who is
racially isolated from the student body at his or her school. Such a
teacher has relatively little experience in teaching, is not on a permanent
contract, is likely to be a classroom teacher, is paid little but is somewhat
economically independent from the teaching salary, disagrees with his or
her principal on the principal's administrative style, feels that he or she is
a target of racial discrimination, is in a school where racial groups of
teachers rarely mix socially, disagrees with administrative policy on
faculty desegregation, and does not want to be at the school to which he
or she is assigned.

Testing Model 2

The initial regression model of the impact of the four groups of
theoretical constructs on the intention to quit teaching involved 28
observed measures. The obtained multiple R was .612, with an R^2 of
.374. Such a model yielded an F of 47.63, which, while statistically
significant, was not parsimonious. Only 13 of the predictors were significant, and when the regression was recomputed using only those predictors, the multiple R dropped only slightly to .610 and the R^2 to .372. The
F associated with the regression was 83.87, again statistically significant
and considerably more parsimonious.

Table 2.2 presents the results of the regression analysis. Burnout is
the most powerful single predictor of the intention to quit, with a b value
of .812. Thus, for each increase in a unit of burnout, there is over 81 percent of a unit of intention to quit teaching. None of the other variables in
the model has such a profound influence on intentions to quit teaching as
has burnout, although all the other measures used in the regression are
significant.

Among actor traits, sex, father's occupation, and locus of control all significantly affect plans to quit teaching. Male teachers are more likely to want to quit teaching than are females. Likewise, teachers whose fathers were entrepreneurs are more likely to want to quit teaching than those whose father's were managers, and those in turn are more likely to want to quit than teachers whose fathers were workers. Finally, as observed in the analysis of burnout, teachers who have an external locus of control are more likely to want to quit teaching than those who are more internal, but the effect is slight.

Three of the building characteristic variables have significant effects on plans to quit teaching. An increase in the racial isolation of a teacher from the students at his or her school (RAISOST) is associated with a small increase in the desire to quit. Likewise, as the percentage of minority students and teachers (PERMINGR) in a school increases, the desire to quit teaching increases (again at the same rate as for racial isolation from students). Elementary teachers are more likely to plan to quit than are junior high school teachers, who in turn are more likely to quit than are high school teachers. As the grade level of the students increases, plans to quit diminish.

Table 2.2
Revised Model of Plans To Quit Teaching

Variable	Total covar. r	b	s.e.	F	Beta
Sex	-.085	-.279	.058	22.93	-.085
Father's class	-.027	-.040	.020	2.34	-.026
External locus	.142	.027	.011	6.18	.045
RAISOST	.048	.002	.001	4.39	.052
PERMINGR	.145	.002	.001	4.55	.053
Grade	-.096	-.066	.017	14.82	-.066
Experience	-.101	-.017	.005	9.37	-.098
Inexperience	.113	.045	.016	8.27	.055
Salary	-.147	-.001	.000	6.73	-.071
Income independence	.014	.001	.000	2.27	.026
Translatability	.023	.113	.038	4.64	.052
Attitude toward Singleton Ratio	-.246	-.060	.026	5.43	-.042
Burnout	.589	.812	.027	859.60	.574
Intercept = 3.289		R = .610	R² = .372	F = 83.87	

Five variables from the side-bet block significantly affect plans to quit teaching. For each year of experience in the classroom beyond the fifth year, there is a small decline in the desire to quit. Among teachers with five or less years of experience (the spline variable"inexperience"), there is a small increase in plans to quit.

Earlier I noted that burnout does not increase yearly through the first five years of teaching but does decline slowly after the fifth year. By contrast, plans to quit teaching escalate through the first five years and then decline after that. Burnout levels are fairly high among less-experienced teachers but do not rise progressively. Plans to quit, which are often the logical outcomes of burnout, do increase during those vulnerable years. It may also be true that the cohorts of teachers with more experience manifest declining burnout and plans to quit not just as their side-bets increase, but as their numbers diminish due to turnover. The failure to detect a significant effect of inexperience on burnout but to detect such an effect on plans to quit suggests that there may be a logical process involved. Burnout, as Maslach (1978a, 1978b), Paine (1982b), Cedoline (1982), and Cherniss (1980) have observed, occurs relatively soon in the career of many public school teachers. Waller (1932) also noted the early loss of idealism, although he of course did not use the term *burnout*. However, a sense of dissatisfaction and of alienation represents just one step in a logical process. The conclusion that action is needed takes somewhat longer. Therefore, the desire to quit teaching may occur only after an individual comes to recognize that the school setting, the students, the administrators, and the nature of the job itself are the sources of one's disillusionment and that the only viable resolution is in making plans to quit the role. Perhaps the process of moving from burnout to the decision to make a role exit necessitates a conclusion that the problem is a generic one, not unique to one school or unique to one's own experiences. Dworkin and Dworkin (1982) suggest in their analysis of racial attitude formation that such processes involve numerous reference group interventions. All these processes take time.

As salary increases, plans to quit diminish. By contrast, as income independence increases, plans to quit increase. The effect of each is measured in one-dollar increments and thus is small per unit of salary or income independence. Again, as in the case of burnout, the cost to a school district of buying the desire to remain in teaching is high. Expressed only in terms of salary, it takes an increase of $18,518 to effect a one-unit change in plans to quit. to move from the sample mean of 2.54, which is a fairly neutral response, to something near the response that is near 1.0, which is a strong desire to stay, would require a salary increase of $27,517 per year in 1977 dollars. (The associated b value for the relationship between the salary and the desire to quit is -.000054.) Income independence displays a much weaker effect on plans to quit. To heighten the desire to quit among teachers, it is necessary for the teahcer to have an outside source of money in excess of $344,828 (b = .0000029) for each unit of increase in the desire to quit. Thus, it is neither inexpensive to buy commitment, nor easy to buy noncommitment. Finally, those with translatable skills are more likely to plan to quit teaching than are those with nontranslatable skills. If one has skills which are convertible into other careers without substantial retraining, then one is more likely to plan to quit.

Among the satisfaction and solidarity variables, only attitudes toward the Singleton Ratio and burnout discussed earlier have a significant effect on plans to quit. For each increment in burnout there is an almost equal increment in plans to quit; but there is a small decrement in plans to quit with each increment of support for the Singleton Ratio. Teachers who feel that the ratio's assignment of teachers to campuses on the basis of race was a good idea and helped morale are less likely to plan to quit than are teachers who object to the ratio.

In conclusion, the teacher who plans to quit is most often burned out, male, and from a higher social class, has an external locus of control, and is racially isolated in the school. The teacher is also likely to be in an elementary school where most of the whole student body and staff are members of a minority group. The teacher is inexperienced, has a low salary but is economically independent, and has skills which are translatable into other fields of employment. He or she also disagrees with the faculty desegregation policy of the school district.

Testing Model 3

The initial regression model of the impact of the four groups of theoretical constructs on actual quitting behavior involved 29 measures. The obtained multiple R was .307, with an R^2 of .094. This regression yielded an F for the whole model of only 7.80. Only nine of the predictors were significant. Recomputation of the regression using only the significant predictors yielded a multiple R of .301, with an R^2 of .090. The F associated with this regression was a more respectable 22.53. In this model, direct and indirect effects can be calculated for the effect of the variables on quitting behavior.[6] None of the indirect effects (paths going from actor traits, building characteristics, side-bets, or satisfaction and solidarity variables through plans to quit to actual quitting) is more than negligible and will therefore not be reported. Most of the effects are direct (see table 2.3). Age and race represented the strongest independent

Table 2.3
Revised Model of Quitting Behavior

Variable	Total covar.r	b	s.e.	F	Direct (beta)	Indirect	Total causal	Non causal
Plans to quit	.102	.015	.005	8.35	.059	None	.059	.043
Age	-.230	-.005	.001	31.91	-.181	-.005	-.186	-.044
Black teacher	-.160	-.101	.017	36.62	-.138	-.001	-.139	-.021
Stereotyping	-.036	-.006	.003	2.01	-.029	.000	-.029	-.007
Grade	-.032	-.011	.005	4.79	-.045	-.004	-.049	.017
Inexperience	.143	.008	.004	2.72	.038	.003	.041	.102
Major duty code	-.098	-.017	.008	3.73	-.040	.000	-.040	-.058
Income independence	.056	.001	.001	12.92	.073	.002	.075	-.019
Translatability	.002	.020	.010	1.98	.036	.002	.038	-.036
	Intercept = .384			$R = .301$	$R^2 .090$		$F = 22.53$	

variables, and income independence represented a weaker third variable. For each year of a teacher's age, there is a 0.50 percent reduction in the likelihood that he or she will quit teaching. Thus, a teacher in his or her forties (slightly older than the average teacher in the district) is 20 percent less likely to quit teaching than a teacher in his or her twenties (when most teachers are first hired by an urban district). Black teachers are associated with slightly more than a 10 percent reduction in the likelihood of quitting than are brown or white teachers. This observation is similar to that reported by Dworkin (1980) and by district experience.

Income independence is associated with increases in actual quitting behavior. However, with a b of .0000033, an independent alternative source of increased income totaling $297,619 would be required to lead a teacher who is currently employed in the district to leave. Thus, it again appears that it is not money per se that drives teachers out of the profession, nor is it money that holds them.

An explanation may be offered to account for the relatively small role that money plays in altering attitudes of teachers, and hence the enormous amount of money that a school district would have to spend to change such attitudes. In 1964 Blauner argued that auto workers, when denied a sense of meaningfulness through work, sought wage incentives to maintain commitment. More recently, Mottaz (1981) studied executives and found a similar phenomenon. In both instances, the individuals were engaged in their line of work for pecuniary reasons—a point noted by Ritzer and Trice (1969) in their study of executive commitment. Thus, even small increases in salaries were capable of altering levels of commitment. The various investigations of side-bet variables in commitment have found that moderate or even small levels of increase in remuneration were enough to get workers to want to quit one job and take another (see, for example, Alutto, Hrebiniak,and Alonzo, 1977; and Shoemaker Snizek, and Bryant, 1977). By contrast, public school teachers tend to be drawn into teaching either by a sense of calling or a desire to help children (Waller, 1932; Becker, 1952; Jackson, 1968; Lortie, 1969, 1975). About 70 percent of the teachers in the National Education Association surveys listed the desire to work with children as their principal reason for entering teaching (1982:72). Through self-selection, a teaching population is one that is not drawn into a career principally by monetary factors. Hence, each unit of monetary reward is less valuable, and enormous quantities of such rewards are needed to compensate for a sense of meaninglessness, inefficacy, and isolation. In chapter 3 I shall probe more deeply into factors which *do* hold teachers and mitigate burnout and plans to quit teaching.

With the exception of stereotyping, no social-psychological measure, including burnout, affects actual quitting behavior. Rather, side-bets and those actor traits which expand career opportunities better account for actual quitting, although even these bear only a weak association with such behavior. Faced with few alternatives, individuals rarely quit careers because of dissatisfaction. People rarely exit roles without entering other roles, and when no other viable roles are available, they are more willing to tolerate a dissatisfying job than abandon a paycheck. This is true despite the finding that money by itself does not promote staying behavior.

It is obvious that quitting behavior is not well predicted. That burnout has no effect on quitting, that the plan to quit has only a small effect, and that the burnout rate is high suggest that there are vastly more teachers who dislike their jobs but stay than teachers who dislike their jobs and leave. The earlier analysis by Dworkin (1982) suggested that teacher entrapment is a more serious problem than teacher turnover. Using a different form of analysis on the teacher data yields the same conclusion. A school district would be naive to believe that teacher turnover is the basic personnel problem that urban schools face. The real problem may well be the consequences for children (which I shall address in an ensuing chapter) of having a significant number of disenchanted teachers in the classrooms.

Commonality Analysis: Retesting the Models

Analysis of the b's and beta's of the significant independent variables permits us to determine the effect of each predictor on the criterion variable. However, such an analysis does not preclude the overestimation of the total variance explained by any single or group of independent variables, since an OLS analysis tends to assign residual shared variance to the strongest predictor, thereby inflating its influence. The alternative, which simultaneously permits us to examine the effect of clusters of independent variables which are theoretically linked, is commonality modeling.

The commonality analysis of the intention to quit teaching was run two ways. In the first analysis burnout was included as a satisfaction and solidarity variable, while in the second analysis it was separated out as an additional construct. In commonality analysis, the number of regressions needed to be run is a function of the number of blocks entered into the equation. Thus, with burnout included as part of the satisfaction and solidarity block, there were a total of four blocks of independent variables (actor traits, side-bets, satisfaction and solidarity, and building characteristics), while with burnout counted as a separate independent variable, there were five blocks. Four blocks yield a total of 15 regression equations, while five blocks yield a total of 31. Table 2.4 presents the commonality analysis of intentions to quit teaching as explained by four blocks of independent variables. A total of 37.225 percent of the total variance in intentions to quit is explained by the regression model. Actor traits account for 5.973 percent of the total variance; however, of this only 0.928 percent is unique variance, attributable to actor traits alone, and the balance is variance confounded by the other blocks of variables. Thus, only a negligible amount of the variance in the intention to quit is explainable by actor traits. Likewise, building characteristics account for 3.438 percent of the variance in the intention to quit, but only 0.583 percent is unique to building variables.

Table 2.4

Summary of Four-Block Commonality Analysis of Plans To Quit

	Blocks of independent variables			
Variance categories	*Actor traits*	*Building characteristics*	*Side-bets*	*Satisfaction solidarity*
Unique variance	.00928	.00583	.00477	.28065
Common variance	.05009	.02855	.01968	.06908
Total variance	.05973	.03438	.02445	.34973
Variance from structural equations (a check)	.05973	.03438	.02445	.34973

Among the commitment measures, side-bets account for 2.445 percent of the total variance, but again, only 0.477 percent of the variance is unique to sidebets, thus seriously casting in doubt Becker's model (1960) of commitment. In fact, even if a more liberal interpretation of side-bets is taken such that side-bets are considered to be the variables encompassed in actor traits and in the side-bet category, the concept accounts for only 1.405 percent of the total variance in intentions to quit.

Satisfaction and solidarity, which includes the burnout measure, accounts for the lion's share of the explained variance—34.973 percent—of which 28.065 percent is unique to satisfaction and solidarity, and thus tends to support the Ritzer and Trice (1969) position on commitment as measured by behavioral intentions (the technique used by Ritzer and

Trice, 1969; Alutto, Hrebiniak, and Alonzo, 1973; and Shoemaker, Snizek, and Bryant, 1977). Less than 7 percent of the variance in intentions to quit implicated in satisfaction and solidarity is shared or confounded variance, and of the total variance in the dependent variable, only about 9 percent is not unique to satisfaction and solidarity (recall that the R^2 in Table 2.2 was .372). Incidentally, the unique variance due to burnout per se is 22.102 percent of the total, or three-fourths of the variance explained only by satisfaction and solidarity.

The second commonality analysis shows more clearly the significant role that burnout plays in intentions to quit teaching (see table 2.5). Actor traits, building characteristics, and side-bets remain as they were. Actor traits explain 5.973 percent of the total variance, of which only 0.928 percent is unique variance; building characteristics explain 3.438 percent of the variance, of which 0.583 percent is unique; and side-bets explain 2.445 percent of the variance, of which only 0.477 percent is unique. However, devoid of burnout, satisfaction and solidarity now explains only 10.030 of the total variance, of which 0.219 percent is unique variance. In contrast, burnout again explains 34.679 percent of the total variance, of which 22.102 percent is unique variance.

Table 2.5

Summary of Five-Block Commonality Analysis of Plans To Quit

Variance categories	Blocks of independent variables				
	Actor traits	Building charac.	Side-bets	Satisfaction solidarity	Burnout
Unique variance	.00928	.00583	.00477	.00219	.22102
Common variance	.05045	.02855	.01968	.09811	.12577
Total variance	.05973	.03438	.02445	.10030	.34679
Variance from structural equations (a check)	.05973	.03438	.02445	.10030	.34679

The concept of burnout has also been subjected to a commonality analysis. Table 2.6 presents the commonality run involving four blocks of independent variables: actor traits, building characteristics, side-bets, and satisfaction and solidarity variables. A total of 32.019 percent of the total variance in burnout can be explained by the model. Actor traits account for 15.504 percent of the variance, of which only 5.514 percent is unique variance and the rest is shared with other blocks of predictors.

Building characteristics account for 11.153 percent of the total variance in burnout, of which 1.582 percent is unique variance. Side-bets explain 5.910 percent of the variance, of which 0.868 percent is unique to side-bets, further weakening the position of Becker (1960). In contrast, satisfaction and solidarity accounts for 20.589 percent of the total variance, of which 9.661 percent is unique. With so little variance to be explained and with the presence of a dichotomous dependent variable, it was decided that no full commonality analysis ought to be conducted on quitting behavior.

Table 2.6

Summary of Commonality Analysis of Burnout

	Blocks of independent variables			
				Satisfaction
Variance	Actor	Building	Side-	Solidarity
categories	traits	characteristics	bets	(less burnout)
Unique variance	.05514	.01582	.00868	.09661
Common variance	.09990	.09571	.05042	.10928
Total variance	.15504	.11153	.05910	.20589
Variance from structural equations (a check)	.15504	.11153	.05910	.20589

The commonality analyses present a clear picture for school policy. To avert teacher turnover, generally speaking, factors outside the constructed model must be manipulated. These are principally economic factors but not salary factors; side-bet variables, especially those reflecting career alternatives or role choices, have the greatest impact on actual quitting. School districts cannot normally manipulate these variables and therefore are unlikely to be able to affect substantially actual quitting rates.

As a matter of fact, even income independence, while significantly associated with the quitting variable, explains only a small amount of the variance. The b associated with income independence is only .008. Translatability bears a b of .020.

It may be true that a substantial increase in teachers' salaries would retard quitting behavior, but a substantial change in the curriculum of the colleges of education might ultimately do the same thing. As I have noted in a previous analysis of dissatisfied teachers (Dworkin, 1982), almost 75 percent of those who were translatable and who were dissatisfied actually quit teaching. In contrast, only about 8 percent of the teachers who were dissatisfied but who did not possess translatable skills left teaching. Since the majority of teachers do not have translatable skills, teacher entrapment rather than teacher turnover seems to be the more serious condition of the public schools. If teacher's colleges would put less emphasis on pedagogy and more emphasis on skills useable by industry, teachers who are dissatisfied with teaching could leave, and presumably a larger percentage of the teachers remaining in teaching would do so because they enjoy their work.

Turning to teachers' intentions to quit and to teacher burnout, we see a distinctively different picture. Here a sense of satisfaction with work and feelings of solidarity with colleagues are essential in retarding the desire to quit and in mitigating burnout. Also important is agreement with the policies of the administration and the administrative style of the principal. In the next chapter I shall examine a sample of teachers who stay in teaching and explore the factors which operate to hold teachers even in the presence of stress-producing variables.

Conclusions and Policy Implications

The models presented in this chapter have attempted to explain teacher burnout, plans to quit teaching, and actual quitting behavior. The analysis clarifies several issues. Teacher burnout, whether it is viewed as a role-specific sense of alienation or a lack of commitment, is selective. While 20 percent or more of the teaching staff in a major urban school district will report burnout, the likelihood is exacerbated if the teacher is young, white, middle class in origin, and assigned to a school in which the individual is racially isolated and which he or she defines as possessing an undesirable student body mix. While burnout is progressive—as Maslach (1978a, 1978b), Cherniss (1980), and Paine (1982b) have noted—the process is sufficiently rapid that it escalates over the first five years of teaching experience and then progressively declines over the balance of one's career. Of course, the relative decline in burnout among older teachers may also be attributed to attrition effects, coping skills, or actual increases in power and control which retard a sense of alienation.

The media have given much attention to the role of teacher salaries in accounting for burnout and alienation. Although teachers are decidedly underpaid for the magnitude of the responsibility they have in our society, economics alone is not the source of burnout. In fact, both salary and economic independence have very little effect on burnout. A school district must spend enormous sums of money on salaries to lower burnout levels among teachers. This is not to say that salaries are unimportant issues for teachers. Duke (1984) suggests that a valuable starting point for the recruitment of new teachers might be more attractive starting salaries. As we shall see in the next chapter, the matter of teachers' salaries is a significant stressor on public school teachers. But an improved salary structure is not a panacea because salaries are not significant in retaining an existing teaching population or in maintaining its enthusiasm. Unless school districts also attend to other concerns—including those directly associated with social support, isolation, and the issues involved in the dimension of satisfaction and solidarity—they are unlikely to be able to buy enthusiasm on the part of their personnel.

Burnout is a significant driving force in the plans of teachers to quit their careers. As in burnout itself, the cluster of satisfaction and solidarity variables plays a more dominant role in the desire to exit the teaching role than does the cluster of side-bet variables. However, as Dworkin (1982) pointed out earlier, the relative explanatory power of the satisfaction and solidarity and side-bet blocks depends upon whether or not the teacher has translatable skills. The models presented in this chapter explain about a third of the total variance in both burnout and plans to quit teaching. Therefore, clearly other more powerful variables have been omitted. The next chapter examines some of those variables which were not available in the initial survey, including administrative support, stress, fear and victimization. It is not expected, however, that any model will account for as much as half of the total variance in burnout. Several decades of personnel research and model building have rarely produced regression models which account for as much as I have explained in the present chapter.

The ability to predict or to explain actual quitting behavior is even more attenuated. Only 9 percent of the total variance in quitting is explained through the use of the models. One reality is that not all teachers who quit actually want to do so, and the majority of teachers who want to quit are unable to do so. In fact, the ratio of those who want to quit to those who actually do quit is approximately 4 to 1, even after the lapse of five years between the enumeration of the attitudes toward quitting and the final data collection of exits from teaching. People do not exit roles unless they can enter other roles. When a teacher has amassed many side-bets and other investments in a career and when that teacher has few other skills which are saleable to employers outside education, he or she is likely to remain in the disliked job.

With such a higher rate of burnout and plans to quit than of actual quitting behavior, we now come to see that the school districts have not been addressing the appropriate question. School districts do lose many new teachers, as Pavalko (1965, 1970), Mason (1961), Brookover and Erickson (1975), and Dworkin (1980) have discussed. In fact, the issue of teacher turnover was the topic of discussion as far back as the 1930s (see Waller, 1932). Nonetheless, the turnover rate does not approach the rate of teacher disenchantment, burnout, and desire to quit. Rather than develop plans to retard turnover, school districts and colleges of education might better concern themselves with matters of retarding entrapment.

Entrapment can be mitigated in several ways. Some, such as the violation of desegration mandates, are clearly unlawful and undesirable. However, school districts and campus administrators who create a social environment which engenders a sense of meaningfulness and effectiveness on the part of teachers as well as a sense of collegiality among teachers (thereby reducing isolation) are likely to retard both burnout and some amount of actual quitting behavior. However, these measures are not enough. A large percentage of teachers enter the profession blindly, unaware of the nature of the job and its expectations. Many quit early in their careers, but many more become entrapped because they can offer no other skills than the teaching of children to prospective employers. One difficulty is that colleges of education, by mandating so many pedagogical courses, heighten the likelihood that their students will be "fit in an unfit fitness" (see Merton, 1968:251–254 for the elaboration of trained incapcity). It is essential that future teachers have majors in academic disciplines such as the sciences, language, literature, or business, and only minors in education. Perhaps, a major in a college of arts and sciences at the undergraduate level, followed by a one-year M.A.T. (master of arts in teaching) program in a college of education is the most viable suggestion. Such an educational policy could go far to ensure that teachers who discover that they have made an error in their career choice will be able to exit one role and enter another.

Clearly, offering academic training which makes teachers more translatable in other markets will heighten the turnover rate in the schools. However, school districts may come to discover that it is preferable to have satisfied and committed employees than ones who feel entrapped. Combining some of the issues to be explored in the next chapter with the policy of career alternatives may ameliorate both the problems of entrapment and of turnover. Teachers who remain because they feel that they are doing meaningful work are likely to be better teachers. Moreover, if the teachers have skills which are in demand by industry, they may also be able to communicate to their students skills which are also in demand by industry. In fact, a teacher who is able to move between industry and teaching is likely to be up-to-date in his or her skills and will better prepare students for their careers. The human relations skills which an administrator may need to maintain teacher commitment may ensure that the teacher who is translatable to other sectors of the economy will always return to teaching.

3

Stress, Burnout, and Support Among Those Who Stay in Teaching

In the previous chapter, a model was presented and tested which explicated the factors which extinguish idealism among public school teachers, produce a sense of role alienation, and under appropriate economic and structural circumstances, yield high rates of voluntary turnover. A sense of estrangement from teaching, brought on by a perception that the work is meaningless and that one is powerless to control either the work or the work setting, weakens an actor's sense of commitment to the work. When such estrangement is joined with a belief that the rules are dysfunctional and that one is isolated from colleagues and clients (students), burnout, or role-specific alienation, is at a maximum (Cherniss, 1980).

In testing the model in chapter 2, it was shown that a significantly greater amount of variance in levels of commitment could be explained than the amount of variance in actual quitting behavior. Thus, despite the arguments of Maslach (1978a, 1978b) Iwanicki and Schwab (1981), and Schwab and Iwaniki (1982), burnout and alienation do not automatically lead to role exits. Economic factors such as job translatability seem to be more crucial. In other words, actors rarely voluntarily exit a role which provides at least financial rewards unless they can enter another role which meets or exceeds those rewards. Role exits tend to be followed by new role entrances.

A major conclusion of the previous chapter was that while teacher turnover is a problem facing many public school districts, teacher entrapment is the central problem that teachers themselves face. Thus, schools are encountering a larger proportion of their teaching staff who remain in teaching even when they are dissatisfied, disliking both their job and their students.

The alienation and burnout factors which weaken commitment have themselves been explained by many investigators as products of stress. Maslach (1978a, 1978b), Cherniss (1980), Cherniss, Egnatios, and Wacker (1976), Iwanicki and Schwab (1981), and Schwab and Iwanicki (1982) have built a cogent case for the link between stress, burnout, and alienation. The prolonged, constant, and intensive interaction which typifies classroom teaching in emotionally charged urban public schools provides a suitable breeding ground for stress.

The attention of the present chapter is focussed upon those teachers who, either because of a sense of continued commitment or because of job entrapment, do not exit the teaching role. In particular, the present chapter assesses the level of stress perceived by a sample of urban public school teachers, many of whom were in a sample collected five years earlier and presented in the previous chapter. The chapter also examines reports of stress-related illness behavior among those teachers and the relationship of stress and illness to alienation and burnout and a weakened commitment to teaching. Finally, an attempt is made to isolate structural and organizational variables which either reduce levels of stress or heighten teachers' ability to cope with the stress prevalent in urban schools. The purpose of this chapter, then, is to discover those categories of variables which are sufficiently malleable and responsive to school policy to reduce stress, burnout and alienation, and to heighten commitment. It is hoped that an enlightened school policy will result from these findings.

Stress and Burnout in Schools

As noted previously, the essential link between stress and burnout is unproblematic. The psychological aspects of burnout, including feelings of exhaustion, depersonalization, and meaninglessness of work, stem from the frequency and intensity of interactions in a teaching setting, and especially from the joint presence of role ambiguity and role conflict (Cherniss, Egnatios, and Wacker, 1976; Schwab and Iwanicki, 1982; Duke, 1984). When inconsistent role expectations are presented to individuals and when there is a lack of clear-cut and consistent information regarding the rights, duties, and responsibilities of the role incumbent, then the role and its performance are laden with stress.

Some elements of the stress imposed upon public school teachers come from a contradiction between the socialization of teachers by colleges of education and the role complexities and ambiguities characteristic of large urban school districts. Preservice teachers come to expect that they will instruct and shape young minds, plan and develop curricula, evaluate students, and manage classrooms and maintain discipline. Some may even recognize that they are expected to serve as role models for children; act as surrogate parents, especially when the children's own parents abrogate such responsibilities; work with students of diverse ability levels, backgrounds, disadvantages, and problems; and combat racism, sexism, child abuse, drug abuse, and learning disabilities. However, they often assume that they will be granted the professional autonomy to exert control over the roles they are assigned to perform. Some investigators—such as Sarason, Davidson, and Blatt (1962), Sarason (1977 and 1978–79), and Duke (1984)—see colleges of education as failing to prepare preservice teachers for the "real world of teaching," in which autonomy is significantly restricted. Others, such as Bartholomew (1976) and Ginsburg (forthcoming), blame the modularization and compartmentalization of knowledge in colleges of education, which separate learning from practice, thus sufficiently "deskilling" teachers (a term in vogue in some colleges of education) so that they are unable to generalize what they have been taught from setting to setting.

Two central issues characterize the instruction of teachers in colleges of education: the development within the role incumbent of an ideology that defines as essential the shaping and molding of young minds, and a methodology (pedagogy) by which such teaching goals may be attained. The training of teachers is predicated upon two conditions: that there is a cadre of eager students and a sufficient degree of control over and autonomy within the interaction setting to plan curricula, instruct and evaluate students, and manage the classroom. Overcrowded, understaffed urban schools with sometimes less than eager students, combined with a complex bureaucracy which separates policy formation from policy implementation, significantly compromise the teachers' capacity to perform effectively. When students in a classroom are functioning at diverse grade levels, partly as a consequence of social promotion policies, the teachers' capacity to exert control over the delivery of a body of information is compromised. When students challenge the authority of teachers in and out of the classroom, control over the methodologies of curricula planning, information delivery, student evaluation, and classroom management is likewise weakened.

Policies which determine textbooks, course content, and even the style by which information is delivered are also removed from teacher's control. Teachers are rarely told much in advance that field trips, in-service activities, or other interruptions to the teaching routine are to occur. Under desegregation mandates, teachers also have no control over where or when they may be assigned to another school. Furthermore, as Cherniss, Egnatios, and Wacker (1976) have observed, there is a difference between the new methodologies created and taught at colleges of education and those permitted by school boards, district administrators, and principals, most of whom are committed to older techniques. Interacting with a multitude of students, parents, colleagues, and administrators, each of whom has different problems and makes different demands, requires that the teacher make quick, personal responses to individuals who may have unpredictable problems. However, because many of the interactions have implications for school policy and even for new policy formation, teachers are rarely permitted to make the required "command decisions" called for by the circumstances. Rather, decisions must work their way down the hierarchy, while the teacher is blamed by the client (student or parent) for being uncaring, inept, or unwilling to make decisions. Compounding this situation further is the movement toward greater student and teacher accountability, which has escalated the number of forms and reports a teacher needs to complete and hence the number of superiors and offices to which the teacher is held accountable. This increase in workload has not been accompanied by an increase in the amount of time in which he or she has to complete such paperwork. Such is the stress-laden environment of the urban public school.

Stress and Illness

Prolonged stress not only leads to role alienation and burnout, but also leads to illness behavior. A vast outpouring of medical sociology has examined the role of stress as an intervening variable in a causal chain between environmental factors (called "stressors") and the onset of disease. Stress has often been implicated in a variety of pathological processes, from heart disease and ulcers to anxiety and sleeplessness (see Jenkins, 1971; Sales and House, 1971; Caplan, 1971; Caplan and French, 1968; and Dohrenwend and Dohrenwend, 1974). The pioneering work of Cannon (1929), Selye (1936), and Meyer (1951) attribute great importance to the sociocultural and social-structural factors as determinants of illness probability. Theoretically, a general adaptation syndrome operates such that environmental factors trigger overreactions in the organism which eventually weaken the body and lead to illness behavior.

Various researchers have found that employees with poor occupational self-esteem, those who find their jobs too dull or too full of unexpected crises, are more likely to seek medical care (French, 1965; Caplan, 1971). Jenkins (1971) found higher rates of coronary risk among workers who had to attend to tedious detail, who received little recognition or praise from their supervisors, or had poor relationships with their co-workers. Additional work by Sales and House (1971) has corroborated these findings, as have Phillips and Lee (1980) in their study of middle school teachers.

That illness behavior is associated with stress among workers who are not given reinforcement by their supervisors strikes a responsive chord among public school teachers in urban settings. In its review of the desegregation literature, the National Institute of Education indicated that urban schools are often characterized by little interaction among teachers and little collegiality between the principal and the teachers (1976). Nobit (1979 contends that the principal is often aloof and neither feels the need to obey the rules he lays down for others to follow nor to praise teachers who are doing their job.

Social Support

Stress need not be overwhelming, nor is burnout automatic in public schools. Social support systems have often been cited in the medical sociology literature as buffers between stressors and the expected outcomes of stress, including illness and burnout. The literature emphasizes a tripartite stress-buffering social support system comprising supervisor support, co-worker support, and family and friend support (see La-Rocco, House, and French, 1980; and Kaplan, 1983). The present investigation emphasizes a model of principal support as the buffer between stress and its negative consequences, although peer influences (from other teachers) will also be examined. The emphasis on the principal is informed by three conditions of urban education.[1] First, unlike supervisors in other work settings where stress studies have been conducted, the principal in urban schools often has considerable power and autonomy in the operation of the school, the selection of faculty, and the control over the work activities assigned to teachers. In fact, schools are often analogous to little fiefdoms controlled by the principal. Second, previous research has strongly pointed to the dominant role of the principal in making a teacher feel wanted or unwanted and in encouraging or retarding turnover (Stapleton, Croft, and Frankiewicz, 1979; Fulcher,

1970; Hearn, 1971, 1974; Conklyn, 1976). Finally, school policies aimed at buffering stress can most economically be focused upon the activities of the principal.

Schools differ in the degree to which the factors producing stress, alienation, and the desire to quit exist. While all schools separate policy formation functions from policy implementation functions, and while every school has a number of students who are uncommitted to their education, there is little reason to expect that stress level or stress management is constant across schools. Dworkin (1980) enumerates the characteristics of teachers who are most likely to want to quit. These individuals tend to be younger than their colleagues who do not want to quit, tend to be white and from middle-class origins, and tend to be assigned to schools whose recial compositions differ significantly from what they desire. Maslach (1978a) and Cherniss (1980) note that younger employees are more susceptible to stress than are older employees because the former bring to the job more enthusiasm and are therefore more likely to have that enthusiasm crushed. Perhaps the waning of ebullience is a coping mechanism which makes stress less devastating. Cherniss argues that older, more experienced employees have learned to work the system to their benefit—have learned to survive. Of course, the difference between the younger and the older cohort could be merely the impact of selection effects, with the older cohort having been attenuated by the loss of its more idealistic members.

It is to be expected that older and more experienced teachers, teachers assigned to schools where they are not isolated, minority teachers, and teachers from working class backgrounds will also report lower levels of stress then their younger, majority-group, middle-class, racially isolated counterparts. It is also expected that illness behavior reported by teachers will vary with the reported stress levels in the school. Finally, it is expected that in schools where the principal is actively supporting the teachers, levels of reported stress will be lower or the negative consequences of stress, including burnout, illness, and lowered commitment, will be mitigated.

The Study

During the 1981–82 academic year, a sample of 291 teachers was collected by Telschow and Dworkin. Ninety-one of the teachers in the new sample had been in the earlier study reported in the previous chapter. The study was sponsored by the Houston Federation of Teachers (HFT) and addressed the union's concern over the levels of stress, illness, and violence against teachers that were felt to exist in the Houston public schools. This chapter is a reanalysis of the data reported to the union by Telschow (1982). In many cases, newly constructed variables are included.

The union sample is not as representative of the whole school district's teaching population as is the sample in chapter 2, nor is it a random sample of public school teachers. Rather, as a study conducted for the union, the sampling is limited to union members. Since it reflects the union membership, the sample of 291 teachers is disproportionately composed of junior high, middle school, and senior high school teachers. These individuals are more likely to have advanced degrees, to be somewhat older, to be male, and to demonstrate a higher level of professional identification and commitment to teaching than their nonunion counterparts (see Fox and Wince, 1976; Donnenworth and Cox, 1978; and Falk, Grimes, and Lord, 1982). Table 3.1 presents the comparisons among the school district population, the 1977 sample discussed in the previous chapter, and the HFT union sample.

The Houston Federation of Teachers provided us with a list of their members. Originally all 1,483 individuals were to be sent questionnaires; however, only 794 were considered by the union to be eligible to receive questionnaires. Ineligibility was based upon four factors: (1) being a member of HFT but no longer a teacher; (2) being a member of HFT but not teaching in the Houston Independent School District; (3) being a member of HFT but not certified to teach classes; and (4) being no longer a member of the union. We would have prefered to include categories 1 and 4 in the sample, but union officials objected. Of the 794 members sent questionnaires, only 37 percent (or 291 individuals) returned them, despite two call-back notices. The union assured us that our return rate was actually better than they normally obtain from their membership. As a result of the exclusions and refusals, the obtained sample is that of Houston Independent School District teachers who are union members and who have not left teaching. Examination of the lists of their exit interviews since the data collection reveals that none of the teachers in the union sample has left teaching. It is therefore a plausible sample upon which to examine the impact of stress, burnout, and social support among those who stay in teaching.

As is evident from table 3.1, the union sample is not representative of the district as a whole or of the initial Singleton Ratio sample. The HFT sample has almost half again as many males as does either the first sample of the district population. However, the membership is representative of the union, which has 31 percent male membership. The HFT sample is also composed of fewer minority group members than district

Table 3.1

Comparison of Teacher Sample with District Population

Variable	District population (N = 11,961)	Singleton Ratio sample (N = 3,444)	HFT sample (N = 291)
Sex, % male	19.8	18.2	31.6
Race* % black	34.9	28.9	27.8
% brown	4.4	3.0	5.2
% white	60.2	67.5	64.9
Age, median	38.6	38.4	35.8
Years teaching, median	10.1	10.0	10.1
Years in HISD, median	8.1	8.0	8.1
Grade level			
% elementary	54.6	55.5	35.7
% junior high	21.7	20.9	19.9
% senior high	22.4	22.5	41.2
% other	1.3	1.1	2.8
Education			
% B.A. or some graduate	74.5	69.7	46.4
% M.A.	25.3	27.6	50.5
% Ph.D., Ed.D.	0.2	0.1	3.1
Contract			
% continuing	64.9	69.9	76.9
% probation	22.8	20.8	23.1
% monthly	10.9	7.8	0
% no contract	1.3	1.3	0

*Oriental teachers are deleted from all analyses because of their small population size in the district.

population, just as is the union itself, which is 63 percent white. The HFT sample is somewhat younger than the district population or the Singleton Ration sample, for the following reasons. Under the Singleton Ratio, a teacher who quits must be replaced by someone of the same race. The district tends to replace teachers who quit with neophytes. Because white teachers are much more likely to quit than black teachers and hence are more likely to be replaced with neophytes, a sample with a higher percentage of white teachers will also be a younger sample. Furthermore, participation in a "somewhat radical" union is more characteristic of younger teachers than of older ones. The total years of teaching experience and the years of experience in the Houston Independent School District, however, are representative of the district population and of the Singleton Ratio sample.

Education and grade level or assignment clearly demonstrate that the HFT sample is a secondary school sample. While the entire district is made up of 54.6 percent elementary school teachers, slightly over one-third of the HFT sample are in elementary grades. The HFT sample is also twice as likely to have the M.A. degree than the district as a whole or the Singleton Ratio sample. Furthermore, the HFT sample is composed of a higher percentage of tenured employees, despite the younger age of the sample.

Although this new sample is not representative of the previous sample or of the district as a whole, it nonetheless provides a valuable opportunity to examine factors which may reduce the negative effects of stress. If it can be shown that stress levels can be moderated or the negative consequences of stress can be mitigated in this sample, which fits the profile of the most vulnerable group of teachers (younger, better-educated, majority-group members; see Dworkin, 1980), then it can be argued that the mechanism of social support will have at least an equal impact upon the larger population of teachers.

The Measurement of Stress

Prolonged intense interaction in settings which are emotionally charged produces stress and ultimately role alienation and burnout (Schwab and Iwanicki, 1982). To generate policies geared toward improving the quality of life for public school teachers, role-specific indices of stress are needed; it is not sufficient to rely upon generalized indicators. Therefore, the widely used inventories of stressful life events (for example, Holmes and Rahe, 1967; Dohrenwend and Dohrenwend, 1974; or Lazarus, 1966, 1971) are illsuited to the present needs. Such generalized measures encompass the experiences of all actors, and do not focus upon the tasks which make up a specific role performance.

A role-specific measure of stress needs to consider the manifold tasks, role-sets, and demands placed upon an actor. It must also itemize the stressors associated with each task, role-set, and demand. The role of public school teacher encompasses much: instructing and socializing students of diverse backgrounds; interacting with colleagues, administrators, and parents; and contending with the consequences of tight fiscal management, including inadequate supplies, relatively low pay, overcrowded classrooms, and a deteriorating physical plant.

Teachers were asked to indicate the personally felt level of stress associated with each of the issues and situations. A forced-choice method was used in which the teacher indicated no stress, a low stress level, a moderate stress level, or a high stress level for each item. The responses were coded from 1.0 for no stress to 4.0 for high stress. Table 3.2 presents the means and standard deviations for each of the fifteen potential stressors.

Table 3.2
Means and Standard Deviations for Each Stressor

Stressor	X	s.d.
Classroom teaching	2.491	0.924
Teaching preparation	2.388	0.991
Teaching off level	2.929	1.015
Teaching load	3.003	1.000
Supplies and resources	2.774	0.948
Discipline in class	2.831	0.951
Discipline out of class	3.056	0.984
Nonteaching duties	2.777	1.000
Interacting with administration	2.870	0.972
Interacting with teachers	1.860	0.806
Interacting with parents	2.326	0.905
Salary	3.194	0.925
Job security	2.042	1.011
Job benefits	2.936	1.036
Building condition	2.587	1.032

Generally speaking, the teachers reported low to moderate levels of stress for the fifteen items. However, the highest levels of stress are associated with salary and benefits; student discipline, especially outside the classroom; teaching load; and interaction with administrators. The lowest level of stress is associated with interactions with other teachers, and to a lesser degree, job security.

That salary and benefits are a source of stress is no surprise because these teachers are members of a union. Furthermore, on the basis of a survey of teacher attitudes enumerated by Gallup for *Phi Delta Kappan*, Elam and Gough (1980) report that school financing and the associated issues of teacher salaries and benefits are the top problems facing American schools (62.2 percent of the teachers in the poll ranked the fiscal area as the number-one problem). That is, teachers are worried about decreasing school resources, as well as salaries which do not keep pace with the cost of living. However, as Chapter 2 demonstrated, low salaries are not the cause of teacher turnover or burnout.

Likewise, issues of student discipline are not unexpected. Teachers have complained that the school board has been unresponsive and unconcerned about attacks on teaching personnel. The mass media have focused attention upon the issue, and *The Safe School Study Report* (1978) presented to Congress by the National Institute of Education describes the public schools in urban areas as dangerous places. Elam and Gough (1980) report that discipline is the second most often cited problem facing American schools, as perceived by teachers (33.2 percent ranked this as the top problem).

Actual teaching duties and the necessary preparation for those duties are not particularly stressful, except in instances involving the teaching of students who are significantly off grade level. Presumably these instances are an indictment of classroom heterogeneity caused by inadequate screening and tracking procedures, social promotion, and the mixing of gifted and slow learners in the same class.

Another source of stress comes from interactions with administrators. Caram (1982) and Caram, Dworkin, and Croft (1983) note that the principal's role as faculty evaluator is significantly associated with teacher alienation and quitting behavior. Likewise, in the previous chapter, a difference score between principal's administrative style and that preferred by the teacher affected burnout, plans to quit, and actual quitting behavior. That principals are charged with evaluating teacher performance and that some principals use every interaction as a data point for evaluation may be a stressor for the teachers in the present sample.

How Uniform Is Teacher Stress?

Are the responses to the stress items homogeneous across teacher groups and school settings? Are certain school environments and teacher categories more prone to experience or report stress? To assess the uniformity of stress, comparisons were run by race, sex, level of assignment, and race of the student body in the assigned school for each of the stress items. To facilitate the analysis, the response categories for the stress items were collapsed into low stress (responses of "none" and "low") and high stress (responses of "medium" and "high"). The race of the student body was determined by the following criteria: schools in which 50 percent or more of the students were black were defined as "black schools;" schools in which 50 percent or more of the students were brown were defined as "brown schools;" and schools in which 50 percent or more of the students were white were defined as "white schools." Schools in which no group of students approached 50 percent of the student body were defined as "balanced schools." Table 3.3 presents the results of the comparisons.

As is shown in table 3.3, female teachers report significantly more stress associated with the total work load and with inadequacy of supplies than do male teachers. The concentration of female teachers in the elementary grades helps to account for sex differences in stress caused by work load. Teachers in elementary schools likewise report more overall stress than do teachers in other schools. In an elementary school the duties of a teacher are less circumscribed. The students are less well socialized, more dependent upon the teacher as a surrogate parent, and have shorter attention spans than do children in higher grades. That supply shortages are more of a stressor for female teachers than for male teachers may not simply be due to differences in teacher concerns over resources. Rather, the differences may again be a function of the concentration of women in elementary grades, since that difference also emerges at the grade level variable. Elementary schools need to supply children with more expendable resources (pencils, paper, paints, etc.) than do higher grades. Higher grade levels use more durable resources, including lab equipment, books, computers, and microscopes, and require the students to provide their own expendables. Since men are more concentrated in secondary schools than in primary schools, sex differences in supplies as a source of stress appears to be a grade level effect rather than a true gender effect.

Significant differences exist among the stress levels reported by different racial groups of teachers. On almost every item, white teachers report more stress than do black or brown teachers, although statistical significance is reached only on the two discipline items. It should be noted that while significant differences are not obtained on the other racial comparisons, many approach significance (p < .10).

On several of the items, significant differences are found in comparisons among grade levels. Usually elementary school teaching is seen as the most stressful, especially in terms of teaching preparation, teaching load, classroom discipline, interaction with administrators, and interaction with parents. Teaching small children, as noted earlier, is draining. They cry, they have a shorter attention span, they are less well socialized, and they continually demand the attention of the teacher. The teacher must work harder at both preparing study materials and amusing the students. Moreover, elementary schools are small in scale, often having no more than twenty faculty and three to five hundred students.

Table 3.3

Significance of Difference within Teacher Category and School Settings for Each Source of Stress

Category or setting	CT	TP	TOL	TL	SR	DIC	DOC	NTD	IA	IT	IP	S	JS	JB	BC
Sex of teacher															
Male	45.6	36.7	64.4	59.6	55.7	61.8	73.3	64.0	64.0	21.6	36.4	82.0	33.3	67.0	50.0
Female	50.3	46.9	67.9	74.6	66.7	68.2	72.3	62.2	65.8	18.3	45.7	75.9	27.6	68.2	55.1
Significance	ns	ns	ns	.01	.05	ns	ns	ns	ns	ns	ns	ns	ns	ns	ns
Race of teacher															
White	55.4	48.1	68.8	74.9	65.9	69.4	76.9	63.8	69.0	19.3	43.5	78.0	28.2	69.9	55.9
Black	37.2	38.5	65.8	59.0	58.4	58.4	61.5	67.1	59.7	20.8	42.3	76.6	29.9	67.1	51.9
Brown	40.0	33.3	53.3	66.7	46.7	60.0	66.7	33.3	53.3	20.0	40.0	80.0	33.3	46.7	33.3
Significance	ns	ns	ns	ns	ns	.003	.015	ns	ns	ns	ns	ns	ns	ns	ns
Grade level taught															
Elementary	56.9	58.3	68.3	71.6	72.6	76.2	71.8	61.4	73.5	24.3	56.3	76.5	34.0	71.6	57.3
Jr./middle	49.1	37.5	82.1	60.7	61.8	73.2	80.4	71.4	59.1	19.9	44.6	78.6	32.1	67.9	45.5
Sr. high	42.0	35.0	58.3	66.7	61.2	56.7	70.6	61.0	61.7	16.0	31.9	78.2	24.2	64.4	54.6
Significance	ns	.01	.03	.05	.05	.002	ns	ns	.05	ns	.002	ns	ns	ns	ns
Race of student body															
Black	44.4	45.1	59.8	65.9	64.6	61.2	65.9	58.8	65.9	30.5	41.5	79.3	28.0	65.0	51.9
Brown	49.1	48.2	82.1	71.4	63.6	64.3	73.2	67.9	63.6	12.7	39.3	75.6	28.6	73.2	58.9
White	46.4	33.9	54.5	73.2	58.2	57.1	72.7	67.3	62.5	17.9	46.4	78.6	28.6	69.6	55.4
Balanced	52.4	48.8	72.1	75.0	65.1	79.1	81.4	78.0	63.6	20.5	45.2	78.0	34.9	58.1	45.5
Significance	ns	ns	.05	ns	ns	ns	ns	ns	ns	ns	ns	ns	ns	ns	ns

NOTE: CT = classroom teaching; TP = teaching preparation; TOL = teaching off level; TL = teaching load; SR = supplies and resources; DIC = discipline in class; DOC = discipline out of class; NTD = nonteaching duties; IA = interacting with administrators; IT = interacting with teachers; IP = interacting with parents; S = salary; JS = job security; JB = job benefits; BC = building condition; ns = not significant.

Thus, administrators have more opportunity to observe teachers, and this observation is a significant source of strain (Caram, Dworkin, and Croft, 1983). The smaller the group, the more frequent the interaction among members; the more frequent the interaction among members, some of whom are charged with evaluation, the greater the likelihood that individual teachers will often be evaluated. In addition, parents of elementary school children are more likely to interact with their childrens' teachers on a frequent basis than are parents of middle school or senior high school children. In elementary schools, children are more likely to have behavior problems which necessitate parent-teacher conferences rather than actions by the vice-principal or other agents of social control. Behavior problems are more often assumed to be related to health or home in the elementary grades. Furthermore, parents are more active in the PTO or the PTA during the elementary grades than in later grades. Increased interaction with parents is likely to lead to an increased sense of stress over such interactions. Finally, elementary school teachers interact intensely with the same small group of children each hour of the school day for an entire year, whereas junior and senior high school teachers have breaks between classes and off periods, and see different students each class period.

Disciplining students is a significant source of stress for junior high school teachers as well as for elementary school teachers. The children are physically strong but still act out their aggressions more often than do their high school counterparts. In fact, interviews with teachers during the Singleton Ratio study revealed that junior high school students are seen as the worst behaved of all students and are characterized with all of the negative imagery of adolescence.

In comparisons among schools with different student body racial compositions, only one difference emerges. Teaching students off grade level, which is associated with teaching in Mexican American schools, and to a lesser degree in balanced schools, is more stressful than in black or white schools. Like a Mexican American school, a balanced school has a sizeable Hispanic population. Schools with large Hispanic populations are often expected to provide a wider range of services for the community, the students, and their parents, many of whom do not speak English. Teachers must perform these greater services and hence have a greater and more stressful work load.

A Unidimensional Scale of Stress

To facilitate further analysis of teacher stress and to provide a single measure of role stress to be used in a model of stress, illness, and social support, the fifteen stress items were subjected to a principal axis factor analysis, with the significance of a factor loading set at $\geq$ .35 (Fruchter, 1954; Harman, 1967). All items loaded significantly on a single factor, and most factor loadings were between .51 and .71. (See appendix C, table C.2, for the results of the factor analysis. (It was concluded that the fifteen items represented part of a unitary construct named "teacher role stress." A scale of stress was constructed using factor score coeficients such that high scores indicated high levels of stress. The obtained Cronbach's alpha value of .855 was well within the acceptable limits for reliability.

Stress and Victimization

A reexamination of the data on victimization reported by Telschow (1982) provides a partial explanation for the higher levels of stress reported by white teachers on the discipline items. It also provides some insights into the higher levels of stress reported by junior high school teachers as compared with senior high school teachers. However, it leaves unexplained the high levels of stress associated with discipline reported by elementary school teachers. Telschow presented the respondents with an item worded, "I hesitate to confront misbehaving students for fear of my own safety." The correlation between agreement with the item and stress associated with disciplining students in one's own class was low but significant ($r = .100$; $b = .162$; s.e. $= .097$; $F = 19.444$). Interestingly, having actually been hurt by a student was not associated with fear of confrontation.

Item analysis confirms that only the teacher's race and grade level are associated with significant differences in victimization experiences, especially threat and assault. More white teachers than black teachers reported having money and other items stolen, being the targets of obscene gestures, being sworn at, receiving subtle threats, receiving overt threats of physical harm, being assaulted, and having their cars vandalized (see table 3.4). The percentage of Mexican American teachers reporting victimization was lower than for whites but higher than for blacks on all items except having money stolen and being assaulted. Clearly, then, victimization or fear of victimization serves as a factor in higher levels of stress more among white teachers than among others. Grade level also produced differences. More teachers in middle and junior high schools reported being subjected to obsenity, swearing, subtle threats, threats of physical harm, and vandalization of their automobiles than did elementary school teachers. Senior high school teachers were approximately midway between the two other groups in such victimizations. Thus, while victimization may explain the higher levels of stress associated with discipline in the junior high/middle schools compared with senior high schools, it cannot explain the even higher levels of stress associated with discipline in the elementary schools. Perhaps a temper tantrum or the crying of a young child is as much a stressor for an elementary school teacher as the fear of retaliation by an older child is for a secondary school teacher.

One must keep in mind that there is no objective measure of actual victimization other than the teachers' reports. Perhaps a mechanism of selective perception or recall may account for the differences between majority and minority teachers. White, black, and brown teachers may actually experience the same amount of abuse, but black and brown teachers may be more likely to define questionable activities as normal student behavior not worthy of reporting, while white teachers may be more likely to be intimidated and offended by such behavior.

The victimization items indicate that there are fewer differences based on sex of teacher and racial composition of schools than on grade level and race of teacher (compare tables 3.4 and 3.5). Although males report victimization on all items more often than females, statistical significance is reached only on three items: obscene gestures, threats of physical harm, and vandalism of a car. Nevertheless, females report higher levels of stress associated with the teaching role than do males, although statistical significance is obtained on only two of fifteen items (see table 3.3). Thus, females are generally more stressed than are males but report lower levels of victimization than do males. Perhaps males, out of concern for their masculinity, are more likely to define the aspects of victimization as less stressful. Given the low percentage of teachers who have suffered injuries needing medical attention (4.5 percent of the males and 4.1 percent of the females), it is also possible that males have a different perception of the actual risks involved in confrontations with students, and are thus less stressed. Furthermore, because a greater percentage of the female teachers than male teachers are physically weaker than their older students, the perception of vulnerability and the fear of victimization may be more powerful to them.

Racial differences between teachers are present on only two of the victimization items: minor assaults (medical attention unnecessary) and vandalism to a car. In both instances, the highest rate of victimization occurs in brown schools. However, the race of the school's student body accounts for only one difference in level of stress reported. Brown and balanced schools are associated with higher stress due to teaching students who are off grade level (table 3.3).

If one selects the victimization items which are most likely to be stressful[2] and divides the sample of teachers according to reports of the

Table 3.4
Race and Grade Level Comparisons of Victimization Items
(Percentage Reporting Victimization by Students in Past Year)

Item	Racial group				Grade level			
	White (N=183)	Black (N=79)	Brown (N=15)	p	Elementary (N=101)	Jr/middle (N=56)	Sr high (N=120)	p
Money stolen	45.1	23.4	46.7	.004	44.0	36.8	39.3	ns
Other items stolen	80.8	46.8	66.7	.000	63.4	71.9	75.6	ns
Obscene gestures	58.7	35.9	40.0	.002	44.6	64.9	51.7	.049
Sworn at	68.3	36.8	46.7	.000	48.5	70.2	64.1	.012
Unspecific subtle threats	62.1	40.0	53.3	.005	39.6	73.2	63.8	.000
Threats of physical harm	41.3	20.5	26.7	.006	25.0	45.6	41.4	.011
Minor assault	14.2	3.8	14.3	.050	9.9	21.4	9.4	.050
Major assault	4.9	2.6	6.7	ns	5.0	3.6	4.1	ns
Car vandalized	43.9	26.0	33.3	.024	30.0	50.0	40.2	.042

Table 3.5

Sex and Race of School Comparisons of Victimization Items
(Percentage Reporting Victimization by Students in Past Year)

Item	Sex			Race of school				
	Male (N=90)	Female (N=194)	p	Black (N=83)	Brown (N=56)	White (N=56)	Balanced (N=45)	p
Money stolen	34.4	42.1	ns	39.5	42.9	29.1	46.5	ns
Other items stolen	77.5	67.9	ns	62.7	78.2	73.2	68.2	ns
Obscene gestures	62.9	46.9	.020	50.6	51.8	51.8	51.1	ns
Sworn at	67.0	55.7	ns	56.1	64.3	65.5	47.7	ns
Unspecific subtle threats	64.8	52.6	ns	56.1	56.4	54.5	55.8	ns
Threats of physical harm	50.6	29.3	.001	35.8	38.2	34.5	29.5	ns
Minor assault	16.1	9.8	ns	12.7	19.6	5.5	4.4	.043
Major assault	4.5	4.1	ns	4.9	5.5	5.4	0.0	ns
Car vandalized	48.8	33.9	.025	31.3	54.5	37.7	35.6	.048

NOTE: ns = not significant.

occurances of these stressors, it is possible to develop an analysis of variance design which examines the roles of victimization, teacher's sex and race, race of school, and grade level taught on the variance in stress. An initial analysis of variance indicated that race of school and teacher's sex accounted for no significant variance in stress. A second analysis of variance and an accompanying multiple classification analysis did display the significance of victimization, race of teacher, and grade level taught for teacher stress. The results of that analysis of variance are presented in table 3.6.

Table 3.6
Analysis of Variance of Stress by Victimization, Race, and Grade Level

Source of variation	S.S.	d.f.	M.S.	F	p
Main effects	13.840	5	2.768	5.115	.000
Victimization	6.021	1	6.021	11.126	.001
Race	3.731	2	1.866	3.447	.034
Grade level	4.689	2	2.345	4.333	.014
2-way interact.	4.734	8	0.592	1.093	ns
3-way interact.	0.228	3	0.076	0.141	ns
Explained	18.802	16	1.175	2.171	.007
Residual	120.139	222	0.054		
Total	138.941	238	0.584		

MULTIPLE CLASSIFICATION ANALYSIS

	N	Unadjusted Deviation	Eta	Adjusted Deviation	Beta
Victimization					
Yes	146	-.14		-.13	
No	93	.21		.21	
			.22		.21
Race					
White	165	.08		.09	
Black	61	-.19		-.20	
Brown	13	-.16		-.18	
			.16		.17
Grade level					
Elementary	91	.08		.16	
Jr/middle	49	.10		.04	
Senior	99	-.12		-.16	
			.13		.19
		R = .316	$R^2 = .100$		

NOTE: ns = not significant.

Significant main effects are found for each of the factors: victimization, grade level and race in descending order. Victims report significantly higher levels of stress than do nonvictims; whites report higher levels
of stress than do blacks or browns; and elementary, junior high/middle
school teachers report higher levels than do senior high school teachers.
However, no significant interaction effects exist. Thus, no combination
of victimization, race, or grade level produces significantly different
levels of stress. It must be acknowledged, however, that the beta's
associated with the independent variables are low (.21 for victimization;
.17 for race; and .19 for grade level), with a multiple R of .316 (R^2 =
.100).

The failure of sex of teacher and racial composition of student body
to account for a significant amount of variance in stress suggests that the
earlier observations, which used single stress items, need to be modified.
Although women reported more stress in the teaching role than did men
on two of the items, the stress measure, when scaled, washed out such
differences. Furthermore, that no significant difference in stress could be
explained by race of school argues strongly against the school district's
plan to give higher "combat pay" to teachers in minority schools
because their work is more stressful and dangerous.

Stress and Illness: The Magnitude in the Sample

The preponderance of evidence from medical sociology, including
that reported earlier in this chapter, suggests that one outcome of stress is
increased levels of illness behavior. On the basis of *The Safe School
Study Report* (National Institute of Education, 1978), a single,
somewhat crude measure of stress-induced illness behavior was used in
the study for the Houston Federation of Teachers. Teachers were asked
whether they had "as a teacher" experienced any illnesses which they
believed were due to "on-the-job stress." The frequency of illnesses
ascribed to stress was determined by a three-point scale of "never,"
"sometimes," and "often." Teachers were also asked to indicate the
severity of such illnesses by indicating how often the illnesses needed
medical attention. The response options were "no medical attention
ever," "sometimes medical attention needed," and "often medical attention needed." The cross-classification of the two sets of questions
provides an index of perceived illness due to stress. The range of
responses then would be from "never ill" and "no medical attention
needed" to "often ill" and "often needing medical attention." It must
be recognized that no attempt was made to determine what kinds of illnesses occurred, nor whether the illnesses actually were induced by work

stress. We could only indicate the extent to which the teachers believed that stress on the job produced illness behavior.

All 291 teachers reported at least some stress-induced illness behavior associated with the teaching role. However, 25.4 percent reported that they were sometimes ill from stress but never needed medical attention; another 55.6 percent indicated that they were sometimes ill from stress and sometimes needed medical attention; 6.3 percent indicated that they were sometimes ill and often needed medical attention; 1 percent reported that they were often ill and needed no medical attention, another 1 percent reported that they were often ill and sometimes needed medical attention; and 10.7 percent indicated that they were often ill from stress and often needed medical attention.

Social Buffering

If stress is created by social interactions, then it can also be mitigated by social mechanisms. Studies cited earlier, especially the work of LaRocco, House, and French (1980) and Kaplan (1983), have demonstrated the crucial role that social support systems play in helping individuals cope with stress and stressors. This section assembles a measure of social support to be used later in a test of the links among social buffering, stress, illness, victimization, and burnout.

An index of social buffering can be constructed from the cross-classification of two sets of indices: a measure of the extent to which the principal provides support to his or her faculty, and a measure of the perceived power and influence of the principal in relations with superordinates. The first is an estimate of the extent to which the principal tries to be helpful and collegial, and the second is a measure of the likelihood that such attempts could ameliorate the stresses reported by teachers. The support items were adopted from a series of scales on teacher morale used by Coughlan (1970). Teachers responded to each item with a five-category Likert format. The items used are presented below.[3]

"My principal shows little initiative in seeking ways to improve our work."

"I think my work performance is appraised and evaluated fairly in this school."

"I'm rarely told whether or not I'm doing good work."

"The principal of this school is active in both the setting and application of rules for students."

"I am given sufficient opportunity to share in planning the instructional program."

"The procedures in this school for dealing with staff grievances and complaints are fair."

The social support items were subjected to a principal axis factor analysis, which yielded one factor, with all items correlated with the factor between .40 and .74. The Cronbach's alpha for the six-item scale was .751, which is within acceptable limits. The factor score coefficients obtained from the factor analysis were subsequently used to construct a perceived social support score for each teacher. (Table C.3, appendix C, presents the interitem corelations and factor loading for the six-item scale.)

The second axis of the social buffering measure involves the perception by teachers that their principal is influential in the management of the school. Teachers were asked, "In general, how much influence do you think that your principal has in determining the daily education matters (curriculum, activities, and policies) in the school in which you teach? Teachers responded by indicating "a great deal of influence" to "no influence at all."

Combining the responses to the influence item with the support scale scores provides four categories of principals: influential principals who are seen as supportive; influential principals who are seen as unsupportive; uninfluential principals who are seen as supportive; and uninfluential principals who are seen as unsupportive. We should expect that a principal who is seen as influential but unsupportive will be associated with the highest levels of teacher burnout, plans to quit teaching, and stress-induced illness. By constrast, the principal who is seen as supportive and influential should be associated with the lowest levels of burnout, plans to quit teaching, and stress-induced illness behavior on the part of teachers. Among principals who are seen as uninfluential, higher levels of burnout, plans to quit teaching, and stress-induced illness should occur among teachers assigned to those who are seen as unsupportive than among teachers who are assigned to those who are seen as supportive.

Before testing the effect of social buffering by a principal, it must be determined whether stress levels are similar across the four groups of principals. If actual stress associated with the teaching role is higher among teachers with unsupportive principals, it would be difficult to determine whether social support influences burnout, plans to quit, and illness behavior or whether differences are due merely to overall differences in stress levels. A one-way analysis of variance, comparing the stress scores for teachers assigned to the four constructed types of principals, resolved the problem. There are no significant differencs in the stress levels reported by teachers assigned to each of the four groups of principals. The obtained F value was 1.96 (d.f. = 3/266), and the associated probability of such differences occuring by chance alone was .123.

Does Social Buffering Reduce Illness?

Since stress levels are homogeneous across the four types of principals, could illness which is stress induced (or perceived by the teachers as stress induced) nonetheless be lower in the presence of social buffering (as the medical sociology literature suggests)? That is, are there differences in the ability of teachers to cope with work-related stress when they have supportive and/or influential administrators? A one-way analysis of variance was computed to determine the significance of differences among the four types of principals. The obtained F value was 2.03 (d.f. = 3/263), and the associated probability of such differences occurring by chance was .110.

Reported stress-induced illness is not reduced by social buffering provided by the principal. There are two explanations for this finding, which runs counter to the studies by LaRocco, House, and French (1980) and many others. First, the reported levels of illness among the teachers were generally low enough and not sufficiently serious enough (needing medical attention) that there may not have been sufficient variance to be explained by social buffering. Second, such a crude index of stress-induced illness may not be sensitive enough to differentiate among illness behavior which is unrelated to job stress (including that which is associated with stress from nonwork roles), illness which is a function of the interactions between work and nonwork stressors, and illness which has nonsocial causes.

Social Buffering, Burnout, and Plans To Quit Teaching

Although the perception of the influence and support of the principal is unassociated with differences in stress levels or with illness behavior, is it associated with teacher burnout and plans to quit teaching? Since burnout and plans to quit are more logically connected to the behavior of principals (see Stapleton, Croft, and Frankiewicz, 1979), we should expect that such work-related attitudes would be significantly affected by the perception of the principal's actions.

Two separate one-way analyses of variances were computed to determine the extent to which differences in burnout and in plans to quit teaching could be explained by social buffering provided by principals. The results of the two analyses are presented in tables 3.7 and 3.8. As these tables reveal, teachers who perceive that their principals are supportive are less burned out and less willing to quit teaching than those who perceive that their principals are unsupportive. However, the perception that the principal is uninfluential does not affect the level of burnout or plans to quit. A show of concern by the principal is sufficient. There are no significant differences in burnout or plans to quit teaching between teachers with principals who are influential and supportive and those with principals who are uninfluential and supportive. Likewise, there are no differences in the two dependent variables between teachers assigned to principals who are unsupportive and seen as influential and those whose principals are seen as unsupportive and uninfluential.

It is the content of the administrative support items which gives a clue to the nature of the impact of support on burnout and the intention to quit teaching. The support measure includes statements of the perception that the principal tries to improve the work and work conditions of

Table 3.7

One-Way Analysis of Variance:
Burnout by Type of Administrative Support

Source of variance	S.S.	d.f.	M.S.	F	p
Between	21.789	3	7.263	9.749	.000
Within	195.937	263	0.745		
Total	217.726	266			

Contrast	Diff.	s.e. diff.	t	d.f.	p
No influence, no support vs. no influence, support	-.489	.164	-2.974	263	.003
No influence, no support vs. influence, no support	-.046	.136	-0.336	263	.737
No influence, no support vs. influence, support	-.667	.145	-4.589	263	.000
No influence, support vs. influence, no support	.444	.169	2.708	263	.007
No influence, support vs. influence, support	-.178	.172	-1.035	263	.302
Influence, no support vs. influence, support	-.622	.145	-4.298	263	.000

Table 3.8

One-Way Analysis of Variance:
Plans To Quit by Type of Administrative Support

Source of variance	S.S.	d.f.	M.S.	F	p
Between	29.545	3	9.848	5.816	.0007
Within	450.453	266	1.693		
Total	479.998	269			

Contrast	Diff.	s.e. diff.	t	d.f.	p
No influence, no support vs. no influence, support	.522	.246	2.127	266	.034
No influence, no support vs. influence, no support	.298	.203	1.468	266	.143
No influence, no support vs. influence, support	.891	.219	4.074	266	.000
No influence, support vs. influence, no support	-.524	.245	-2.138	266	.029
No influence, support vs. influence, support	.368	.257	1.431	266	.154
Influence, no support vs. influence, support	.592	.217	2.724	266	.007

the teachers, sets and enforces discipline for students, evaluates work fairly, provides adequate procedures for airing grievances, and supplies the teachers with feedback on how well they are doing. Even if the principal is seen as ineffective in overcoming problems introduced administratively from above, the principal who makes an effort for the teachers is telling them that he or she considers them significant individuals and considers their work important. Furthermore, by involving teachers in curriculum planning, the principal affords them some control over pedagogy. By working for their benefit and showing interest and respect for their efforts, the principal informs teachers that he or she thinks they are doing meaningful work. In essence, the supportive principal stems the loss of the ideology and methodology given to teachers in their college training, as discussed earlier, and thereby mitigates burnout. As I noted in the last chapter, a sense of meaninglessness, coupled with a sense of powerlessness, exacerbates the desire to quit teaching. If a sense of isolation is also present, the effect can be devastating on morale. The supportiveness of a principal retards both these destructive factors.

Disaggregating the Burnout Dimensions

How uniform is the effect of social buffering upon each alienating element of burnout? Are meaninglessness, powerlessness, isolation, and normlessness all affected in the same way by social support? One might think not. Table 3.9 presents the contrasts among types of principals for each of the elements of burnout. For meaninglessness, significant differences are found between supportive and unsupportive principals, regardless of their effectiveness. The simple act of support, regardless of effectiveness, is sufficient to retard a sense of meaninglessness. However, the pattern is less pronounced for a sense of powerlessness. Powerlessness levels are as high for the principal who is supportive but uninfluential as for the principal who is unsupportive but influential. Control over the various aspects of teaching is vested not only in the campus, but also in the area superintendent, the district administration, and the school board. Thus, the reduction of a sense of powerlessness depends not merely upon the principal's support, but also on some evidence of his or her effectiveness. In addition, the difference in the sense of powerlessness among teachers assigned to principals who are influential and supportive compared to uninfluential and supportive approaches statistical significance. Support may help reduce a sense of powerlessness, especially on local issues, but because school policy is controlled at many levels, a major reduction in the sense of powerlessness among teachers necessitates an effective and powerful administrator.

Isolation behaves in a similar manner as meaninglessness. Significantly lower levels of isolation are reported by teachers whose principals are supportive, regardless of the reported effectiveness of such principals. By including teachers in planning and by evaluating them fairly and praising their achievements, the principal is informing them that they are not alone—that someone cares.

Normlessness deviates somewhat from the pattern found for meaninglessness and isolation. Teachers who work for unsupportive principals report greater normlessness if the principal is uninfluential than if the principal is influential. Since the influential principal is likely to be able to control the school setting and thereby make the workplace more predictable, it is likely that the rules in such a setting are clearly delineated and predictable. Moeller (1964) reported that teachers often prefer to work in settings where the principal is highly bureaucratic and where the rules are clearly defined because such a setting produces greater predictability and minimizes surprises. In a similar vein, no significant difference in normlessness is found in comparisons between

Table 3.9

*Contrasts from the Analysis of Variance of the Elements of
Burnout and Alienation by Type of Administrative Support*

	Diff.	s.e. diff.	t	p
Variable: meaninglessness (d.f. = 267)				
-I, -S vs. -I, S	. .4011	.187	2.144	.027
-I, -S vs. I, -S	.0393	.156	0.252	ns
-I, -S vs. I, S	.4780	.168	2.849	.002
-I, S vs. I, -S	-.3752	.186	-2.017	.030
-I, S vs. I, S	.1634	.196	0.833	ns
I, -S vs. I, S	.4386	.167	2.628	.004
Variable: powerlessness (d.f. = 266)				
-I, -S vs. -I, S	. .4134	.170	2.438	.015
-I, -S vs. I, -S	.1593	.140	1.135	ns
-I, -S vs. I, S	.6825	.151	4.521	.000
-I, S vs. I, -S	-.2541	.169	-1.505	ns
-I, S vs. I, S	.2691	.178	1.514	ns
I, -S vs. I, S	.5232	.150	3.485	.001
Variable: isolation (d.f. = 265)				
-I, -S vs. -I, S	. .4162	.183	2.272	.024
-I, -S vs. I, -S	-.1420	.152	-0.934	ns
-I, -S vs. I, S	.5961	.163	3.656	.000
-I, S vs. I, -S	-.5581	.183	-3.054	.005
-I, S vs. I, S	.1800	.192	0.937	ns
I, -S vs. I, S	.7381	.631	4.963	.000
Variable: normlessness (d.f. = 266)				
-I, -S vs. -I, S	. .5891	.190	3.095	.002
-I, -S vs. I, -S	.3633	.156	2.324	.021
-I, -S vs. I, S	.6605	.168	3.928	.000
-I, S vs. I, -S	-.2258	.190	-1.191	ns
-I, S vs. I, S	.0714	.199	0.358	ns
I, -S vs. I, S	.2972	.167	1.777	ns

NOTE: I = influence; -I = no influence; S = support; -S = no support; ns = no significant difference.

the principal who is uninfluential and supportive and the principal who is influential and not supportive, nor in comparisons between the principal who is influential and unsupportive and the principal who is influential and supportive. Clearly, influence implies control over the school environment and in turn the likelihood that there is regularity and predictability in that environment. Regardless of whether or not the teachers feel that the rules operate to ease their jobs, the preference is for predictability.

A Causal Model of Social Buffering

I have demonstrated that the supportive principal significantly reduces the level of alienation and burnout and of intentions to quit teaching among his or her staff. This is true even though the level of stress was similar across each of the four constructed types of principals. However, what is the effect of the principal's support on the link between stress and burnout and stress and the desire to quit teaching? Is it possible that a supportive principal engenders a school environment in which stress is sufficiently buffered and dispersed so that it leads to minimal negative consequences for teachers?

To ascertain the impact of social support by the principal upon the link between stress and negative job attitudes, I shall offer four regression models, each using the variables presented in this chapter and also including one variable from the previous chapter that was found to be a significant factor in burnout: the locus of control index, externality. Each model controls for one of the four constructed types of principals. I assume that the constructed types represent a qualitative distinction not necessarily assignable to a continuum. Hence, four separate regressions are computed. This differs from the single, moderated regression approach in which a social buffering variable is added as an additional predictor and an increment of R^2 is assessed (see LaRocco, House, and French, 1980; and Kerlinger and Pedhazur, 1973).

The variables included in the models are teacher's race, sex, and locus of control (all actor traits), grade level and race of school (building characteristics), victimization, fear of confrontations with students, stress, stress-based illness, burnout, and plans to quit teaching. It is assumed that the actor traits and building characteristics act as exogenous variables which affect victimization and fear, and that these two variables in turn create stress. Stress then leads to burnout and intentions to quit teaching. Tested in a preliminary model was the variable of stress-based illness. However, it is unassociated with burnout, plans to quit teaching, and, as we observed earlier, even with stress.

Figure 3.1 displays the path models for the four types of principals. (The decomposition of the path models are presented in appendix E, table E.1.) As the path analysis were computed, variations developed in the structure of the models because links between variables changed for each type of principal. Separate path models are presented for illness behavior and for the link between burnout and plans to quit teaching. Nonetheless, there are certain similarities across models. In each model, burnout affects plans to quit teaching more than does any other variable. Illness behavior is not influenced by stress in any model, nor does illness affect burnout or plans to quit teaching. Finally, victimization is not a factor in creating stress. However, except where the principal is influential but unsupportive, victimization has a significant effect on illness.

The most dramatic aspect of the four models is the difference which emerges between supportive and unsupportive principals. When the principal is supportive, there is no significant path linking stress to burnout or plans to quit teaching. However, when the principal is unsupportive, burnout and plans to quit are influenced by stress. In addition, when the principal is supportive, a variable such as locus of control (external) rather then stress affects burnout and plans to quit teaching. Locus of control plays no role in burnout and plans to quit in instances where the principal is unsupportive.

The path models clearly point to another role that a supportive principal plays in the attitudes of teachers. A supportive principal not only reduces the level of burnout and the desire to quit teaching among the faculty, as we observed in tables 3.7 and 3.8, but also effectively breaks the link between stress and its negative consequences. This is true despite the similarity of stress levels across groups of teachers assigned to the four types of principals.

It is intriguing that stress is influential in creating burnout and the desire to quit teaching in settings where the principal is unsupportive, and that locus of control[4] triggers both attitudes when the principal is supportive. Expressed differently, some level of teacher burnout and the desire to quit teaching is likely to occur regardless of the behavior (or perceived behavior) of the principal. However, burnout is higher and more stress driven when the principal is seen as unsupportive. It is lower and more attributable to the personalities of the teachers and to confrontations with students when the principal is seen as supportive. Although burnout cannot be entirely eradicated by a supportive principal, it can be significantly reduced, and teachers can better cope with the stresses of the teaching role when the principal is supportive.

The Role of Peer Group Support

Earlier in this chapter I contended that the central agent of social buffering is the principal and that other teachers provide at best minimal assistance. Some researchers, including Stinnett and Henson (1982) and

FIGURE 3.1

PATH MODELS OF THE EFFECTS OF PRINCIPALS ON TEACHERS

TYPE I: PRINCIPAL UNINFLUENTIAL AND UNSUPPORTIVE

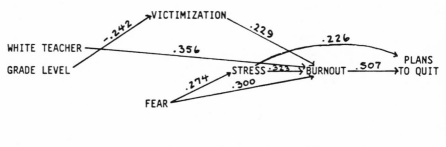

GRADE LEVEL —.242→ VICTIMIZATION —.439→ ILLNESS

TYPE II: PRINCIPAL UNINFLUENTIAL AND SUPPORTIVE

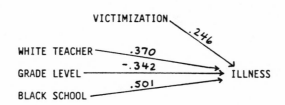

Duke (1984), suggest that in many settings peers (other teachers) and unions may play similar social buffering roles. Since a majority of the states in the Sun Belt, including Texas, limit the power of unions and grant them no legal right to take job actions, it is unlikely that unions

TYPE III: PRINCIPAL INFLUENTIAL AND UNSUPPORTIVE

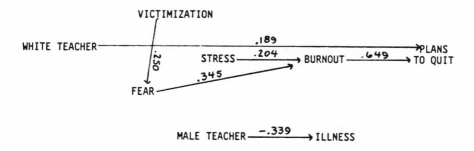

TYPE IV: PRINCIPAL INFLUENTIAL AND SUPPORTIVE

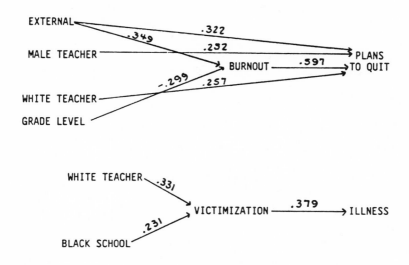

could play much of a buffering role. In fact, Dworkin et al. (1977) reported that the majority of teachers in the Houston Independent School District did not even depend upon their unions to inform them about school policies or the interpretation of those policies.

The study presented in this chapter did not have as rich a range of measures to assess buffering by peers as by principals. However, two items assessed the perceived level of cooperation and mutual support among teachers. When burnout was regressed on principal support, the effect was significant (beta = -.416) but when burnout was regressed on peer support, the effect was insignificant (beta = -.060). Entering both forms of support (principal and peer) into a regression caused the peer variable to fail to be included. Likewise, comparing the effect of stress on burnout under conditions of supportive and unsupportive peers led to a conclusion that peer support could not break the functional link between stress and burnout. The effect of stress upon burnout under the condition of a supportive peer was .329, and under an unsupportive peer it was .361. Both effects were significant. We must therefore conclude that peer support is a poor surrogate for principal support.

One reason for the failure of peer support to break the functional link between stress and burnout can be found in the dynamics of peer groups. If individuals are under considerable stress and feel alienated, and if they turn to individuals of the same status who are also under stress and feel alienated, each will reinforce and validate the perceptions of the other. Much research in the sociology of reference groups has shown that when one relies upon an internal reference group (a group of the same status as oneself), one tends to blame the system and call it illegitimate ("the school and principal are no good," "teaching is a crummy occupation"). By contrast, a trusted superordinate, as a supportive principal often is, can diffuse or buffer the stress and alienation (see, for example, Chafetz and Dworkin, 1986, for an elaboration of this issue in the development of social movements).

Summary And Policy Implications

The data collected on members of the Houston Federation of Teachers reveal that stress levels in the public school district tend to be moderate. However, stress is not uniformly felt by all groups of teachers or in all aspects of the teaching role. Teachers report that much of the stress they experience is associated with some intrinsic job factors such as student discipline and teaching students who are off grade level, as well as with extrinsic factors of the job such as salary and benefits. Black teachers tend to report stress less often than do white teachers, especially in matters of student discipline. There is a weak, but significant, association between fear of physical harm and stress over student discipline reported by all teachers, but especially by white teachers, even in white schools. Whether white teachers are more often singled out for abuse by students than are minority teachers is unknown. What is known is that they more often feel that they are the targets of abuse, especially obscene gestures, threats of assault, and actual assaults. Women are likewise more stressed by the need to discipline students than are men. Teachers who are racially isolated are more stressed than those who are not isolated. Finally, high school teachers are the least stressed of all groups of teachers.

Since a fear of abuse and victimization is central to the feelings of stress among many groups of teachers, a school policy directed toward mitigating aggression against teachers may help to reduce both the stress levels reported by teachers and the fear that some teachers have of disciplining their students. However, there is a caution. Telschow (1982) reported that teachers are most fearful of violence in schools where there is actually very little violence directed against them. She explained the apparent contradiction by a reference to the cognitive dissonance literature and the sociology of rumor (Shibutani, 1966). Boggs (1971) observed in her study of attitudes toward the police that fear of crime was most rampant in those neighborhoods which had little crime. When one is fearful and yet has no objective evidence to corroborate one's fears, rumors emerge to rationalize the fears. Teachers hear from the mass media and from their unions that school violence has escalated. If this violence has not occurred in the teachers' own school, rumors that it is imminent are likely to arise. In schools which have experienced violence against teachers, the administration has usually taken positive steps to control future violence. Furthermore, in these schools teachers are more likely to recognize situations which are potentially violent and to avoid them.

A key finding in this chapter has been the impact of the supportive principal on the relationships between stress, burnout, plans to quit teaching, and locus of control. When a principal is supportive and concerned and treats the teachers as colleagues, teacher burnout and plans to quit are reduced. Principal support is also crucial in breaking the link between stress and burnout, even if the principal is unable to influence policymakers to ameliorate the conditions faced by the teachers. Although some of the teachers assigned to a supportive principal may still experience burnout, they will do so because of more idiosyncratic variables, including personality factors (locus of control) and victimization. A supportive principal has the greatest effect on a teacher's sense of meaninglessness, reducing it significantly. A supportive principal who is also seen as influential with superordinates significantly reduces a teacher's sense of powerlessness.

I have argued in this and the previous chapter that burnout is an extreme form of role alienation in which the actor feels a sense of meaninglessness in the performance of his or her role and a sense of powerlessness to effect changes which might make the role performance more meaningful. The bureaucratization of urban public schools, with its separation of policy formation and policy implementation, takes from teachers a sense of their personal efficacy as professionals. The absence of enough students, parents, and other teachers who seem to care about education deprives the job of meaning. The principal who is supportive of teachers informs them that their work is appreciated. If that principal is also influential in making changes, then teacher idealism may linger, and a sense of meaningfulness and powerfulness may be afforded them. The principal who treats teachers as valuable colleagues retards burnout even if there remain significant levels of stress associated with the teaching role.

It is fortuitous that principals can affect teacher burnout with better management and human relations skills. There is an economy of scale afforded by this circumstance. It is easier for a school district to provide the necessary training for a few hundred principals to help them retard teacher burnout than to have to provide coping skills for thousands of teachers. It must be recognized, however, that burnout cannot be entirely eradicated. Some teachers, because of personality factors which I have enumerated or because of confrontations with students and parents, may still experience burnout. Thus, to expect very high rates of rekindled or continued enthusiasm among teachers is naive.

The teachers in this study reported that some of the stress they feel is a function of low teacher salaries. As Blauner (1964) and Mottaz (1981) have both observed, when workers feel that their work has no meaning and when they feel powerless, they turn to economic considerations to drive their work commitment. Although I do not offer a supportive principal as a functional alternative to better teacher salaries and working conditions, I would point out that in times of tight school fiscal policies, districts can ill afford to neglect teachers' need to feel that they are making a valuable contribution to their world and that they can affect some academic policies. There is, after all, a cost efficiency in retarding burnout and lost commitment.

Finally, it must be recognized that providing human relations skills to principals and encouraging them to be more supportive of their teachers may be too facile a solution. Principals are likely to treat teachers as colleagues if they actually respect those teachers and trust that they are competent. School boards and school districts are only willing to encourage collegiality among principals and teachers if they trust that the teachers merit respect. Citizens are likely to be supportive of greater power, control, and salaries for teachers as long as they are confident in the abilities of the teachers. Opinion polls have repeatedly shown that the public has an ever-declining trust in the schools and the abilities of teachers. As long as teachers are not trusted, they are likely to burn out, to be less committed to their students, to desire to quit teaching, and actually to quit teaching. In so doing, however, teachers reduce public trust in public education. There is a certain circularity to the problem.

4

The Impact of Teachers on Students

In the previous two chapters the focus of the analysis was upon the factors which affect teacher behaviors. I have developed and tested models which explain some of the variance in teacher burnout, plans to quit teaching, and actual quitting behavior. I have also explored support mechanisms which can break the link between teacher stress and teacher burnout. The present chapter represents a significant change in focus but is nevertheless a logical outgrowth of the preceding chapters. The unit of analysis now shifts from the teacher to the student who is instructed by that teacher. The goal of the present chapter is to develop and test models which will account for the impact of teacher burnout, intentions to quit, and actual quitting behavior upon student behavior. Specifically, I shall explore the role of the blocks of teacher and building variables developed previously upon students' academic achievement and attendance behavior.

It must be noted at the outset that the goal of the present chapter is not to account for all or most of the variance in student achievement and attendance behavior. Aside from a few polemicists, no investigator has proposed that teachers account for most or none of the variance in student behaviors. Rather, some argue that teacher attitudes and expectations are significant, while others argue that they are less so. Since I do not include peer variables and have not enumerated student attitudes and commitments to education, it is unlikely that I can do more than assess the magnitude of the role that teacher burnout plays in student achievement and attendance behavior. If that assessment can be made, then this chapter will have been successful.

Despite the plethora of research devoted to the effects of teachers and schools upon student achievement, there appears to be almost no

103

work which addresses the impact of teacher work commitment upon students. Previous research has either aggregated teacher demographics across campuses, thereby ignoring individual attitudes, or has examined the tendency of teachers to label certain children as more "preferable" (labeling behavior). Both approaches have assumed a homogeneity in teachers' commitment to their work. Nevertheless, a survey of school and home effects upon achievement will guide the development of my models.

Teachers and Their Students

The assessment of teacher and school effects on student performances has had an extensive history. Since the release of the Coleman report in 1966, few other questions have had such a profound influence on the direction of educational research. Generally speaking, this research has attempted to explain why poor people and members of racial and ethnic minorities do not perform as well on achievement tests as do more affluent people and members of the dominant group. Two stances have characterized the research on the effects of the school on student achievement. The first stance reflects a human capital–status attainment–meritocratic approach, which views the resources and abbilities that a student brings to a school as most essential and school and teacher variables as least essential. The second stance places the blame for minority and low-income students' diminished achievement on the education system—specifically, on labeling processes by teachers, tracking by counselors, and the insuffciency of the school resources offered to the poor.

Status Attainment–Human Captial–Meritocratic Explanations

The status attainment and human capital approaches to educational attainment bear a relationship to the theories by the same name used to explain labor market stratification and class mobility. The link between processes in the school and processes in the larger society has been well established, and represented a major impetus behind Title IV of the 1964 Civil Rights Act, the Brown Brothers decisions of 1954 and 1955, and the national study conducted by Coleman and his associates (1966). According to the status attainment and human capital model, individuals bring to the school setting human labor, resources, and abilities which are differentially valued and valuable. Children from low-income families, whose parents provide few educational resources and little enrichment, enter schools with real disadvantages which continue to hinder their academic development. Furthermore, these individuals may also have diminished abilities, either inherited or acquired as a function of poverty. Thus, differences in student achievement between rich and poor children and between minorities and majorities are seen as caused by the absence of human capital brought to school by the child. In essence, as Ryan (1971) has noted, the model blames the victim.

Coleman et al. (1966) observed that some of the differences in achievement between rich and poor and between black and white diminished in desegregated school settings. It was argued that by changing the environment for disadvantaged children, differences in human capital could be somewhat ameliorated. Unfortunately, subsequent studies have failed to confirm consistently Coleman's observations, especially when one removes the influence of living in an integrated neighborhood from the model (St. John, 1975). Nonetheless, the Coleman study encouraged a considerable increase in school busing for the purpose of attaining racial desegregation. (Ironically, the intent of the 1964 Civil Rights Act was not to encourage the transfer of students from school to school in order to attain racial balance, but to establish a color-blind assignment policy.) Busing was mandated and given the force of the Supreme Court's approval in the 1971 Swann et al. v. Charlotte-Mecklinburg decision. Also inspired by the human capital assumptions was the ideology of the War on Poverty advanced by Lyndon Johnson in the 1960s. Thus, there is a double consciousness associated with the human capital–status attainment model of educational attainment. On the one hand, it is argued that differences in educational achievement are not a function of the activities of the school, but rather endemic to poverty and minority status and to the "weaknessess" a child brings to school. On the other hand, those who endorse the model feel that it is the obligation of the school to ameliorate these inequalities, despite their continued observation that school effects account for little variance in student achievement (see, for example, Coleman, 1966; Hanushek, 1972; Mosteller and Moynihan, 1972; Alexander, Cook, and McDill, 1978; Alexander and Cook, 1982; Mayeske et al., 1969; Haller and Davis, 1981; Murnane, 1975; Jencks, 1972; and Jencks et al., 1972).

Labeling and Teacher Definition Explanations

Those studies which stress the role of labels and self-fulfilling prophecies on student achievement tend to rely upon microethnographic techniques or upon very small data sets. This research tradition began with the work of Rosenthal and Jacobson (1968) and includes studies by

Dusek (1975), Braun (1976), Cooper (1979), Rist (1970), Bowles and Gintis (1976), and Bowles and Levin (1968), as well as the work by Clifton (1981), Haller and Davis (1981), and Clifton et al. (1986). All these studies explore the extent to which teacher labels create self-fulfilling prophecies. Rist's (1970) work best portrays the approach. Rist argues that teachers have tastes for particular types of students; that is, they have certain preferences and tend to view students who best match those preferences more positively. Teachers prefer students who are well behaved, neat, and quiet. Since affluent and majority-group members tend to possess more of these characteristics, teachers often ascribe a "halo" to such individuals. Because teachers are also hedonistic, they tend to spend more time interacting with such "preferable" children. Increases in teacher interaction lead to more learning. Children who are ignored tend to have less exposure to educational enrichment and hence tend to perform less well on achievement tests. Once students manifest differences in achievement, teachers tend to increase interaction with high test scorers, to the detriment of the low scorers. Thus, an initially labeled disadvantage is exacerabated by decreased interaction and instruction. Real educational disadvantage issues from the process and thereby perpetuates lower achievement and encourages dropout behavior.

When such a scenario for teacher labeling has been subjected to testing, the results have been less than conclusive. In fact, the overwhelming evidence has suggested that teachers play a relatively minor role in accounting for student achievement, especially as compared with home and student effects. Nonetheless, the issue is far from resolved. Much of the macrodata has relied upon surrogates for teacher effects, including aggregating teacher educational attainment (for example, percentages of teachers with M.A. degrees) or other teacher characteristics across all teachers in a school or even a district, and then using that aggregated measure as the teacher input. In these situations, regression effects obliterate the contributions of individual teachers to individual students. However, as Jencks (1972) and Jencks et al., (1972) observe, one cannot discount school (and teacher) effects completely. There is evidence that black children who do not attend summer school record either no increase in achievement over the summer or a slight drop in achievement. By contrast, white children (who may be exposed to alternative learning experiences that are school-like in nature) do show an increase in achievement over the summer. When black children who go to summer school are compared with white children, no significant difference in achievement gain is noted. Thus, exposure to school does make some difference in achievement.

In the original Rosenthal and Jacobson study (1968), teachers were randomly assigned students. Half the students were defined a priori to the teachers as "high achievers" and half as "low achievers." Despite this random assignment, the children labeled as "high achievers" recorded at the end of the year significantly higher achievement and IQ scores than the children labeled as "low achievers." However, Clifton (1981) and Haller and Davis (1981) report that there has been little success in replicating these significant findings. Hurn (1978) suggests that one reason is that the Rosenthal and Jacobson study is so famous that it has altered teacher behavior toward low scorers. With the increase in federal and state programs directed specifically toward low achievers it is also plausible that such children are more likely to receive extra attention and assistance from their teachers. Furthermore, with the increase in middle-class and white flight from urban schools (see Armor, 1980), there may be a homogenizing of teacher ascriptions, which in turn produces more uniform treatment of students and a more uniform set of student learning outcomes.

Finally, Luce and Hoge (1978) observe that the labeling perspective implies a causal link between teacher definitions, teacher actions on behalf of those definitions, differences in student behavior (commitment to school work) occasioned by those teacher actions, and differences in student performances on standardized tests because of student behaviors in response to actions by teachers. These writters contend that there is no evidence that students become less enthusiastic about learning because of teacher difinitions. Luce and Hoge attempt to demonstrate that when one controls for actual differences in student ability (as measured by an independent pretest assessment of intelligence), the association between teacher labels and student performances becomes spurious. In short, although teachers tend to label students who are in fact less able as "lower achievers," it is the students' actual abilities that produce the learning outcomes. Quite recently, Duesek (1985) has compiled an impressive set of articles on teacher expectancy, including a summary of the many critiques of the research by Rosenthal and Jacobson (1968). The reader is referred to this volume for a more detailed anaysis of the issues.

Comparison of Techniques

The status attainment–human capital approach relies extensively upon macrodata that are often based upon numerous school districts and thousands of students. In fact, Coleman's own data involved information on 645,000 students and 3,100 schools. Student data included standardized test scores and assessments by principals regarding the social class backgrounds of the students. The measures used in these analyses were in general easy to obtain and count. Teacher and school characteristics were aggregated across campuses or even districts; sometimes test scores were entered into a regression as a campus mean score. For these reasons, it is impossible to ascertain the effects of individual teachers on individual students. Frequently, as in the case of Coleman and his associates, stepwise regression was used and home effects were entered first, thereby attributing to those variables all confounded and communal variance. By contrast, studies which have stressed self-fulfilling prophecies on student achievement and have emphasized labeling effects have tended to rely upon small samples and microdata on individual classrooms. With these data sets, generalizability has been problematic.

Ideally, a test of the relative importance of human capital and status attainment effects and teacher effects on student achievement and student attendance behavior would correct several deficiencies in previous work. It will be necessary to locate the unit of analysis at the level of the individual child and incorporate data on that child's own teacher, rather than aggregate teacher effects across a campus or a school district. Prior achievement data ought to be available to assess a gain score. Additional outcomes other than achievement, especially some measure of student attendance behavior, ought to be viewed as dependent variables. Some assessment ought to be made regarding teacher attitudes toward the school and children in the school to avoid a priori assuptions that teachers will automatically hold favorable attitudes toward students who share their own class and ethnic background and therefore will provide more intense and better teaching to those students. Likewise, there ought to be a measure of teacher commitment to separate teachers who like their jobs from those who do not. Prior status attainment and human capital research has assumed a uniform level of commitment among teachers. In contrast to the studies of self-fulfilling prophecy effects, data should be collected across a large number of campuses and classrooms so that findings can be generalized.

In addition to model building which aggregates teacher effects across all groups of children, separate analysis ought to be conducted on subgroups of children to determine whether racial groups, gender groups, and grade levels are affected differently by the various blocks of independent variables. Ideally, the achievement scores should also be disaggregated into their respective components, including arithmetic skills, reading skills, and other elements.

Whither Teacher Commitment?

Common to both the human capital–status attainment–meritocratic models and the teacher-labeling models has been an assumption that individual classroom teachers are relatively similar in their work commitment, implying that teachers' attitudes toward their jobs play no role in student academic performance or student attendance behavior. In fact, an ERIC clearing house search and a search of current articles in education and sociology have yielded no links between teacher commitment, alienation, or teacher burnout and student academic outcomes, other than preliminary work done by myself and my graduate students on the current data set. There are a few impressionistic studies which suggest that teacher enthusiasm influences how well the students perform in class, but conclusive data on the topic are missing.

However, one can establish a logical link between teacher burnout, intentions to quit teaching, and actual quitting behavior, and diminished student achievement and attendance behavior. A characteristic of burnout is a reduced willingness to expend extra efforts for clients (Cherniss, 1980; Maslach, 1978a). If burned-out teachers are less willing to invest much into their teaching, one would expect to find lower achievement gains. Furthermore, as the evidence from the labeling perspective has suggested, teachers who have a low regard for the abilities of certain groups of students tend to offer those students less encouragement, less support, and less attention than they do to students evaluated as promising (see, for example, Rosenthal and Jacobson, 1968; Rist, 1970; Jackson and Cosca, 1974; United States Commission on Civil Rights, 1973; Cooper, 1979; and Bowles and Gintis, 1976). Hence, if attention and support are associated with increased achievement, then any teacher motive (be it based on prejudice or the lack of commitment) ought to diminish student learning outcomes.

By a more circuitous route, one can conclude that quitting behavior among teachers diminishes student achievement. In this argument, the effects of quitting are not recorded on the students exposed to a given teacher, but to the students exposed to his or her replacement. It is known that inexperienced teachers tend to be associated with lower levels of student achievement than more experienced teachers (Jencks, 1972; Jencks et al., 1972; Murnane, 1975; Coleman et al., 1966; Hanushek, 1972; McNamara et al., 1977). Teachers who are racially isolated and unfamiliar with the culture of their students also tend to diminish student achievement (Brookover and Erickson, 1975; Schaffer and Schaffer,

1970; Rist, 1973; Larkin, 1975; Percell, 1977; Drury, 1980). Likewise, racial prejudice toward students has been implicated in diminished achievement (Rist, 1973; Jackson and Cosca, 1974; Wiles, 1970; Clark, 1965; Entwistle and Webster, 1974; Johnson, Gerard, and Miller, 1975; Drury, 1980;). Under the aegis of federal faculty desegregation mandates, teachers who quit are replaced by teachers of the same race. Since school districts tend to replace a teacher who quits with a neophyte teacher, turnover tends to keep the teaching pool inexperienced. As Dworkin (1980) has observed, turnover is highest among young white teachers, especially those assigned to schools whose student body characteristics they define as undesirable—usually black schools. Since replacements are more likely to be white teachers sent to black schools (the pattern has been noted since Becker's work in 1952), it can be hypothesized that those schools will experience diminished student achievement because of teacher turnover.

Current Research Questions

The present chapter examines the effect of teacher burnout, intentions to quit teaching, and actual quitting behavior upon student achievement and student attendance. It also examines the relative roles of each of the blocks of teacher variables enumerated in chapter 2, which explain the three groups of teacher job attitudes and behaviors. Three sets of dependent variables will be examined. The first is a composite achievement score on the Iowa Test of Basic Skills (ITBS) for each child assigned to sampled teachers. The second is a gain score on achievement constructed from the comparison between the achievement score noted previously and the achievement score for that child from the year before. Finally, I shall examine the impact of the teacher variables on student commitment to education. In the absence of a measure of attitudinal commitment, student attendance will serve as a viable surrogate.

Four research questions will be probed in this chapter. The first three speak to the impact of teacher attitudes and behavior upon student achievement and attendance behavior, while the last examines the role of each of the blocks of teacher commitment variables (side-bets, satisfaction and solidarity) upon student achievement and attendance. The questions are as follows:

(1)   Do students with burned-out teachers make different academic gains than students assigned to teachers who are not burned out?

(2)   Do children with burned-out teachers attend class less often than children assigned to teachers who are not burned out?

(3)   Are there differences in achievement gains and attendance behavior between students assigned to burned-out teachers who subsequently quit teaching and children assigned to burned-out teachers who do not quit?

(4)   Does the source of one's commitment or burnout (side-bets, satisfaction and solidarity, or translatability) influence the achievement gains and attendance behavior of one's students?

Models To Be Tested

The construction and testing of models for this chapter will involve progressive disaggregations of the sample. The initial model examines the impact of each of the three teacher blocks of variables presented in chapter 2 (actor traits, side-bets, and satisfaction and solidarity variables), the variables of teacher burnout, intentions to quit teaching, and actual quitting behavior, plus the block of building characteristic variables on student performances and behaviors (represented by an achievement score, an achievement gain score, and student attendance behavior). Where significant student differences are noted in terms of grade level, race, and sex, the models will be disaggregated and separate regression runs will be presented for each category of those variables. As in chapter 2, following the examination of the effect of the teacher variables on student performances using OLS modeling, separate commonality analysis runs will be presented which explore the unique and shared variance of each conceptual block of variables on the student measures.

The final disaggregation of the data sets involves an analysis of the differential effects of the exogenous variables upon the performance variables for high achievers and low achievers. Jencks (1972) and Jencks et al. (1972) have observed that the impact of school and home effects is different for high-achieving and low-achieving children. By constructing statistical categories of high and low achievers, the relative influence of each block can be explored.

Since there is some reason to believe that the various elements of achievement which comprise the Iowa Test of Basic Skills may be affected differently, separate regression runs will also be conducted on each of the elements; the results of those runs are presented in appendix F. (For a discussion of the manner in which different aspects of achievement are determined by student, teacher, and school effects, see the presentations by Jencks et al., 1972; Murnane, 1975; Hanushek, 1972; and Winkler, 1972.)

Conceptual Variables in the Model of Teacher Effects

Although my concern is the effect of specific teacher attitudes and behaviors on student performance, I recognize that other aspects of the teacher, the school, and the child are significant in estimating the effect of teachers on students. If regressions were computed using burnout, plans to quit, and actual quitting behavior as the only independent variables in explaining student achievement and attendance, then the tested model might well overestimate the role of those predictors. Incorporating variables which are known either to affect student performances or to affect the central independent variables will alleviate this concern.

As in chapter 2, the model building involves the analysis of the additive effects of blocks of independent variables. Three general models are advanced. Model 1 is offered to explain the impact of the blocks of variables on one year's gain in student achievement, during which time the student has been exposed to the sampled teacher. The score reflects a year's growth in academic achievement. The following equation represents that model:

$$Y_g = bX_{at} + bX_{sb} + bX_{ss} + bX_c + bX_{stb} + bX_{atn} + e,$$

where Y_g = a year's gain in the achievement of a student, as measured by the difference between the achievement between year one and year two;

bX_{at} = the actor traits of the teacher, as discussed in chapter 2;

bX_{sb} = the side-bets of that teacher;

bX_{ss} = the satisfaction and solidarity attitudes of that teacher;

bX_c = the commitment of that teacher, expressed as burnout, plans to quit, and actual quitting behavior;

bX_{stb} = the background variables of the student;

bX_{atn} = the attendance behavior of the student; and

e = measurement error.

Model 2 represents the effect of the blocks upon the total achievement level of the students rather than upon a gain score. Because the model does not incorporate a gain score, prior achievement becomes an independent variable, expressed as bX_{a-1}, and present achievement is expressed as the dependent variable, Y_a. The model is expressed as follows:

$$Y_a = bX_{at} + bX_{sb} + bX_{ss} + bX_c + bX_{stb} + bX_{atn} + bX_{a-1} + e.$$

With the exception of Y_a and bX_{a-1}, all the terms in the equation are measured as they were in the first model.

Model 3 presents the effects of the blocks of variables on attendance behavior. Because attendance may be effected by prior success or failure in school as well as by present level of success, achievement variables will also be entered into the equation. The model is as follows:

$$Y_{atn} = bX_{at} + bX_{sb} + bX_{ss} + bX_c + bX_{stb} + bX_{a,a-1} + e.$$

The predictors in this model are the same as in previous models; however, Y_{atn} refers to the dependent variable attendance behavior, and $bX_{a,a-1}$ represents the achievement scores for the first and second year. Specific operationalizations of each of the blocks are presented in the next section, along with hypotheses indicating their expected effect.

Predicted Effect of Each Variable
in Each Block of Conceptual Variables

Actor Traits

As I discussed in chapter 2, actor traits represent those characteristics, both attitudinal and demographic, which a teacher brings to a school setting. Included in the block are the age, sex, race, and educational attainment of the teacher, plus a measure of teacher stereotyping and locus of control. On the basis of Hanushek's (1972) observations it is predicted that the age of a teacher will be negatively associated with student achievement gain and actual achievement level but positively associated with student attendance behavior. Hanushek argues that older teachers tent to stress discipline, thereby mitigating absenteeism, but do not offer innovative and modern instruction. The race and sex of the teacher have an inconclusive effect on student performance. Gold and Reis (1982) find that males are generally less able to teach reading than are females. However, Murnane (1975) and Michelson (1970) contend that black male teachers are able to produce higher achievement in math among black students than are female or white teachers. Some investigators have argued that students generally perform better if an attempt is made to match student and teachers by sex and race. McNamara et al. (1977) and Sanders (1978) report no such sex or race effect on student achievement. In light of these inconclusive findings, the directions of the effects of sex and race will not be predicted. However, three dummy variables will be computed and the dependent variables regressed on them. The three dummy variables are student and teacher of same race; student and teacher of same sex; and student and teacher of both the same race and sex.

Coleman (1966), Jencks et al., (1972), Alexander and Cook (1982), and Alexander, Cook, and McDill (1978) have all argued that teachers with master's degrees produced higher achievement scores than those without master's degrees. Thus the educational level of the teacher should be positively associated with student achievement, and presumable with student attendance behavior as well. Teacher stereotyping is expected to reduce achievement levels, as the labeling hypothesis has maintained (see Bowles and Gintis, 1976; Clark, 1965; Wiles, 1970; Rist, 1973; Jackson and Cosca, 1974; and Johnson, Gerard, and Miller, 1975). Two of the messages of education, especially for children in the inner city, are that children can attain personal mobility through their own efforts, and that those efforts involve good school attendance behavior and hard academic work. To the extent that teachers are less confident in the message of personal effectiveness, it is predicted that they will be less successful in promoting high attendance and high achievement. Because by definition externals are less able to effect changes in their world and are less able to inflict their will upon others, it is predicted that student achievement levels will be lower when students are assigned to teachers who are externals. It is through this argument that one would expect the most negative effect of externality among teachers to be on minority children and children with lower socioeconomic status (SES).

Side-Bets

Among the side-bet variables which are expected to impinge upon student achievement and attendance behavior are teacher experience, tenure, mobility, salary, translatability, and income independence. Murnane (1975), Hanushek (1972), and Sanders (1978) have each maintained that student achievement is affected by teacher experience, and that the association is nonlinear. That is, teachers with less than five years of experience tend to produce higher test scores for each additional year of experience they achieve, while teachers with more than five years of experience tend to produce either no different level of achievement as their experience increases, or to produce somewhat lower achievement at the extreme end of the experience level. This relationship is similar to the effects predicted for age.

Tenured teachers presumably are more experienced, more confident in their own skills, and more likely to have advanced degrees than untenured teachers. Thus, tenure will produce the same effects as increased experience and higher levels of academic attainment among teachers. However, there may be an independent effect of tenure. Job stability, which is associated with tenure, may make teachers less tentative in demanding achievement of their students. Unfortunately, tenure could also make the teacher lazier and less willing to expend efforts for the child. On balance, however, it is proposed that tenure is positively associated with student achievement and attendance.

Higher salaries and mobility in teaching are indicative of higher levels of organizational achievement. It is hypothesized that such higher levels of personal achievement among teachers will translate into higher levels of student achievement and student attendance behavior. It is possible that the measures of income independence and translatability could be associated with lower student performances because teachers who do not need to remain in teaching may be less willing to invest efforts in the job. However, it is more likely that these variables acutally heighten student acheivement and attendance behavior. Teachers who remain with their careers even when they have another option may be more likely to think of their work as a calling, to be more enthusiastic about their work, and to be more willing to make the necessary additional efforts which kindle enthusiasm on the part of the students.

Satisfaction and Solidarity

It is assumed here that any variable which increases teacher enthusiasm and commitment is also likely to heighten the effectiveness of that teacher. Thus, among the satisfaction and solidarity variables, it is argued that a positive assignment attitude, a favorable transfer experience, support for faculty desegregation, and minimal discrepancies between the principal and the teacher's evaluation of the principal's administrative style will be associated with heightened achievement and attendance behavior, while perceptions of discrimination will be associated with diminished achievement and attendance (Collins and Noblit, 1976; National Institute of Education, 1976).

To the extent, then, that factors which diminish commitment and satisfaction are associated with lowered achievement and attendance behavior, we may also hypothesize that burnout, intentions to quit teaching, and actual quitting behavior will also be associated with lower levels of student achievement and student attendance behavior.

Building Characteristics

Although Coleman et al. (1966) and Jencks et al. (1972) find little support for the claim, it is widely believed that lower achievement levels among low-income and minority children can be traced to the kind of school in which the child is located. Low-income schools are assumed to have a smaller share of resources and less ability to provide quality education than schools in more affluent neighborhoods. Little research has substantiated that claim, since inner-city schools are actually more likely to have a larger share of state and federal funds for their programs. Despite the evidence, the claim regarding low-income and affluent schools persists (Jencks et al., 1972; Hurn, 1978). Nevertheless, noneconomic factors may differentiate schools. Large schools and those with overcrowded classrooms have been associated with lower achievement and poorer attendance (St. John, 1975; Hanushek, 1972; Haller and Davis, 1981). Thus, it is hypothesized that classroom size and overall school size are negatively associated with student performance.

The Houston Independent School District has used a magnet school plan to attain school desegregation. Although not all magnet schools are aimed toward increased academic achievement (some elementary magnets stress ecology, others physical education, and still others careers), they have received greater scrutiny by the district. More funds are allocated to the magnet schools, and attempts are made to screen faculty to match faculty abilities and student needs. It is therefore proposed that the dummy variable of magnet schools should be positively associated with student achievement and attendance behavior.

Schools in which a high percentage of the students are bused have been associated with both lower achievement and with higher achievement. The paradox is simply that minority children are more likely to be bused and that such children tend to perform less well on standardized tests. However, the receiving schools tend to be racially balanced or majority schools, which are associated with higher achievement levels. The percentage bused refers to the percentage of students coming into the school who are bused, rather than the percentage of children being bused out of a given school. Minority schools, except for those which are magnets, tend to be sending schools, while majority schools tend to be receiving schools. Thus, receiving schools may experience a greater reduction in achievement than majority schools who are not receiving students. Moreover, minority schools with magnet programs may receive majority students and therefore ought to experience a greater increase in achievement than minority schools without magnet programs. The potential for the effects balancing one another out suggests that no hypothesis ought to be offered here.

It should be reported, however, that Drury (1980) observes that black children who are bused to white schools are often rejected by white students and teachers and do poorly in such schools. A consistent finding from all previous research is that student achievement and attendance behavior are suppressed in schools with higher percentages of minority students. The expectation that school desegregation would produce better educational outcomes for minority students has not been fully realized. St. John (1975) reports as many cases where desegregation has made no impact as cases where some small impact has been registered. Winkler (1972) reports that the achievement rate of minority students who attend all-black elementary schools falls when the children are transferred to a desegregated junior high school. The contention by Pettigrew et al. (1973) that integration takes much longer than desegregation may account for Winkler's results. Minority children experiencing desegregation for the first time may need an extended period of adjustment to the new setting. Likewise, before such children are accepted, their white classmates and teachers may also need time to adjust. Short-term studies may be insensitive to the necessary period of adaptation.

The evidence on the impact of desegregation has been mixed. The more well-controlled studies, such as those conducted by Murnane (1975) and those reported by Greenblatt and Willie (1980), Stephan and Feagin (1980), and Hurn (1978), show some advantage for minority students attending majority schools. This is particularly true if the minority students live in the neighborhood and are not bused into the neighborhood. I therefore propose that schools whose student bodies are predominantly black or brown will be associated with lower achievement levels and attendance behavior than schools with a predominantly white student body. As in the analysis of the data on teachers in chapter 2, I shall define a black school, a white school, and a brown school as one in which more than 50 percent of the students in that school are black, white, or brown, respectively, and a balanced school as one in which no group attains 50 percent of the student body.

Katzman (1971), McNamara et al. (1977), Murnane (1975), and Hanushek (1972) have found that teacher stability is associated with higher student achievement and attendance behavior. Schools which have a stable teaching population tend to have low percentages of neophyte teachers. They are also less fraught with teacher discontent—discontent that is likely to spill over into the classroom. Using my measure of teacher turnover from a previous chapter, I hypothesize that student achievement and student attendance behavior will diminish with increases in teacher turnover.

Finally, although all schools in the district have some degree of desegregation—if only faculty desegregation—not all schools have norms for interracial cooperation. Schools which have such norms ought to be associated with less interpersonal hostility. Furthermore, interpersonal hostility is likely to be disruptive and hence is likely to reduce student achievement and attendance. I therefore hypothesize that student achievement and attendance will be positively associated with positive interaction norms of cooperation.

Student Characteristics

The final block of variables represents the demographic and behavioral aspects of the students in the sample. Included in this block are the student's age, grade, race, sex, socioeconomic status and prior achievement level.

It has been argued that older children are more likely to have longer attention spans; therefore, as a child grows older, achievement is also likely to increase. There is also some evidence that ability levels increase with age independent of either intelligence or exposure to education. Therefore, I propose that there is a positive association between a student's age, achievement, and attendance.

Related to age variables is the impact of additional exposure to education and the issue of a "fan effect." Coleman's data and the reanalysis by Okada, Cohen, and Mayeske (1969) point to the tendency for children to make gains at increasing rates with increases in grade level. Hence, children who enter a school with a disadvantage in learning and children who enter a school with an advantage in learning grow more dissimilar in grade-equivalent ability with time. In other words, the groups fan out. Murnane (1975), on the other hand, finds no such fanning. If there is a fan effect, then grade level will be positively associated with achievement gain scores. Of course, since grade level ought to be associated with actual achievement level, it will not be included in a regression predicting total achievement. Grade level may also be positively associated with attendance behavior, as a function of school socialization over time, plus decreased illness behavior with age.

There is some evidence that girls have a better attention span than do boys in grades 4 through 6; therefore, we may find higher achievement and attendance behavior among girls than among boys. In addition, girls are socialized to conform to teacher's wishes more than are boys; therefore, to the extent that conformity produces higher achievement levels, girls will again have an advantage. Compliance behavior will also lead girls to attend school more often than boys.

It has been a consistent finding that minority children perform less well on standardized tests than do majority-group children. Likewise, children from lower socioeconomic statuses are likely to perform less well than those from higher socioeconomic statuses. Whether this difference is a function of differences in academic enrichment afforded to children or of teacher expectations and prejudices is unknown. However, the total model will be able to tease out some of the differences in effects. I hypothesize that black and brown children will perform less well than white children and that lower-SES children will perform less well than higher-SES children. Likewise, higher attendance behavior should be found for majority-group members and for higher SES students.

Some have asked whether the school makes a difference. The question couched in that manner is facetious. Evidence presented by Jencks et al. (1972) on the impact of summer school on minority achievement establishes that exposure to school does elevate achievement. McNamara et al. (1977) and Sanders (1978) have observed that absenteeism is a significant predictor of lower achievement. It is therefore hypothesized that attendance behavior will be positively associated with achievement.

The pivotal conceptual variable in the assessment of home and school effects is a measure of native ability. Nearly every model of student achievement incorporates a measure of personal competence into the equation. Coleman et al. (1966), Jencks (1972), System Development Corporation (1977), Hanushek (1972), Winkler (1971), Blau (1981), Murnane (1975), and Alexander, Cook, McDill, and their associates (1976, 1978, 1979, 1982) have each used some measure of ability. But although an independent measure of student ability is preferable, the use of an intelligence score for each child is not possible. The Houston Independent School District, under a combination of political and economic constraints, does not conduct wholesale intelligence testing of its students. The only measures available are reading readiness tests, indicators of minimal facility with English, and prior achievement test scores.

In the present research I wish to determine the effect of teacher commitment upon student achievement and attendance behavior. I therefore need a measure of student performance which can capture the effects of ability and prior exposure to education. Reliance upon an intelligence test would have given an indication of native ability—disregarding at this point the validity of the construct 'intelligence'. However, since the effect of intelligence on achievement is only moderate (Blau [1981], reports a beta of 0.40), it cannot be used as a baseline to assess the contribution of the current teacher. It is for a similar reason that Hanushek (1972), working on a microdata set in Richmond, California, recommends capturing past ability and learning environment through the use of prior achievement scores. The original Singleton research team for the Houston schools, who collected the student data used in the current study, used this line of reasoning to select prior achievement as its indicator of ability in the absence of other measures. Prior test scores permit the computation of a gain score to assess the role of each block of predictors upon increments in achievement. The present research uses past achievement as a baseline predictor of present achievement, with the intent of discerning (1) how much variance in achievement can be explained by the other blocks of student, teacher, and school variables, once past achievement has been controlled; (2) the effect of the predictors on academic gain over a year's exposure to the teacher block; and (3) the assessment through commonality analysis of the unique contributions of each block of variables, including prior achievement and learning environment, on present achievement. I recognize that prior achievement provides advantages, disadvantages, and compromises. It is my hypothesis that prior test scores will be positively associated with present achievement levels and with attendance behavior.

It is Murnane's (1975) observation that studies of student outcomes ought not to concentrate only on achievement variables. Although Murnane never uses attendance as a dependent variable but rather as an index of student commitment, it is reasonable to view attendance also as a product of school, teacher, and student inputs. In other words, if attendance is a surrogate for student commitment, then it not only ought to affect student achievement, but it also ought to be affected by those blocks of variables which affect student achievement. As an independent variable, student attendance measures the likely exposure that a student will have to school effects. Therefore, it is arguable that the greater the exposure of students to school effects, the greater the impact of those effects upon student learning outcomes. By contrast, school, teacher, and home effects may determine the willingness of the student to be exposed to continued school and teacher effects. Thus, if teacher and school variables are punishing, one recourse for the student is to diminish interaction with the school and the teacher. Hence, we would expect that the teacher commitment would affect student commitment. As I maintained in chapter 2, it is also plausible that student commitment and student achievement may serve to reward or punish teachers; therefore, such variables are also influential in teacher commitment.

Sample Design and Sampling Methodology

The population of students from which the original student sample was drawn by the Singleton Ratio consulting team consisted of children in grades 4, 5, and 6 who attended the Houston Independent School District's 169 elementary schools during the 1976–77 academic year. This original sample consisted of 8,203 pupils and matched almost exactly the district population parameters.[1]

From this highly representative sample, computer matches were made with the teacher data reported in chapter 2. Matches were achieved between 2,287 students and 518 teachers. The unit of analysis for this chapter is the student. The Singleton Desegregation study team elected to study only grades 4 through 6, for several reasons: complete test score records were available on those grade levels, including records on the previous year's test scores; since the impact of school effects accumulate (Murnane, 1975; Mosteller and Moynihan, 1972), earlier grades would have confounded home and school effects; and later grades would have effects of student exposure to multiple teachers, thereby confounding the impact of a given teacher on the student. Table 4.1 compares the demographic characteristics of the matched sample with the larger Singleton Ratio sample. In general, there is a substantial concordance between the two samples. The exceptions are a slight overenumeration of 4th graders and a corresponding underenumeration of 6th graders. Likewise, there is an underenumeration of black teachers. In the latter case, black teachers represent 47.7 percent of the Singleton Ratio sample and 40.1 percent of the matched student sample. This difference may reflect a lower percentage of black elementary teachers for whom full attitudinal data are available. If so, some caution might be prudent in generalizing race effects to the district as a whole, but not in generalizing about teacher effects on students in urban school districts. The rest of the structural variables are a very close match with the larger sample, and in terms of student test scores and attendance behavior, the matches are nearly identical.

Appendices A and B present the operationalizations and the means and standard deviations of each of the independent and dependent variables included in the testing of the models. These appendices provide an overview of the measures of central tendency for each of the predictor and criterion variables. It should be noted that because of their scarcity in the Houston school system, Oriental teachers and students are omitted from the present analysis. There were only twelve Oriental students in the sample, and of these, only five had available test scores for both years of observation. To compute gain scores, it is obviously necessary to have

Table 4.1

Comparison of Matched Student Sample with Singleton Ratio Sample

Variable	Singleton Ratio Sample (N = 8,204)		Matched Sample (N = 2,287)	
Grade level				
% 4th graders	34.3		37.1	
% 5th graders	33.7		32.9	
% 6th graders	32.0		30.0	
Sex				
% Males	50.1		50.2	
% Females	49.9		49.8	
Race				
% Black	42.1		40.4	
% Brown	22.4		22.1	
% Oriental	0.8		0.5	
% White	34.2		36.9	
SES index score, $\bar{X}$ (s.d.)	10.53	(0.75)	10.57	(0.75)
Days absent, $\bar{X}$ (s.d.)	12.10	(12.64)	11.54	(12.14)
Membership days, $\bar{X}$ (s.d.)	163.40	(40.07)	163.42	(40.10)
Absenteeism (days absent), $\bar{X}$ (s.d.)	0.079	(0.088)	0.080	(0.090)
Sex of teacher				
% Male	12.6		11.5	
% Female	87.4		88.5	
Race of teacher				
% Black	47.7		40.1	
% Brown	2.6		1.5	
% Oriental	0.5		0.9	
% White	49.1		57.5	
Experience of teacher, $\bar{X}$ (s.d.)	11.94	(9.47)	11.46	(9.01)
% teachers tenured	80.0		81.1	
% students bused at school	3.3		4.0	
% in magnet schools	14.7		15.1	
Composite Iowa scores	$\bar{X}$	s.d.	$\bar{X}$	s.d.
Grade 4				
1976 score	3.640	(0.990)	3.641	(1.032)
1977 score	4.508	(1.160)	4.466	(1.174)
Gain score	0.869	(0.568)	0.858	(0.568)
Grade 5				
1976 score	4.446	(1.152)	4.594	(1.185)
1977 score	5.334	(1.322)	5.506	(1.366)
Gain score	0.875	(0.567)	0.901	(0.557)
Grade 6				
1976 score	5.250	(1.303)	5.360	(1.345)
1977 score	6.205	(1.449)	6.201	(1.483)
Gain score	0.990	(0.603)	0.924	(0.630)

available an achievement score for both time periods. In the original Singleton Ratio student sample, scores were available for both years on 5,258 children, or 64.1 percent of the sample. In the matched student sample, test scores for both years were available on 1,505 children, or 65.8 percent of that sample. Clearly, then, the matched sample and the Singleton Ratio sample differ only slightly on this characteristic. District personnel report that two consecutive test scores are available on approximately 65 percent of the population of Houston students. In and out migration of students is the principal reason for the unavailability of two consecutive test scores on students in urban public schools. Thus, while the matched sample has a size of 2,287, the analysis of gain scores can be conducted on 1,505 students. As Murnane (1975) suggests, only gain scores ought to be analyzed with the attenuated sample; for total achievement level and attendance behavior, data on as many of the 2,287 students as possible will be analyzed.

To interpret what follows, the reader should understand the interpretation of the effects of the b, or unstandardized regression, coefficients. The unit of analysis for academic gain scores is measured in terms of one-year intervals. Thus a b of .2 means two-tenths of a year's gain based upon a ten-month school year, or a gain of two months. Likewise, a b value of -.05 represents a decline in achievement of approximately one-half month, or two weeks. When the dependent variable is total achievement rather than a gain score, the unit of analysis remains one year. Thus, any b value for this measure can be interpreted in the same fashion as can the b value for gain scores. In the instance of absenteeism, the dependent variable is measured in terms of percentage points of a year absent. If the b value for absenteeism is .2, then the student has been absent 20 percent of the time that he or she was carried on the class rolls. On a 180-day school year, that would represent 36 days absent.

Testing the Model of Achievement Gain

The first model to be tested examines the role of the five blocks of predictors upon children's gains in achievement over a year's time. Five blocks of variables comprise the independent variables in the model; they include those depicting teacher traits (actor traits), teacher side-bets, teacher satisfaction and solidarity, building characteristics, and student characteristics. A total of 42 predictors were involved in the initial test of the model, and a substantial number neither met the minimal F values for retention nor had b's which were at least twice the magnitude of their standard errors. This extended model produced an R of .358, an R^2 of .128, and a disappointing F of 3.53, given the preponderance of non-significant predictors.

The model was retested using 16 surviving variables. This model is presented in table 4.2. The obtained R is .344, with an R^2 of .118. The F value for the model rose to 7.84. Slightly under 12 percent of the total variance in achievement gains can be explained by the five blocks of variables entered into the model. In the absence of prior achievement or some other measure of ability (which will be incorporated into the next model), structural and social-psychological variables do little to explain student achievement. This result is consistent with the observations of Murnane (1975), Jencks et al. (1972), Coleman et al. (1966), Mayeske et al. (1969), and Sanders (1978).

Table 4.2

Revised Model of Student Achievement Gain

Variable	Total covar r	b	s.e.	F	Beta
Stereotyping	.056	.029	.008	10.93	.101
External locus	-.134	-.015	.007	3.08	-.056
Inexperience	.164	.052	.014	13.95	.133
Experience	-.043	-.007	.003	3.44	-.064
Assignment attitude	.149	.062	.027	5.46	.074
Discrimination	-.095	-.090	.045	4.04	-.064
Quitting	.007	.110	.051	3.82	.061
Teacher turnover	-.176	-.675	.239	7.97	-.097
Busing	.057	.326	.160	3.27	.054
Brown school	-.080	-.107	.053	2.44	-.071
Age of student	.043	.043	.021	2.26	.076
Black child	-.183	-.261	.064	16.21	-.218
Brown child	-.089	-.109	.054	3.38	-.081
Student grade	.019	.056	.026	2.37	.079
Student SES	.048	.052	.024	2.07	.041
Absenteeism	-.089	-.582	.254	5.25	-.068
Intercept = .856		R = .344	$R^2 = .118$	F = 7.84	

Those independent variables which have the largest effects include teacher stereotyping, teacher inexperience, teacher assignment attitude, turnover rates among faculty on the campus, student absenteeism, and race of student. Teacher's locus of control, teacher's quitting behavior, and student attendance at a brown school also affect achievement gain.

Two variables from the actor trait block of teacher characteristics are significantly associated with academic achievement gain scores. For each unit of increase in teacher stereotyping, there is an accompanying increase in student achievement of approximately one week. These findings run directly counter to the labeling model of Rosenthal and Jacobson (1968), Bowles and Gintis (1976), and Rist (1970); however, they could be explained by two rival models, as we will see later. The second variable in the block of actor traits is locus control. Here, external teachers, who feel that their destinies are not controlled by their own actions, are responsible for one week less in achievement for each external response they make to the locus of control measure. American education is predicated upon a belief that through individual initiative, particularly in terms of educational attainment, people may attain upward mobility. The teacher who does not believe that message may not be as likely to stimulate students to try harder academically, and may therefore be less able to effect real educational growth. To the extent that urban schools are composed of large numbers of students who are economically disadvantaged, a teacher who is more fatalistic about life's chances may be less effective in conveying to students that they need to study diligently to attain upward mobility.

Two side-bet variables are associated with student achievement gain scores. For each year of additional teaching experience that a new teacher attains through the fifth year, students register two weeks of additional achievement gain. However, for each year of additional teaching experience beyond five years, students register a few weeks less of achievement. Thus, the variable for years of teaching experience, expressed in spline analysis, operates in the same fashion that it does in predicting burnout and plans to quit teaching. Years of experience is related in a nonlinear fashion both to teacher morale and to student achievement. Ideally, then, the best teachers in terms of commitment and student achievement gains are those relatively new enough to bring a freshness to their teaching but sufficiently experienced not to be overwhelmed by the demands of the job. This finding suggests that when teachers quit, they should be replaced with teachers with approximately five years of experience in the classroom, not with neophytes or with those tired from years of exposure to the classroom.

Among the satisfaction and solidarity variables, assignment attitude, discrimination perceptions, and quitting behavior are significantly associated with student achievement gains. Teachers who are assigned to schools whose student body's racial composition they define as desirable heighten achievement gain by more than two weeks. However, teachers who feel that they are targets of discrimination at their school are associated with nearly a month less of achievement by their students. It is interesting that teachers who ultimately quit teaching produce over one month of greater achievement gain than those who do not quit teaching. Burnout and intentions to quit, however, have no effect upon academic achievement gains for students.

The links between teacher stereotyping and student achievement and between assignment attitude and student achievement are also interesting. Teachers who stereotype their students, it will be recalled, elevate student achievement. However, teachers who do not want to teach at a school with a particular student racial composition are associated with lower achievement.

That burnout and intentions to quit teaching are unassociated with student achievement suggests that programs designed to mitigate teacher dissatisfaction in the hope of improving test scores may be misdirected. As the commonality analysis of the teacher variables later in this chapter suggests, it may be inappropriate to emphasize improvement of teacher morale as a means to improving the quality of education. Although not directly measured, it is suspected that improving the quality of teachers may be a better way to improve student education.

While burnout and intentions to quit teaching are unassociated with student achievement gain, actual quitting behavior elevates student achievement by more than one month in gain scores. In chapter 2, it was indicated that teachers who quit tend to be disproportionately drawn from a group who have translatable skills. The translatability of these skills may also indicate greater competence. School personnel have often maintained that the most creative and ablest individuals find the bureaucratization and routinization of the teaching role constraining and often quit before they can amass side-bets to become entrapped or before they become burned out. Earlier I maintained that a significant problem facing urban schools is teacher entrapment, not simply teacher turnover. This statement seems to need some modification. Teacher entrapment per se does not lead to diminished outcomes for students because burned-out and entrapped teachers do not necessarily diminish achievement. But if the teachers who quit are the ablest, and turnover accompanied by a replacement policy that hires neophytes insures that the teaching population will be inexperienced, the combined effects of turnover are to diminish student achievement.

One of the building characteristics which is associated with achievement gain is the turnover rate of faculty at the school. An elevation in teacher turnover rates is associated with six-and-three-quarter months of lower achievement gains, despite the fact that the individual teacher who quits may be linked to higher achievement gains. The apparent discrepancy is a function of the difference between individual effects and group rates. Schools which have high faculty turnover rates tend to be those in which two elements operate. Because of faculty desegregation mandates, they tend to replace departing faculty with individuals who are also likely to find the school undesirable (negative assignment attitude) and to be recent graduates without experience in teaching. Both of these factors are associated with diminished student achievement gains. By contrast, an individual who leaves may not necessarily teach at a school which suffers from high rates of turnover. Schools which have high rates of turnover are likely to be disorganized and troubled schools. However, even in schools which have lower turnover rates, a few individuals may elect to leave teaching.

Schools into which higher-than-average numbers of students are bused (another building characteristic) are associated with a one-third year of increase in achievement gain. These schools tend to be of two kinds: magnet schools and schools in which the dominant population is white and/or middle class. Black schools and brown schools in urban districts tend to be sending schools that bus their students out to white schools, while white schools tend to be receiving schools. Except when going to particularly excellent magnet programs in minority schools, whites prefer to leave the public school system rather than enter predominantly minority schools (Armor, 1980). By contrast, minorities are most likely to be sent to white schools. Consequently, many black schools are in excess of 90 percent black, whereas no white schools have more than 70 percent white students, and most have percentages nearing 50. Therefore receiving schools tend to have higher achievement gain scores than do sending schools.

Only brown schools are associated with a significant impact on achievement gain scores. Attendance at a brown school is associated with one month of lower achievement gain than attendance at any other type of school. Brown schools tend to be ones in which a higher-than-average percentage of the students are not fluent in English. Since the achievement tests are in English, difficulties with the language will be associated with diminished gain. Coleman et al. (1966) and Mahard and Crain (1980) report the same achievement disadvantage for students attending brown schools. Likewise, Bridge, Judd, and Moock (1979) note that there are no observable disadvantages associated with attendance at a black school, nor advantages associated with attendance at a white school. This is not to contend that differences in the achievement levels of black, brown, or white children are absent.

Among the variables in the student block, the student's age, grade level, race, socioeconomic status, and attendance behavior are all implicated in achievement outcomes. Older children, because of maturation, tend to be associated with an increase in achievement gain. With each year of age, the gain increases at an increasing rate, by one week per year. Likewise, for each increase in grade level, the students record an increase in achievement gain of two weeks. The combination of these observations lends credence to the fan effect reported by Coleman et al. (1966) and by Okada, Cohen and Mayeske (1969). Gains in achievement increase at increasing rates. Children who lag behind their classmates over time will fall further and further behind. Disadvantages compound, and the likelihood that they will be overcome approaches greater levels of improbability.

As has usually been found in previous research, minority children gain at a slower rate then do majority-group children. In fact, black children are associated with more than a two-and-one-half-month decrease in academic gain as opposed to whites, while brown children are associated with a month's decrease in academic achievement compared to whites. Children of higher socioeconomic status, independent of race, are associated with an increase in achievement gain of approximately two weeks. Finally, as the percentage of absenteeism from school increases, student achievement gain diminishes. For each percentage increase in absenteeism (as a proportion of the total school year of attendance) there is a nearly six-month reduction in achievement gain scores. This evidence clearly suggests that schools do make a difference. Failure to attend school retards achievement gain.

It is interesting to examine the variables which are not included in the model. Each of the following variables has no significant effect on student achievement gain. At the aggregate level, neither race nor sex of teacher makes a difference. It is also unlikely that this difference will emerge as we match children and teachers, because the dummy variables of same race and same sex are not significantly associated with gain scores. None of the side-bet variables of the teachers are associated with student gain scores. Tenured teachers, teachers who have experienced mobility within the school, teacher's salary levels, and those variables which lead to career alternatives, such as income alternatives and translatability, are unassociated with gain scores.

Among satisfaction and solidarity variables, disagreements with a principal over administrative style—including academic style—as well as attitudes toward desegregation, are unassociated with gain scores. As I mentioned earlier, the commitment variables of burnout and attitudes toward quitting are also unassociated with gain. Thus, many of the variables which account for teacher commitment seem to have little impact on students. One reason may be that the routinization of lesson plans and the similarity of teaching content materials minimize the role of teacher enthusiasm on students. However, there may be differences in the disaggregated subsamples, especially when students of differing ability are examined or when different racial groups of students are explored.

Many of the building variables also have little effect. Racial norms in the school are unassociated with student achievement gains. Likewise, just as Murnane (1975) has found, class size and school size have no impact. Thus, the argument that overcrowding in schools hinders achievement gain is not supported. Of course, since the variance in school size in the sample is minimal, there is no significant overcrowding.

Testing the Model of Total Achievement

In this section my concern is for the impact of the blocks of variables on the achievement level of the students rather than on a gain scores. Entered into the regression in the student block is a measure of ability and prior achievement, merged as a test score from the previous year. I shall assess the role of the other independent variables in light of prior achievement level, which is usually an extremely powerful predictor. It is expected that the total R and R^2 will approach unity, but my concern is for the relative effect of the teacher and building blocks in the model. Since total achievement is the dependent variable and since a "fan effect" is present, the model tested omits grade level as a predictor.

The initial model contained 42 predictors, producing an R of .936 and an R^2 of .878. The F value associated with this model was 154.42. Table 4.3 presents a revision of the model, deleting all variables with nonsignificant F values and variables whose b's are less than twice the size of their standard errors. Fifteen variables are used in that model, producing an R of .931 and an R^2 of .867. The associated F value for that model is 408.40. In general, the model which describes current academic achievement is similar to that which described academic gain, with the obvious exception that prior achievement radically inflates the amount of variance explained. Other differences reflect the cumulative effect of achievement level rather than of gain.

High turnover rates, while detrimental to actual achievement level, have a greater negative effect on gain scores. In contrast, total achievement is more heavily influenced by the student's race than is a gain score. Perhaps the stress on "back to basics" initiated only two years earlier in the school district had the impact of equilibrating gains while still not permitting minorities to catch up. Although there are differences in gains associated with race, the differences are not as pronounced as those reported by Coleman and his associates in 1966, or by Okada et al. in 1969. Actual disadvantage would continue to be recorded in the achieve-

Table 4.3

Revised Model of Total Student Achievement:
Second-Year Achievement

Variable	Total covar r	b	s.e.	F	Beta
Stereotyping	.020	.024	.009	7.44	.033
External locus	-.128	-.154	.008	3.48	-.023
Inexperience	.182	.054	.014	14.80	.053
Experience	-.051	-.006	.003	4.92	-.030
Assignment attitude	.261	.055	.026	3.78	.025
Discrimination	-.057	-.086	.041	3.91	-.024
Quitting	.071	.122	.057	4.85	.026
Teacher turnover	-.223	-.499	.227	4.85	-.028
Busing	.115	.468	.180	6.74	.030
Brown school	-.256	-.156	.070	5.01	-.040
Age of student	.257	.060	.029	4.47	.042
Black child	-.382	-.339	.066	26.61	-.109
Brown child	-.171	-.135	.054	6.16	-.037
Absenteeism	-.117	-.707	.255	7.65	-.032
First-year achievement	.922	.927	.018	2,614.57	.833
Intercept = .592		R = .931	R^2 = .867	F = 408.40	

ment level scores, but the gain scores would reflect the narrowing of disadvantage. That socioeconomic status is not significantly associated with actual achievement level but only with gain scores appears on the surface to present a challenge to this argument. However, the impact of socioeconomic status on gain is minimally significant, while its impact on actual achievement just fails of significance. Chance factors alone can explain the failure to include socioeconomic status in the revised model of total student achievement.

The prominent feature of the total achievement model is that prior achievement accounts for an enormous proportion of the total variance. The associated r for prior achievement, which stands as a surrogate for ability and prior experience, is .922, with a b of .927 and a beta of .833. The F value associated with a value of that magnitude is 2,614.57. In the absence of a commonality analysis of the model (to be conducted later in this chapter), the reader is left with the conclusion that student ability, a seminal aspect of student effects, is so powerful that school variables are of no importance. The conclusion would thus be drawn, as it has been by

Coleman and his associates (1966). Hanushek (1972), Jencks (1972), Alexander and Cook (1982), and others who employ the human capital–status attainment–meritocratic paradigm, that schools and teachers account for very little. To reach this conclusion is also to argue that if a child does poorly in school, it is because he or she brings to school too little human capital to be transformed into learning outcomes. Later in this chapter, however, I shall reexamine these findings in light of a commonality analysis to determine whether prior achievement effects are as profound as they appear to be here.

Testing the Model of Student Attendance

The measurement of student commitment to education is a difficult variable to assess. In the absence of interview data on students (not permitted by the Board of Education), surrogates for commitment need to be constructed. One viable possibility is a ratio computed from unexcused absences and total days of membership in a class. Here one assumes that a student who is absent without an excuse is less committed to education, or at least to the school experience, than a student without such absences. By dividing the total number of days with unexcused absences by the total number of days in attendance, a ratio is obtained which can permit comparisons of students, controlling for days enrolled.

The above ratio represents a preferable estimation of student commitment. Unfortunately, district records on attendance are merely a record of days in attendance and days absent, rather than a consistent record of excused and unexcused absences. Thus, as I began to work with the attendance records, it became apparent that they were affected by more than commitment factors. The measures served better as an index of the exposure students had to classroom instruction than as a true index of student commitment, as had been maintained by Sanders (1978) and McNamara et al. (1977). As such, one would expect that attendance or absenteeism would be poorly explained by teacher commitment.

The initial model of student absenteeism involved 41 predictors. The obtained multiple R was .286, with an R^2 of .082. The associated F value with that number of predictors was only 2.19. Clearly, the model neither acounted well for student absenteeism nor was parsimonious. Reduction of the model to 7 variables which have both significant F values and sufficiently high b's retains an R of .277 and an R^2 of .077, but increases the F value to 9.62 (see table 4.4).

Among the variables which have significant effects are three from the teacher blocks (teacher stereotyping, age, and experience); one from

Table 4.4

Revised Model of Absenteeism

Variable	Total covar r	b	s.e.	F	Beta
Stereotyping	.059	.002	.001	3.59	.057
Age of teacher	-.022	-.001	.000	3.20	-.099
Experience	.026	.022	.001	8.24	.180
Black school	.041	.018	.008	5.19	.123
Age of student	.080	.010	.002	23.70	.153
Black child	-.033	-.030	.008	24.56	-.210
Second-year achievement	-.177	-.118	.002	51.67	-.260
Intercept = .092		R = .277	R² = .077	F = 9.62	

the building block (black schools); and three from the student block (student age, being a black child, and present achievement level). Stereotyping by teachers heightens absenteeism by .2 of 1 percent of a school year (one-third of a day) for each increment in the level of stereotyping. Teacher age lowers student absenteeism by .1 of 1 percent of a school year for each year of increase in teacher age. Teacher experience heightens absenteeism by 2.2 percent of a school year for each additional year of teacher experience beyond the fifth year in the classroom. Thus, each additional year of teacher experience after the fifth year is associated with nearly three days of student absenteeism. Since absenteeism is a significant factor in achievement and since teacher experience heightens student absenteeism, we may posit the mechanism by which more experienced teachers retard achievement: they drive students away and thereby minimize student exposure to instructional materials. This argument is consistent with Murnane's (1975) observations regarding the lower achievement levels of students who are assigned to teachers with more than five years of experience. Murnane suspected that they may be more concerned with discipline and less concerned with instructional content. An emphasis on discipline may also make school more punishing and heighten absenteeism.

Reexploring the Data Sets Using Commonality Analysis

The analysis conducted so far in this chapter has relied upon OLS regression modeling. However, as I noted in chapter 2, an alternative model of analysis explores the amount of unique and shared variance accounted for by conceptual blocks of independent variables. The tables presented in this section only summarize the results of the commonality computer runs. For a display of the individual commonalities and the algebraic equations used to arrive at those commonalities, the reader may consult appendix D. The analysis begins with the issue of the relative explanatory power of the blocks of conceptual independent variables upon student achievement gain scores.

Reanalysis of Academic Gain Scores

In the revised model presented in table 4.2, the obtained R^2 was .118, meaning that a little under 12 percent of the total variance in achievement gain could be explained by the variables in the regression model. Reanalysis of the model using commonality equations reveals that even this view is overly optimistic. Table 4.5 presents the result of the commonality analysis. No block of variables can account for even 5 percent of the total variance in gain scores, or even account uniquely for more than 2 percent of that variance. In every instance, the variables in the blocks are so intertwined that no block is left unconfounded. Thus, because of the interconnectedness of the blocks, policies which seek to effect change in one of the conceptual blocks cannot be assumed to effect significant changes in student achievement gain scores. There is little support in table 4.5 for either a human capital or a labeling approach to explain student achievement gain scores.

Table 4.5

Summary of Commonality Analysis of Academic Gain Scores

| Variance categories | Blocks of independent variables | | | | |
	Actor traits	Side-bets	Satisfaction solidarity	Building characteristics	Student characteristics
Unique variance	.01506	.01994	.01593	.01874	.01237
Common variance	.01517	.01425	.01827	.03066	.01126
Total variance	.03023	.03419	.03420	.04940	.02363
Variance from structural equations (a check)	.03023	.03419	.03420	.04940	.02363

Reanalysis of Total Achievement Levels Using Commonality Analysis

More dramatic results are obtainable in the commonality analysis used to explain current achievement level than in that used to explain achievement gain. As presented in table 4.3, the total variance explained was very high (R^2 = .867), and with the inclusion of a prior test score, the models of human capital and teacher labeling can be given full opportunities to have an impact. As table 4.6 reveals, teacher variables account for only a very small amount of unique variance. Likewise, although building characteristics explain slightly over 20 percent of the variance in achievement, this block of variables uniquely explains only one-third of 1 percent of the total variance. In contrast, the student block (including past achievement) uniquely explains nearly 59 percent of the total variance in achievement. Nearly 27 percent of the total variance in student achievement initially explained by the student block, however, is confounded variance and is intertwined with the other blocks, including the teacher blocks.

Table 4.6
Summary of Commonality Analysis of Total Academic Achievement

Variance categories	Blocks of independent variables				
	Actor traits	*Side- bets*	*Satisfaction solidarity*	*Building characteristics*	*Student characteristics*
Unique variance	.00245	.00316	.00251	.00350	.58695
Common variance	.03489	.04908	.08997	.19915	.26494
Total variance	.03734	.05224	.09212	.20265	.85189
Variance from structural equations (a check)	.03734	.05224	.09212	.20265	.85189

If the past test scores are deleted from the student block and entered separately, it becomes possible to calculate the unique variance explained by past academic achievement upon present academic achievement. Although the obtained R for past achievement is .922, with an accompanying R^2 of .850, this is an inflated value. Suprisingly, commonality analysis reveals that the unique variance in present test scores which can be attributed to past test scores is .346 (with an additional unique variance of .241 attributed to other variables in the student block). Thus, of the 86.7 percent of total variance in present achievement explained by all blocks of variables, and the 85.2 percent explained by the student block, all but 34.6 percent of that variance is so interwined and confounded by other predictors that it cannot be attributed to a single variable or to a single block. Coleman et al. (1966) and Murnane (1975) and overstate their cases by attributing so much uniquely to past achievement.

This is not to contend that past achievement is a weak predictor of present achievement. Past achievement is the most powerful single predictor. However, much of its robustness is a function of its mutual impact on other blocks. The demographics of schools and the nature of teacher assignment and teacher reactions to students tend to become interlinked so as to exacerbate the apparent impact of the past on the present. What the results suggest, then, is that students who have performed poorly on standarized tests in the past continue to do so because of the absence of corrective mechanisms within the home, the neighborhood, and the school. Likewise, disadvantages obtained through the mutual interactions of home, neighborhood, and school tend to perpetuate and even exacerbate themselves in successive years of schooling. Thus a child who performs badly in year one does so because of a combination of home and school disadvantages. These disadvantages increase and are linked with teacher assignment, teacher attitudes and labeling procedures, and school and home resources. The combined effect is one of diminishing the likelihood of future performance. The commonality analysis indicated that only about three-eighths of the total explained variance in present achievement is a function of past achievement; this fact suggests that increased achievement levels for students necessitate taking the student from a school-neighborhood-home environment that interactively and multiplicatively accentuates their disadvantage. Altering only one of the variables is inadequate; it may be necessary to rearrange many variables to affect academic performance.

An additional element in an equation of the effects on present achievement is native ablility or intelligence. These data were not consistently accessible and therefore were not included in the model of the original Singleton Ratio study. Thus, some of the variance in achievement explained by past achievement may actually be a function of intelligence; some of the variance unexplained by any other factor may also be due to ability.

It is arguable that the role of past test scores in present achievement tends to increase with exposure to the educational system. Logically, if school effects are cumulative, as Murnane (1975), Okada et al. (1969), and Hanushek (1972) maintain, then for each year of prior exposure to schooling, the impact of prior academic achievement will increase. Logically, the impact of school on a 1st grader's achievements are minimal, since only the kindergarten experience is involved. By contrast, the impact of school effects and especially prior achievement should be maximal for the 12th grader. Optimally, one would need to assess the impact of these effects in a time series and track students over several years. The data in this study do not afford us that opportunity. However, if we can demonstate that the unique contribution of past test scores to the total variance in achievement level does not differ with each grade level, we can discount the claim that the relatively smaller amount of unique variance explained by past achievement for the entire sample is a function of the suppressing effect of merging younger and older students.

The commonality analysis of prior test scores on present test scores was run singly for the 4th, 5th and 6th graders. As will be recalled, the unique contribution to the total variance accounted for by past test scores for the aggregate was .346. For the 4th graders analyzed alone, the value was .348, while for the 5th graders it was .344, and for the 6th graders it was .345. Applying the Kerlinger and Pehazur (1973) test of the increment of R^2 to the extreme differences yields no significant differences. Thus, we can conclude that the effects of past test scores on the unique contribution to R^2 in present test scores do not incresase significantly from year to year, and therefore we need not reject the prior observation that past test scores do not uniquely contribute more than a third of the variance in present test scores.

Reanalysis of Student Absenteeism Using Commonality Analysis

As I observed earlier, the measure of absenteeism includes both unexcused and excused absences. The former may be a function of student commitment and the latter a measure of student health. As an independent variable, absenteeism adjusted for membership in the school has a significant effect on achievement. As a dependent variable, the meaure is weakly explained by the predictors. Only 7.69 percent of the total variance in absenteeism was explained by the model. Few blocks uniquely explained even 1 percent of the total variance, with the student block explaining 3.74 percent of the variance uniquely (see table 4.7). Clearly, student absenteeism is not affected by teacher behavior or attitudes, and is only weakly affected by any of the other student background characteristics. It is thus concluded that basic health, the emergence of flu epidemics on a campus, and other factors unassociated with student commitment or teacher commitment affect actual attendance behavior.

Table 4.7
Summary of Commonality Analysis of Student Absenteeism

Variance categories	Blocks of independent variables				
	Actor traits	*Side-bets*	*Satisfaction solidarity*	*Building characteristics*	*Student characteristics*
Unique variance	.00073	.00824	.00492	.00410	.03739
Common variance	.00365	.00578	.00411	.01053	.01653
Total variance	.00438	.01402	.00903	.01463	.05392
Variance from structural equations (a check)	.00438	.01402	.00903	.01463	.05392

High- and Low-Achieving Students

It may be argued that children of different prior achievement levels may be affected differently by teacher burnout, intentions to quit teaching, and actual quitting behavior. It will be recalled that on the aggregate, the effect of those variables was small. Burnout and intentions to quit had no significant effect on gain scores, while actual quitting tended to elevate gain scores slightly. To ascertain the effect of the three teacher actions and attitudes on students of differing ability or achievement levels, the composite achievement scores for the first year (1976) were trichotomized at plus and minus one standard deviation from the mean. High scorers were defined as students who in the previous year had scored one standard deviation or more above that of their grade level; low scorers were defined as those scoring one standard deviation or more below that of their grade level; and average scorers were those within one standard deviation above or below their grade level.

The cutting points for high, average, and low scorers for each of the three grade levels are presented below.

Grade level	Low scorer	Average scorer	High scorer
4	<2.65	2.65 to 4.63	>4.63
5	<3.24	3.24 to 5.59	>5.59
6	<3.95	3.95 to 6.55	>6.55

The values represent achievement levels in years. It is immediately apparent that achievement levels in the Houston Independent School District are not noticeably high. Low scorers, at least one standard deviation below the mean, are generally at least one-and-one-half years below their grade level, while high scorers need be not much more than a half year above their grade level to exceed the point of one standard deviation above their grade level.

Table 4.8 presents the associations and effects of the three teacher attitude and behavior variables on the academic gains of the three groups of scorers. Among low scorers, neither the intention to quit teaching nor actual quitting behavior has an effect on achievement gains between the first and second year. Interestingly enough, burnout has a small but statistically significant positive effect. An increase in teacher burnout produces about a three-week gain in the achievement of low scorers (b = .077). One might speculate that the demands upon teachers made by low-achieving students heighten burnout but that the expenditure of such efforts, while they exhaust the teachers, produces some results in the students. An alternative explanation is that burned-out teachers may not be as intimidating to low-achieving students and therefore many not press them to work at faster rates than that at which they can assimilate information.

Among average students, neither burnout nor actual quitting behavior has an impact. The intention to quit teaching has a small negative effect on achievement. The obtained b of -.029 suggests that a teacher who intends to quit produces one week less in achievement in the average scorers.

A more pronounced effect can be seen in the impact of the teachers variables on high-scoring students. While no significant effect is registered for plans to quit or actual quitting behavior, the role of burnout is pronounced. The obtained b is -.169, indicating that for a high-scoring student, every unit of increase in burnout among that student's teacher produces a decline in achievement of one-and-two-thirds months within the year.

The explanation for the overall findings regarding the impact of burnout on each group of scorers is reasonably clear. With standarized lesson plans, average and low-achieving students are likely to get a fairly constant and perhaps average education regardless of the enthusiasm level of their teachers. The same is not true for higher achievers. High-achieving students are also likely to be bright students. To stimulate them to greater achievement and not bore them by routine instruction, the teacher must be enthusiastic about his or her work. Burned-out teachers are less likely and less willing to go beyond the requirements of the

Table 4.8

*Impact of Teacher Commitment on Gain Scores of Low-,
Medium-, and High-Scoring Children*

Gain	Total covar. r	b	s.e.	F	Beta
Low scorers					
Burnout	.079	.077	.042	3.39	.143
Plans to quit	-.048	-.049	.031	0.04	-.120
Quitting	-.003	-.199	.100	2.46	-.013
		R = .131	R² = .017		
Average scorers					
Burnout	-.040	-.008	.027	0.08	-.011
Plans to quit	-.063	-.029	.020	2.17	-.056
Quitting	-.035	-.059	.070	0.72	-.029
		R = .017	R² = .005		
High scorers					
Burnout	-.167	-.122	.038	10.40	-.197
Plans to quit	.003	.032	.027	1.37	.072
Quitting	.023	-.006	.093	0.005	-.004
		R = .182	R² = .033		

minimal lesson plan and are less likely to provide the necessary enrichment, stimulation, and challenge that bright students desire. Burned-out teachers are therefore more likely to suppress potential achievement among high-achieving students and even to be threatened by such children, who demand challenge and stimulation. But they are less likely to be threatened by average or low-achieving children, and thus do not adversely affect the achievement of those groups. It is therefore imperative, when selecting faculties for above-average and gifted children, to match technical competence requirements for teachers with a sufficient degree of enthusiasm for teaching. Otherwise, such programs are likely to produce disappointing results.

One caution must be applied to the conclusions in this section. The amount of achievement variance accounted for by the teacher attitude and behavior variables is small. The highest amount of variance explained was for the high-achieving group; however, even that was slight. Among low scorers, the three teacher variables I have discussed produce and R of .131 and an R^2 of .017; for average achievers, the R is .071 and the R^2 is a tiny .005. For high scorers, the obtained R is .182 and the R^2 is .033.

Racial Differences in the Models of Student Achievement Gain, Total Gain, and Absenteeism

Earlier, I noted that many of the teacher variables played a negligible role in determining student achievement gain, total achievement, and attendance behavior when the models were analyzed at the aggregate level. However, I also indicated that where significant differences between catgories of students existed, I would disaggregate the effects of the independent variables on student academic outcomes, controlling for student categories. Do the patterns discerned at the aggregate level persist when the models are tested on separate racial subgroups of students? For example, teacher stereotyping is consistently associated with achievement gains. Is this true for black students, brown students, and white students equally? In the present section, the models are recalculated and separate regression runs are conducted for each racial group of students. The next three tables present the results of the models of gain, total achievement, and absenteeism for black students, brown students, and white students.

Black Students

Table 4.9 presents the test of the models of gain, total achievement, and attendance behavior computed only for black students, regardless of the school setting in which they are located. For achievement gain, each of the significant predictors is drawn from the teacher and the building blocks. Teacher stereotyping continues to exert a positive influence on achievement gain, elevating the score by about two weeks. Interestingly enough, however, teachers who like the racial composition of the school to which they are assigned also elevate gain scores, in this instance by about a month-and-one-half. Teachers who feel that *their own group* is the target of discrimination depress gain scores by more than two-and-one-half months.

For each year of additional teacher experience (up through five years), students' gain scores increase by three weeks. A one-year increase in a teacher's age is associated with only a three-day increase in student gain, partly because there is more variance in teacher age than in years of experience, and also because the substantial gains in achievement are associated with the less-experienced teachers. Teachers who quit are associated with an increase of more than two-and-three-quarter months gain. Likewise, teachers who are burned out elevate gain scores by well over one month. Black students attending white schools gain two-and-one-third months more achievement than black students in other schools.

Table 4.9

Disaggregation of Gain, Achievement, and Absenteeism Scores:
Black Students

Gain	Total covar. r	b	s.e.	F	Beta
Gain scores					
Stereotyping	.035	.043	.017	5.98	.131
Age of teacher	.156	.012	.005	5.37	.213
Assignment attitude	.189	.151	.044	11.57	.172
Discrimination	-.093	-.261	.082	10.13	-.184
Inexperience	.213	.070	.024	8.59	.185
Quitting	.008	.280	.095	8.69	.158
Burnout	.023	.121	.042	8.13	.173
White school	.079	.233	.164	2.00	.074
	Intercept = -.284		R = .393	$R^2 = .154$	
Total achievement					
Stereotyping	.018	.037	.017	4.62	.064
Age of teacher	.054	.010	.005	3.67	.099
Assignment attitude	.123	.155	.044	12.53	.099
Discrimination	-.093	-.259	.080	10.46	-.102
Inexperience	.141	.078	.024	10.22	.115
Burnout	.083	.096	.042	5.17	.077
Quitting	.095	.224	.095	5.59	.071
First-year achievement	.837	.875	.034	677.82	.831
White school	.210	.334	.164	4.12	.057
	Intercept = 1.136		R = .864	$R^2 = .747$	
Absenteeism					
Experience	.037	.002	.001	2.93	.169
Age of student	.088	.009	.003	6.60	.125
Second-year achievement	-.163	-.012	.003	15.39	-.198
Teacher turnover	.125	.085	.036	5.41	.114
	Intercept = .189		R = .272	$R^2 = .074$	

The same teacher and building variables come into play, with total achievement levels and the magnitude and direction of the effects are also about the same. Teacher burnout continues to be linked with slightly higher levels of achievement for black children. Because black children are disproportionately found among the group of low achievers, it is possible that they may heighten teacher stress and feelings of personal failure, which predispose professionals to burnout. In other words, working with low achievers, of whom a disproportionate number are black, may produce burnout, rather than burnout acutally producing higher achievement. There is no support, however, for a claim that high-achieving black students also benefit from a teacher who has burned out. Rather, these children suffer low achievement levels from such exposure $(b = -.155;$ s.e. $= .041;$ beta $= -.186)$. Thus, it is being a low achiever, rather than being black, which is involved in gains due to exposure to burned-out teachers.

Student absenteeism for black children is heightened most by teacher turnover rates at the school. The other variables exert a much weaker effect (although the b's are significant). High teacher turnover, an especially chronic problem for black schools (Dworkin, 1980), is associated with an increase in black student absenteeism of twelve days (.085 of a school year). Presumably, if there is high turnover in a school, then teacher morale (as opposed to individual teacher burnout) may be so low that attendance norms are not being enforced. Clark (1965), Remsberg and Remsberg (1968), and Noblit (1979) have all commented that when white teachers in black schools are unable to maintain order, they simply allow students to do as they please—including cutting classes.

Mexican American Students

As is shown in table 4.10, only teacher and building characteristics exert a significance influence on Mexican American student achievement gain and total achievement levels. Teacher stereotyping elevates achievement gains for Mexican American children by three-quarters of a month, while an external locus of control held by teachers diminishes achievement gains by two weeks. It is plausible that teacher stereotyping is directed toward the use of Spanish. A teacher who believes that Mexican American children start more trouble, get undeserved special treatment, and are not targets of discrimination is less likely to condone bilingual teaching and bilingual classroom speech. Given that the Iowa Test taps a facility with English, a teacher who is biased in favor of the monolingual use of English in the classroom would be expected to produce higher achievement gain scores. Regardless of the social and political issues involved in bilingual education, these data suggest (keeping in mind that the total amount of explained variance is small), that a bias toward Anglo conformity in speech style is associated with registered achievement gains when measured by an instrument with a decided bias toward English as a language and Anglo norms.

Table 4.10

Disaggregation of Gain, Achievement, and Absenteeism Scores:
Brown Students

Variable	Total covar. r	b	s.e.	F	Beta
Gain scores					
Stereotyping	.252	0.074	.019	15.46	.255
External locus	-.205	-0.044	.018	5.91	-.166
School size	-.069	-0.0002	.0001	3.92	-.129
Intercept = .408 R = .342 R² = .117					
Total achievement					
Stereotyping	.054	0.066	.019	12.40	.100
External locus	-.063	-0.041	.018	4.89	-.067
Busing	.119	1.295	.620	3.24	.077
Magnet school	-.003	-0.288	.140	3.70	-.081
Intercept = .249 R = .911 R² = .831					
Absenteeism					
Sex of teacher	.053	0.027	.015	3.34	.128
Assignment attitude	-.149	-0.022	.008	7.57	-.173
Attitude toward Singleton Ratio	-.053	-0.012	.006	3.30	-.128
Teacher turnover	.114	0.183	.089	4.17	.134
First-year achievement	-.172	-0.017	.005	10.45	.261
Teacher and student of same sex	.052	0.022	.011	2.91	.143
Intercept = .018 R = .366 R² = .134					

The role of an external locus of control in diminishing achievement gains and total achievement has been addressed earlier. A teacher who does not believe that upward mobility is attainable through personal effort nor that people control their own destinies is unlikely to encourage minority and low-income children to strive for higher levels of achievement. A certain degree of optimism toward self-improvement is evidently necessary for a teacher to elevate achievement levels for minority children.

Total achievement scores are affected considerably by busing. The higher the percentage of students bused to a school, the higher the academic achievement of Mexican American children. Most of the *barrio* elementary schools are not receiving schools. Therefore, being sent out of a Mexican American school is associated with heightened achievement. In fact, the total achievement level associated with increases in busing is more than one-and-one-quarter years. This is not necessarily to contend that a black or a white school is better. Perhaps the achievement differences are between children sufficiently fluent in English that they can attend a school out of the *barrio* and those not so fluent; thus the differences are between English speakers and non-English speakers, again on a test that is biased in favor of English speakers.

Attending a magnet school is associated with lower achievement levels of almost three months. At the time of the study, the majority of magnet schools at the elementary level focused on such subjects as physical education, conservation and forestry, or foreign languages rather than upon academic excellence. Therefore, attending a magnet school might track a Mexican American child into either a nonacademic curriculum or into a school which sharpens that child's facility with Spanish. Again, given the bias towards English, attending a magnet school is not beneficial for achievement as measured by the Iowa Test.

Absenteeism among Mexican American students is raised by nearly five days by having a female teacher. This finding suggests that the children (and probably their parents) are more likely to conform to school attendance rules if a male teacher issues those rules than if a female issues them. That teacher's sex is not significantly associated with absenteeism for any other group of students is intriguing. The ethic of *machismo* may still linger in the behaviors of these students.

Teachers who like being assigned to the school at which they teach depress absenteeism by about two days. Schools which have high rates of teacher turnover increase student absenteeism to 18.3 percent of a school year, or over thirty days. High levels of prior achievement are associated with low absenteeism, either because children who do well in school find school more rewarding and so are absent less often, or because good school attendance promotes higher achievement. Here, the effect is one of about four-and-one-half days. Since most teachers are women, the variable operates as follows. Mexican American parents value the education of their daughters less than that of their sons. Because most of the teachers are women, insistence on attendance imposed by a female teacher is honored less often by girls—some of whom are expected to stay home and care for younger siblings—than by boys, who are expected to be somewhat better educated (Ramirez and Castanada, 1974). Girls therefore attend school less than boys, and female teachers are less effective in maintaining attendance for girls than for boys.

White Students

Generally speaking, white students are affected by teacher and school variables in a similar fashion as are minority students; however, the effects are not always as pronounced. As is displayed in table 4.11, a teacher with an external locus of control reduces the gain in white achievement by a third of a month, compared with the nearly half-month for Mexican American students. Older teachers reduce achievement gain by slightly over two days for each year of increase in the teacher's age. By contrast, achievement gains for black students increase by three days for each additional year of the teacher's age. Income independence of teachers tends to heighten achievement for white students. The teacher who does not have to work but does so heightens the academic achievement of white students by approximately one hour for each dollar of income independence. Since the teachers in the study averaged over $13,000 in income independence, with a standard deviation of over $9,000, teachers at the upper end of the income independence continuum could account for as much as a third of a year of additonal gain among white students.

Teacher turnover in schools affects white students more profoundly than it does black or Mexican American students. While teacher turnover has no statistically significant effect on black or brown achievement gain, it reduces white gain scores by over eight-and-one-half months. Because high turnover rates for teachers in predominantly white schools are not common, they may reflect some of the influence of white teacher turnover on white children attending minority schools, in which case it is not merely turnover that is being measured, but racial marginality as well.

Among the student variables which affect white students' achievement gain are age, grade level, and absenteeism. Older students gain at a rate that is nearly one month more than younger students. Students with high absenteeism rates lose a year-and-one-quarter in gain scores. Since white absenteeism is actually quite low, this magnitude of loss reflects the impact of a relatively small percentage of students who are regularly absent. For each year of increment in grade level for white students (comparing 4th, 5th, and 6th graders), there is a corresponding increase in the magnitude of gain scores of one-and-one-third months. It is clear, then, that white students supply the greatest evidence for a fan effect. That black and brown students do display this fan effect suggests that some of

Table 4.11

*Disaggregation of Gain, Achievement, and Absenteeism Scores:
White Students*

Variable	Total covar. r	b	s.e.	F	Beta
Gain scores					
External locus	-.132	-0.036	.011	11.35	-.166
Age of teacher	-.133	-0.007	.002	11.03	-.172
Income independence	.128	0.0001	.0000	3.07	.086
Teacher turnover	-.093	-0.849	.343	6.13	-.119
Age of student	.055	0.110	.043	6.73	.222
Grade	.044	0.136	.052	6.98	.230
Absenteeism	-.167	-1.278	.406	9.89	-.150
	Intercept = 1.714	R = .369	R² = .136		
Total achievement					
External locus	-.096	-0.036	.011	11.25	-.057
Age of teacher	-.019	-0.007	.002	10.00	-.056
Income independence	.139	0.0001	.0000	3.01	.029
Teacher turnover	-.069	-0.827	.344	5.79	-.039
Age of student	.322	0.112	.043	6.58	.077
First-year achievement	.940	0.996	.022	1,984.40	.910
Absenteeism	-.213	-1.212	.408	8.82	-.049
	Intercept = 1.213	R = .948	R² = .899		
Absenteeism					
Stereotyping	.068	0.002	.001	2.36	.080
Income independence	-.113	-0.0001	.0000	3.05	-.084
Black school	.109	0.034	.014	5.93	.118
Teacher and student of same sex	.070	0.008	.004	3.08	.076
First-year achievement	-.171	-0.013	.006	4.35	-.293
Second-year achievement	-.213	-0.019	.006	11.52	-.476
Student SES	-.150	-0.012	.004	8.24	-.137
	Intercept = .266	R = .344	R² = .118		

the differences between majority and minority educational outcomes are due to the fact that majority group members' gain scores increase at an increasing rate, while those of minorities do not. It is not that minorities fall farther and farther behind because of diminishing returns from education, but that majorities pull farther and farther ahead. Minority groups also display a slight fan effect, but the b values are not statistically significant. Better-quality schools, more teacher encouragement, and better home resources thus seem to help white students extract more out of the educational scene than they do minorities. In terms of actual achievement levels, each of the variables operative in white gain scores plays the same role. An external locus of control, teacher age, teacher turnover, student age, and student absenteeism all reduce achievement levels to approximately the same extent that they reduce gain scores. Teacher income independence heightens achievement levels to the same magnitude that it heightens gain scores. Of course, prior achievement remains the most powerful predictor of present achievement levels.

White students exposed to stereotyping teachers are absent slightly more often than those who are not so exposed. An increase in teacher stereotyping is associated with an elevation in absenteeism of merely a few hours. However, attending a black school heightens white student absenteeism by a third of a month. Thus, those few white students who attend predominantly black schools or who are in magnet schools attached to black schools are absent much more often than those who are not in such schools. Having a teacher of the same sex as the student also increases absenteeism, but the impact is less than one day. By contrast, student absenteeism for whites is reduced by assignment to a teacher who is economically independent of the teaching salary, by past and present high achievement levels, and by higher socioeconomic levels.

Disentangling the Effect of Teacher Stereotyping on Student Achievement

An entirely unexpected finding in this chapter has been that students seem to achieve more academically if they are assigned to a teacher who stereotypes them pejoratively than if they are not. This finding runs exactly counter to the labeling model advances by Rosenthal and Jacobson (1968), Rist (1970), and Bowles and Gintis (1976). In that model, teacher bias against low-income and minority children is manifested in reduced interaction between the teacher and such children, and therefore diminishes teaching and help directed toward those children. As a consequence, the children benefit less from the educational experience than children labeled as desirable. While much of the subsequent research has failed to support the labeling hypothesis, nowhere have data previously suggested that pejorative labeling may actually heighten achievement. The current findings cry for further investigation and a revised model. Two rival explanations for the findings can be offered, and a further disaggregation of the data sets will be conducted to test the rival explanations.

The first explanation, termed the "embourgeoisment hypothesis," stems from the observations by Charters (1963), Ogbu (1974), Levy (1970), Fuchs (1969), and Collins and Noblit (1976) that middle class teachers in inner-city schools often come to define their role as socializing agents who can bring middle-class values to their students. These teachers believe that in adopting middle-class values and mannerisms, the children will be able to raise themselves out of their lower-class existence. One way to accomplish this change is to encourage the children to change their language usage and speech styles (Dworkin, 1968). To the extent that standardized achievement tests tend to be biased toward middle-class vocabularies and learning experiences, attempts to make minority and low-income children conform to middle-class norms, combined with teacher rejection of multicultural ideologies, may have the effect of escalating student achievement. The embourgeoisment thesis does not contend that middle-class or majority-group values and behaviors are preferable, nor does the model condone stereotyping. It simply states that since the tests are biased in favor of the middle classes, a teacher who rewards middle-class ideas and is not supportive of working- and lower-class values may elevate achievement scores. By contrast, the teacher who is multicultural in outlook, stressing the legitimacy of a variety of ethnic and class orientations, may be less critical of vocabularies and behaviors which are counterproductive to high achievement scores, given the biased nature of the tests.

The rival to the embourgeoisment model is that which Maykovich (1972) has termed the "reciprocal prejudice" model. In this model, which Maykovich attributes to the work of Adelson (1958) and Dworkin (1965), minority group members rebut dominant stereotypes with negative imagery directed toward the majority group. The major share of the variance accounted for by stereotyping would be attributed to negative images minority teachers hold of majorities, which serve to sustain and provide self-pride to minority students. Thus, minority teachers, in an attempt to foster ethnic pride, may deride the majority group. Success in developing minority self-pride in turn elevates achievement. In such cases, then, stereotyping does not elevate achievement in the target group, but only in groups for whom the stereotypes serve as rebuttals. Presumably, black or brown teachers who hold negative images of whites but no such images of students of their own race may actively stimulate minority children to be proud of their ethnic heritage. This activity serves as a reverse labeling procedure which elevates achievement of minority children labeled as "preferable" and "superior."

Support for an embourgeoisment model requires that the negative stereotypes are directed at the child's own ethnic group. Support for the reciprocal prejudice model requires that the stereotypes are directed toward a dominant outgroup. It should be noted in advance that so few teachers in the study held negative images about their own group that only outgroup stereotying could be assessed. However, whenever a teacher asserts that a group is more likely to cause trouble, to receive undeserved advantages, and to break school rules, that teacher is also asserting that other groups are less likely to commit such acts. A minority teacher who attributes negative motives and behaviors to majority students on a questionnaire format which requires comparisons and permits an option to consider all groups as equal is attributing to minorities less negative imagery.

Table 4.12 presents the results of the regression analyses of the impact of teacher stereotyping on students, controlling for the race of the teachers and the students. The data provide some support for the reciprocal prejudice model but only circumstantial support for the embourgeoisment model. Black and brown achievement levels are significantly higher statistically when a teacher of the same race as the students is stereotyping whites pejoratively, but white achievement levels are unaffected by pejorative images of them held by nonwhite teachers. However, when white teachers stereotype minority students negatively, there is no statistically significant effect, although all of the b's are in the direction supporting an embourgeoisment hypothesis. For white students, negative stereotyping of minorities is not associated with heightened achievement, although the b is negative.

In conclusion, considering the small amount of total variance explained, the reciprocal prejudice model is the more viable one. Teacher stereotyping elevates achievement for minority children when the teacher is of the same race as the children and the target group is white. When the teacher is white and pejoratively stereotypes minority children, the effect on minority children is rather negligible (even though it is also in the direction of elevating achievement), no doubt because majority images of minorities are not considered legitimate by minority group members (Dworkin, 1965; Maykovich, 1972; McCarthy and Yancey, 1971).

Table 4.12

*Effect of Teacher Stereotyping on Achievement Gain,
Controlling for Race of Student and Teacher*

Race of child/ Race of teacher	Total covar. r	b	s.e.	p	F	Beta
Black/black	.120	.093	.039	.001	5.51	.250
Black/brown	.000	.000	.000	ns	0.00	.000
Black/white	.097	.040	.021	ns	2.03	.132
Brown/black	.382	.122	.074	ns	2.71	.395
Brown/brown	.201	.217	.108	.05	1.99	.296
Brown/white	.147	.023	.028	ns	0.65	.079
White/black	.146	.004	.023	ns	0.03	.019
White/brown	.000	.000	.000	ns	0.00	.000
White/white	-.054	-.005	.015	ns	0.10	-.021

NOTE: ns = no significant difference.

Summary and Policy Implications

It is now possible to provide answers to the four original research questions posed at the beginning of this chapter. Generally speaking, teacher burnout has a minimal effect on student achievement and attendance. The only notable exceptions are that low achievers and some groups of black children register slight gains in the presence of burned-out teachers, while high achievers tend to register lesser gains when assigned to such teachers. However, other variables in the models have greater effects.

The first question dealt with differences in academic gains between students assigned to burned-out teachers and those assigned to teachers who were not burned out. I contend that the effect is minimal, possibly even nonexistent. I have noted that teacher burnout has the most negative effect on children who are high achievers and who need a teacher who is enthusiastic and willing to make extra efforts for them. However, the stability offered by standardized lesson plans insures that most students (all but 16 percent) will be unaffected by teacher burnout directly. Indirectly, however, teacher burnout may play a role, since it can contribute to staff instability at the school level. This instability is implicated in lower achievement levels for all students.

Turning to the second question—the association between teacher burnout and attendance behavior—I find no evidence that burnout affects student absenteeism. This finding is consistent across all groups of students. Thus, a measure of teacher commitment is unassociated with the estimate of student commitment. Again, the only link is found through the variable of staff stability. The forces which make for an unstable teaching staff also make for higher student absenteeism. However, unlike the model of student achievement, the variables used in accounting for student absenteeism very poorly explain that construct. There is no doubt that attendance is affected by many factors outside the control of the school or the behaviors of the teachers. In the absence of attitudinal measures of student motivation, attendance is the only available index of student commitment. However, such a measure is confounded by parental attitudes and behavior, health factors, and a multitude of other variables, many of which may not be related to student attitudes regarding school.

The third question addressed the effects of assignment to a teacher who subsequently quits teaching on student achievement and attendance. Although quitting behavior on the part of teachers has a small impact, it is nonetheless significant. Teachers who later quit tend to produce higher achievement levels among their students than teachers who do not quit teaching. No such effect can be found on the dependent variable of attendance. It must be recalled that quitting behavior is defined not in terms of exiting the school district, but of exiting teaching. The teacher who quits does so either to exit the labor market (most often because of marriage) or to obtain another job. Earlier work on translatability (Dworkin, 1982) has indicated that role exit behavior among teachers who want to quit teaching is most often accomplished by those with translatable skills. The academic gains of students assigned to teachers who subsequently quit may in part be attributed to exposure to teachers with higher skill levels, especially communications skills demanded by industry, and perhaps a better grasp of current subject matter. Such teachers may also have more recent training and therefore more current knowledge of their subject matter, but may still be experienced enough to avoid the counterproductive mistakes characteristic of neophyte teachers.

A distinction must be made between the effect of the quitting behavior of an individual teacher and of the wholesale turnover of faculty at a school. While the behavior of an individual teacher may affect the turnover rate, higher-than-normal quitting rates are likely to indicate administrative disorganization and generally low morale among all participants. Therefore, while higher rates of teacher turnover are associated with depressed levels of student achievement, the teachers who quit in any given year may be individuals who are sufficiently competent or motivated enough at the time when the students took the Iowa Test to elevate student achievement.

The fourth question asked about the varying roles of the components and predictors of burnout, taken separately and in combination, on student achievement and attendance. Student outcomes are poorly explained by teacher burnout. Burnout per se has no effect on the achievement gain, total achievement level, or attendance behavior of the aggregate of students. It does have an elevating effect upon the achievement level of low achievers and many black students, heightening their achievement by nearly a month for each increment in burnout. The more profound effect of burnout is upon students who were identified as high scorers (their achievement scores are one or more standard deviations above the mean for their grade level). Such high-achieving students within a year recorded achievement gains that are well over one month less for each unit of increment in teacher burnout.

The predictors of burnout—including actor traits, building characteristics, side-bets, and satisfaction and solidarity—account uniquely for small portions of student achievement gain, total achievement level, and attendance. The commonality analysis strongly suggests that no aspect of the burnout model is dominant in its ability to explain student outcomes. In fact, no aspect of the model is any more or any less powerful in accounting for student achievement gain than are the student background variables. Each accounts uniquely for only about 1 to 2 percent of the variance in gain scores. Likewise, once prior achievement is removed, total achievement is weakly explained by all the components of burnout, and even by the background characteristics of the students. Less than 1 percent of total achievement can be explained uniquely by any teacher block, building block, or the student block with the removal of previous achievement. Nonetheless, the commonality analysis persuasively illustrates the confounded nature of school, teacher, and student variables in accounting for achievement. Most of the variance in present achievement is communal—shared and intertwined with teacher, student, and school variables in such a way that it cannot be teased out.

5

Conclusion

School districts in urban areas expend a significant portion of their resources in attempts to reduce the level of teacher turnover. It has not been uncommon for a large urban school district, such as the one studied in this report, to spend six to ten million dollars annually in programs such as the "Second Mile Plan," which are designed in part to create incentives to retard quitting behavior among teachers. These funds are spent in spite of the scarcity of empirical evidence that significant student gains can be created by such indirect means.

This research began with an inquiry into the extent to which teacher alienation and burnout propel quitting behavior and, in turn, the extent to which such burnout adversely affects students. Although the central theme of the research was the impact of teacher burnout on student learning outcomes, it soon became apparent that an analysis of the factors which create and retard burnout among teachers was needed before the effect of burnout on children could be studied. The three previous chapters have demonstrated that teacher burnout does not adequately account for teacher turnover; that an enlightened administrative style on the part of the principal can do much to mitigate the negative aspects of stress and teaching; and that the majority of students are not adversely affected by a burned-out teacher. In light of the impact of burnout on some groups of students, the allocation of school resources to reduce burnout may be extravagant. However, it is possible to create an informed and comprehensive educational policy which may go far to reduce burnout; ultimately to reduce turnover, or at least entrapment; to reduce significantly the negative aspects of stress associated with teaching; and to provide for increased educational gains, especially for high-achieving children. Such an educational policy should be informed by the findings of the studies presented in this book.

Summary of Empirical Generalizations (Supported Propositions)

What follows in this section is a presentation of the research find-ings from each of the three research projects. The findings are expressed in terms of supported propositions and are ordered by study, by model within study, and by block within model. The reader should note that the findings reported are from the regression analyses and thus are essential-ly multivariate in nature. All relationships reported are supported, even controlling for the effects of other variables. A brief overall discussion of the findings for a particular model is given before the presentation of each group of supported propositions. The intent of this section is to per-mit the reader to examine in abridged fashion the findings presented in the three previous chapters of the report.

I. Teacher Burnout, Plans To Quit, and Quitting Behavior

The first study, based upon the questionnaire data on 3,444 public school teachers in the Houston Independent School District in 1977 and the follow-up exit records through 1982, examined the role of actor traits, building characteristics, side-bets, and satisfaction and solidarity upon burnout, plans to quit teaching, and actual quitting behavior. The model of burnout accounted for 32.0 percent of the variance in that con-struct. Commonality analysis revealed that the strongest unique variance was explained by the satisfaction and solidarity block, followed by the building characteristics, actor traits, and side-bet blocks. Much more support was garnered for a social psychological theory of burnout and commitment then for a social-structural one.

The model which was designed to account for plans to quit teaching accounted for 37.2 percent of the total variance in that construct. Here, commonality analysis revealed that satisfaction and solidarity explained the preponderance of the variance in plans to quit, with actor traits, building characteristics, and side-bets following weakly behind. When burnout was extracted from the satisfaction and solidarity block, it uni-quely accounted for 22.1 percent of the variance in plans to quit.

Actual quitting behavior was not particularly well explained by our model. Whether or not a teacher quits, even if he or she was dissatisfied with teaching, seemed to be much more a function of opportunities and alternatives often out of the actor's control. Most teachers have relative-ly few skills which are translatable into other careers without substantial retraining. The model of quitting behavior explained only 9.0 percent of the total variance in the construct. No commonality analysis was run on this model because the total explained variance was much too small to partition. However, individual variables which indicated greater career alternatives were the strongest predictors of quitting Behavior.

A. Supported propositions pertaining to teacher burnout:
1. The older the teacher, the less the likelihood of burnout.
2. The more external the teacher's locus of control, the greater the likelihood of burnout.
3. Black teachers are less likely to burn out than any other racial group of teachers.
4. The more that a teacher is racially isolated from the student body of a school, the greater the likelihood that the teacher will experience burnout.
5. The likelihood of teacher burnout diminishes with each additional year of teaching that a teacher gains beyond the fifth year in the classroom.
6. Tenured teachers are less likely to burn out than untenured teachers.
7. The greater the income independence of a teacher (having alternative sources of income), the greater the likelihood of burnout.
8. The greater the discrepancy between a teacher's perception of the preferred role of a principal and his or her own principal's perception of that role, the greater the likelihood that the teacher will experience burnout.
9. Teachers who report experiences with racial discrimination are more likely to burn out than teachers who do not.
10. The more that the norms in a school are seen as supporting interracial cooperation among faculty and staff, the less likely is the experience of teacher burnout.
11. The greater the support for the Singleton Ratio, which assigned faculty to schools on the basis of their race, the less the likelihood of burnout.
12. The more a teacher defines the racial composition of the student body of a school as desirable, the less likely it is that the teacher will report having experienced burnout.

B. Supported propositions on plans to quit teaching:
1. Male teachers are more likely to want to quit teaching than female teachers.
2. The higher the social class origin of a teacher, the more likely it is that the teacher will plan to quit teaching.
3. The more external a teacher's locus of control, the more likely it is that the teacher will plan to quit teaching.
4. The more that a teacher is racially isolated from the student body of a school, the more likely it is that the teacher will plan to quit teaching.

5. The larger the percentage of minority groups in a school, the greater will be the desire of teachers to quit teaching.
6. The higher the grade level that a teacher is assigned to teach, the less that teacher will want to quit teaching.
7. The likelihood that a teacher will plan to quit teaching diminishes with each additional year of teaching experience that a teacher gains beyhond the fifth year in the classroom.
8. The likelihood that a teacher will plan to quit teaching increases with each additional year of teaching experience that a teacher gains up through the fifth year in the classroom.
9. The higher the salary of a teacher, the less likely it is that the teacher will plan to quit teaching.
10. The greater the income independence of a teacher, the more likely it is that the teacher will plan to quit teaching.
11. Teachers with skills that are translatable into careers in other sectors of the economy without substantial retraining are more likely to plan to quit teaching than teachers without such translatable skills.
12. The more a teacher supports the Singleton Ratio, which assigned teachers to schools on the basis of race, the less likely it is that the teacher will plan to quit teaching.
13. The greater the level of burnout of a teacher, the more likely it is that the teacher will plan to quit teaching.

C. Supported propositions on actual quitting behavior:
1. Older teachers are less likely to quit than younger teachers.
2. Teachers who hold negative stereotypes about members of other racial groups are less likely to quit teaching than teachers who do not hold such stereotypes.
3. Black teachers are less likely to quit teaching than white or brown teachers.
4. Teachers in higher grades are less likely to quit than teachers in lower grades.
5. The likelihood of actual quitting increases with each additional year of teaching experience that a teacher gains up to five years in the classroom.
6. The higher the status of a school employee's job title in the school district, and hence the responsibilities of that employee, the less likely it is that the employee will quit.
7. The greater the income independence of a teacher, the more likely it is that the teacher will quit teaching.
8. Teachers who have planned to quit are actually more likely to quit teaching than those who have not planned to quit.
9. However, burned-out teachers are no more likely to quit teaching than those who are not burned out.

In summary, teacher burnout and plans to quit teaching were exacerbated by punishing settings and were reduced by rewarding settings, status attainments, and social support systems. However, the conversion of burnout and plans to quit into actual quitting behavior is not so much a function of dissatisfaction and punishing settings as of opportunity. Teachers do not often quit their jobs, even if those jobs are unfulfilling, unless there are alternative sources of employment or economic support. Therefore teacher turnover is less of a problem facing public schools than is entrapment a problem for the teachers.

II. Teacher Stress and Social Support Mechanisms

The second study was conducted under the aegis of the Houston Federation of Teachers and involved a new questionnaire distributed to its members, some of whom were in the sample of the first study in 1981 and 1982. The sample size was 291, all of whom were then current members of the union. Stress levels were low to moderate across the sample of teachers. There were observable differences in stress level associated with the race and sex of the teacher, the grade level taught, the race of the school of assignment, and the experience of victimization reported by the teacher. Teachers who reported that their principals were supportive and treated them as trusted colleagues were less likely to be burned out and to plan to quit teaching than those who did not report such support. Furthermore, for such teachers stress was not functionally linked to burnout. The significance of this finding is enhanced when one realizes that the level of stress was homogeneous across groups of teachers assigned to supportive and unsupportive categories of principals. Furthermore, the actual effectiveness of the principal in minimizing stress on teachers was unimportant compared with the perception by the teachers that the principal was attempting to reduce stress levels. By contrast, peer support (the support of other teachers) did not affect burnout, plans to quit teaching, or the link between stress and burnout. The supported propositions are presented below.

1. Minority group members are less likely to report minor student offenses as stressful than majority group members. (The more often in the past that individuals experience situations as everyday activities, the less stressful will they define those activities to be.)
2. Teachers assigned to teach in elementary grades or in grades where student behavior is likely to be less predictable are more likely to report school occurrences as stressful than teachers assigned to teach in higher grades, especially in high school.

3. The more that a teacher perceives that he or she has been victimized by students or knows of teachers who have been victimized by students, the greater the probability that that teacher will report a high level of fear of students.
4. The greater the level of fear of victimization, the greater the level of reported stress.
5. Teachers who see their principals as supportive are less likely to report feelings of burnout than teachers who see their principals as unsupportive. However, levels of stress do not differ between the two groups of teachers.
6. Teachers who see their principals as influential among higher-level administrators are no less likely to report feelings of burnout than teachers who see their principals as uninfluential.
7. The more that teachers define their principals as supportive, the less likely it is that those teachers will report burnout or plans to quit teaching, regardless of the level of stress they report in their schools.

The 5th through 7th propostition suggest a clear path for an enlightened school policy. Teacher burnout may be reduced, and plans to quit teaching may in turn by retarded, by administrative policies which make principals more supportive, caring, and collegial toward their faculities. (Of course, as we have seen in the second chapter, actual quitting behavior may be unaffected by any such strategy.) The implementation of such policies should begin at the campus level. Principals must be provided with more adequate management training, either in colleges of education or in schools of business administration. "Theory X" approaches to administration (where policies are issued from the top down) are clearly not conducive to staff morale. As I have noted in the third chapter, the principal who treats his or her teachers as valued professional colleagues breaks the functional link between the stress which accompanies teaching and burnout. By breaking this link, the principal weakens the desire to quit teaching. School districts should not only require such administrative skills and styles of their principals, but they should reward principals who are able to lower burnout and turnover rates among their teaching staff. Of course, some controls are needed to prevent a principal from subverting educational goals in order to appease those teachers who might be dissatisfied under any circumstances. However, when a school has an excessive burnout rate, not just an excessive turnover rate, it is essential that the principal be held accountable.

Many investigators who have studied burnout have advocated counseling and personal therapy as viable strategies for helping affected human service professionals, including teachers (see Maslach, 1978b; Freudenberger, 1982; Sparks and Hammond, 1981; Cedoline, 1982; and Cherniss, 1980, who also advises "management support"). However, there is an economy of scale afforded by a structural policy which encourages principals to be more collegial and supportive of their teachers. In a school district as large as Houston's, it is only necessary to provide in-service training for less than three hundred principals to affect their management style; it is not necessary and more costly to provide individual and group assistance to several thousand teachers.

There is an additional reason why counseling and personal therapy for teachers may be less desirable than modifying the administrative style of principals. The problems which I have cited in public education are structural ones, and the failure of principals to treat teachers as respected colleagues is an administrative and organizational issue. Counseling and therapy stress coping skills and presume that the reasons for peoples' difficulties lie within themselves: either because they cause the problems directly or because they overreact to the problems. Teaching people to cope with organizational problems does little to correct those problems; it only ensures that the problems will continue, albeit with possibly fewer consequences. There is already a considerable tendency for teachers to blame individuals rather than the system. Ginsburg and Newman (1985) have found that most preservice and new teachers used meritocratic, human capital, and status attainment explanations to account for poor achievement by minority students. Rather than pointing to discrimination, educational disadvantage, or poverty as relevant factors, these teachers assume that poor achievement is caused by laziness. However, as we have seen in chapter 3 in the analysis of the four types of principals, the link between job stress and burnout is external to the teacher and is vested in the administrative behavior of the principal.

As I observed in the first study, teacher burnout and entrapment are more serious problems than is actual teacher turnover. Therefore, policies which reduce the harmful effects of stress on morale may actually be preferable to those solely monetary policies which attempt to entice teachers to stay in teaching when they want to leave. This is especially true given the consistent National Education Asssociation finding that teachers view their low salaries as less of a major educational problem than several other issues which more directly affect morale (Elam and Gough, 1980). I shall pursue the salary issue further in the last section of this chapter.

III. The Impact of Teacher Burnout upon Student Achievement Gain, Total Achievement, and Attendance

The third study involved merging the data sets from chapter 2 with data collected by the Singleton Ratio consulting team on student learning outcomes. In the student study presented to the school district in 1977, a random sample of 8,203 students was drawn, representing one out of every six children in grades 4, 5, and 6 of the district. Computer matches between the student data and the teacher data yielded a student sample size of 2,287 children who were taught by 518 of the teachers. Individual children represented the unit of analysis. In exploring the results of this substudy, two caveats must by acknowledged. First, the data are only on elementary school children; we do not know the nature of the effect of teacher burnout on junior and senior high school students. Second, test score data were available for only a two-year period; we cannot estimate the cumulative impact on children of having a burned-out teacher year after year after year.

The study counterpoised two prevailing models of school, teacher, and home effects upon three forms of student outcomes: achievement gain scores, overall achievement level, and attendance behavior. Models which propose that school effects are minimal argue that all or most of the variance in student performance can be accounted for by past achievement or some other measure of student ability and experience. Models which stress school and teacher effects emphasize labeling processes, which diminish the amount or quality of instruction that certain children receive. The blocks of teacher and building variables used in creating the models of burnout, plans to quit teaching, and quitting behavior were enhanced by the addition of a block of student variables. In addition, the block of student variables was analyzed with and without the inclusion of a commonly used measure of ability: a prior test score. Analyses included regression models of the agregate data sets, subsets comprising racial groups of students, and analyses of the separate components of the criterion of achievement—the Iowa Test of Basic Skills.

Less than 12 percent of the total variance in achievement gain scores could be explained by the entire model—a figure similar to that obtained by recent investigators when prior achievement is omitted. Commonality analysis revealed that no block of variables, not even the student block, could uniquely account for more than 2 percent of the variance in achievement gains. Achievement gain scores were so intertwined among the predictors, each of which was weak, that it was not possible to disentangle the effects. Teacher, school, and student effects were sufficiently intermixed that a modification of one would not ensure that achievement gains would be radically affected. Teacher burnout did not mitigate achievement gains for most children. Only in the subset analyses did we find any impact of teacher burnout upon children. Children who were low scorers on the Iowa Test of the previous year and black children (except for high-scoring black children) seemed to benefit slightly from assignment to a burned-out teacher. By contrast, children, regardless of race, who were high scorers in the previous year were quite adversely affected by such an assignment.

It is clearly advisable to screen out teachers who are burned out from assignment to programs for gifted and talented children. Bright children need stimulation and enrichment to heighten their achievement gains. The burned-out teacher is more likely to follow a uniform lesson plan approved by the principal and is unlikely to go beyond that plan or to make extra efforts for children whose abilities demand more complicated material. To assign burned-out teachers to children with high previous test scores may ensure that such children will not achieve as much as they might otherwise. Other groups of children, particularly those who are average scorers on prior tests, are not adversely affected by a burned-out teacher. Given the uniformity of lesson plans in the school district, a burned-out teacher neither benefits nor harms an average scorer.

The propositions which were supported for achievement gain were also supported for total level of achievement. The latter measure assessed the impact of the blocks of variables on the cumulative achievement of students. This measure was less sensitive to the impact of a single teacher but more sensitive to the accumulated effects of home, school, and teacher factors. The most significant finding in this analysis came from the commonality models. The model comprising the teacher, building, and student blocks accounted for 86.7 percent of the variance in achievement level when prior achievement was introduced into the regression equation. However, the commonality analysis revealed that, while prior achievement was the strongest predictor, it uniquely explained 34.6 percent of the variance. More than one-half of the toal variance in achievement was confounded variance, intertwined among the blocks. Thus, prior achievement was not as powerful a predictor as was previously argued by those using more conventional regression approaches.

Finally, the model accounted for only a tiny portion of the total variance in attendance behavior. In the absence of measures of student attitudes about their schooling, it was not possible to assess student commitment in any other fashion. Only 9.2 percent of the variance in absenteeism could be explained by the model. In fact, as an independent variable, absenteeism was a stronger predictor of achievement gain and total achievement level than were the variables used to predict absenteeism. Student absenteeism was probably more a function of idiosyncratic factors, including health and parental variables, than of any school or teacher variable.

The supported propositions involving the predictors of achievement gain, total achievement level, and absenteeism are presented below.

A. Supported propositions on achievement gain:
1. Teachers who hold negative stereotypes about members of other racial groups are more likely to be associated with higher gain scores among their students than teachers who do not hold such stereotypes.
2. The more external the teachers' locus of control, the lower the achievement gain of their students.
3. The more years of teaching experience that a teacher has up through the fifth year in the classroom, the greater the achievement gains of that teacher's students.
4. The more years of teaching experience that a teacher has beyond the fifth year in the classroom, the smaller the achievement gains of that teacher's students.
5. The more a teacher defines the racial composition of the student body of a school as favorable, the greater will be the achievement gain of that teacher's students.
6. Teachers who report having experienced racial discrimination are more likely to be associated with lower levels of achievement gain among their students than are teachers who do not report experiencing such discrimination.
7. Teachers who subsequently quit teaching are associated with higher levels of achievement gain among their students than teachers who do not quit teaching.
8. The higher the level of teacher turnover in a school, the lower the achievement gain of students assigned to that school.

Propositions 7 and 8 appear at first to be contradictory. However, proposition 7 refers to individual quitting behavior, which may be motivated by career alternatives. Proposition 8 refers to quitting rates, an indicator of structural and organizational problems at the school which weaken all areas of school effectiveness (see Shoemaker and Fraser [1981] for a summary of case studies on this issue).

9. The higher the percentage of students bused to a school, the higher the achievement gain at that school.
10. Brown schools are associated with lower achievement gain scores than other schools.
11. Older students gain more in achievement per year than younger students.
12. Black children are associated with lower achievement gain scores than white children.
13. Brown children are associated with lower achievement gain scores than white children.
14. The higher the socioeconomic status of the students, the higher their achievement gain scores.

15. The more days that a student is absent from school, the lower is that student's achievement gain score.

B. Supported propositions on total achievement level:

1. Teachers who hold negative stereotypes about members of other racial groups are more likely to be associated with higher total achievement levels in their students than teachers who do not hold such stereotypes.

2. The more external the teachers' locus of control, the lower the total achievement level of their students.

3. The more years of teaching experience that a teacher has up through the fifth year in the classroom, the greater the total achievement level of that teacher's students.

4. The more years of teaching experience that a teacher has beyond the fifth year in the classroom, the smaller the total achievement level of that teacher's students.

5. The more that a teacher defines the racial compostition of the student body of a school as desirable, the greater will be the total achievement level of that teacher's students.

6. Teachers who report experiencing racial discrimination are more likely to be associated with lower total achievement levels among their students than teachers who do not report experiencing such discrimination.

7. Teachers who quit teaching are associated with higher total achievement levels among their students than teachers who do not quit teaching.

8. The higher the level of teacher turnover at a school, the lower the total achievement level of the students at that school.

9. The higher the percentage of students bused to a school, the higher the total achievement level of the students at that school. (This finding is a result of the fact that majority schools are more often receiving schools and minority schools are more often sending schools. Furthermore, higher-achieving minorities are more likely to request busing than lower-achieving minorities.)

10. Brown schools are associated with a lower total achievement level than other schools.

11. Older students have higher levels of achievement than younger students.

12. Black and brown children are each associated with lower total achievement levels than white children.

13. The more days that a student is absent from school, the lower is the total achievement level of that student.

14. The greater the prior achievement level of a student, the greater are the present achievement level and the total achievement level of that student.

C. Supported propositions on attendance behavior:

1. Teachers who hold negative stereotypes about members of other

      racial groups are associated with higher levels of student absenteeism.

2. The older the teacher, the less the absenteeism among that teacher's students.
3. Absenteeism among a teacher's students increases with each additional year of teaching experience that the teacher has beyond the fifth year in the classroom.

The discrepancy between proposition 2 and 3 is primarily a function of low but significant associations between student absenteeism and teaching experience, and student absenteeism and a teacher's age. Likewise, the association between the age of teachers and their years of teaching experience is a great deal less than perfect.

4. Black schools have higher levels of student absenteeism than other schools.
5. Older students are absent more often than younger students.
6. Controlling for SES, black students are absent less often than other students.
7. The higher the current level of a student's achievement, the lower the absenteeism of that student.

    The supported propositions of the three studies and the overall conclusions of each appear to reflect some policy contradictions. Chapters 2 and 3 would lead one to strongly urge school districts to adopt a much more humane administrative stance with regard to teachers. Such a posture would do much to reduce the level of teacher burnout and the intentions to quit teaching (although it may not affect actual quitting behavior). Those chapters also argue that teacher colleges train their students poorly for the ambiguities and role strains of urban teaching, and even worse, provide them with few saleable skills which they can use in another career should they elect to leave teaching. Toward the end of chapter 4, however, these conclusions regarding the problems of teacher burnout appear to have been modified. It was shown that burned-out teachers do not adversely affect the great majority of students in the elementary grades studied. It is impossible to comment upon the impact of teacher burnout on junior and senior high school students, because there are no data from which to draw a conclusion. Student achievement and attendance seem to be affected by relatively few teacher variables, even though the achievement gains of students assigned to teachers who quit teaching imply a link between teacher competency and student achievement. Nonetheless, if teacher morale is of relatively little consequence to the learning outcomes of most children, then school resources ought to be redirected toward factors which contribute directly to better student achievement, and not toward making teachers more contented.

In reality, however, the two perspectives are not contradictory. Although enthusiasm for a teaching job is not a sufficient condition for quality instruction, without such teacher enthusiasm some of the school district's children will not learn as much or as well as they might otherwise. No school district that depends upon test score results to curry the support of voters can afford to ignore the needs of its brightest students. In fact, urban public school districts which are attempting to maintain desegregated education through a magnet school strategy must provide all the enrichment possible for promising black, brown, and white children if such a strategy is to succeed. The reduction in levels of teacher burnout is one such means to success.

A Not-So-Modest Proposal

The problems facing public school teachers are numerous, and there appear to be no panaceas for the difficulties. However, three categories of changes ought to be considered seriously by American educators. There must be changes in the recruitment and training of preservice teachers by colleges of education; there must be significant changes in the employment and deployment of public school teachers by school districts; and there must be changes in the manner in which public school teachers are managed by school administrators, especially by school principals.

Changing the Colleges of Education

The studies cited in the first chapter—including those by Schlechty and Vance (1981), Vance and Schlechty (1982), the National Commission on Excellence in Education (1983), and the Rand Corporation (Darling-Hammond, 1984)—have confirmed Ornstein's (1981) contention that colleges of education tend to attract students who score significantly lower on standardized tests than do other colleges in the universities of this country. In a society where career opportunities for women are expanding and where teachers' salaries continue to lose ground to inflation, it is unlikely that the most able will elect to become education majors (Vance and Schlechty, 1982:25). However, these colleges ought not to accept such a disproportionate number of the least able. Entrance requirements should be as stringent as they are in other colleges within a university. Of course, attracting better students will depend upon some factors outside the control of colleges of education; these factors will be addressed later.

The training of preservice teachers must also resemble more closely that of other students in a university. In 1983, the National Commission on Excellence in Education reported on a survey of 1,350 teacher training institutions. The commission noted that elementary education majors allocated 41 percent of their course work to "educational methods," thereby detracting from academic hours which might be spent in substantive courses (1983:22).

Not only do education majors tend to take a litany of pedagogy courses in lieu of substantive academic courses, but they also tend, when selecting courses outside education, to take a larger share of introductory and lower-division courses than do traditional arts and science majors. This was the contention of the Southern Regional Education Board as reported in *The Chronicle of Higher Education* (see Evangelauf, 1985:11). Furthermore, as the board observed, education majors were less likely to have earned credits in several important disciplines, including the sciences, mathematics, economics, philosophy, and foreign languages, than were majors in the arts and sciences. A group of education deans at twenty-four of the nation's top research universities (The Holmes Group, 1986) has decried the quality of teacher training and has urged vastly stricter entrance and training standards for teachers (see also Currence in *Education Week*, June 12, 1985:5).

In the first chapter, I noted that the last years of the 1980s and some of the 1990s will see a teacher shortage, especially in several critical fields. In the past, schools that were faced with critical shortages responded by encouraging colleges of education to relax admission standards and to weaken the academic requirements for a degree in education (Stinnett and Henson, 1982). The result of the educational crises of the 1950s and 1960s has been a less qualified population of teachers and a loss of public trust in public education. It would be unwise to make that mistake again in the name of expediency. Stinnett and Henson (1982), Gideonse (1982), The Holmes Group (1986), the National Commission on Excellence in Education (1983), the Rand Corporation (Darling-Hammond, 1984) and the Carnegie Task Force on Teaching as a Profession (1986) have all called for radical changes in the training and certifying of teachers. Some have contended that during the first four years of training, prospective teachers should take the same courses as liberal arts students. In fact, before receiving the baccalaureate degree, preservice teachers ought to have majors in the arts and sciences and only an education minor. With a broader education that involves the range of courses found lacking by the National Commission on Excellence in Education (1983) in the training of preservice teachers, future teachers might have more saleable skills. Of course, as we have observed, the initial consequence of providing teachers with more saleable skills may be that the turnover rate could increase in the decade or so after the institution of these new training procedures. However, the long-term benefit would be a teaching staff who elect to remain in teaching because they find it rewarding, not entrapping.

Only after having completed their undergraduate training should preservice teachers concentrate on "educational methods" and other pedagogical courses. During those postgraduate semesters, they should also serve as interns in school districts, serving under the guidance of master teachers. These internships would differ from practice teaching in that the teacher candidates would be supervised closely by the master teachers and socialized into the organizational environment of the school. In short, the internship would approximate the resident training of medical school graduates or the clerkships of law school graduates.

A few years ago, when there was still talk of a teacher "glut," Stinnett and Henson (1982) and Gideonse (1982) proposed that the training of teachers should take six years and result in a graduate degree such as an M.A.T. or an Ed.D. With a postgraduate credential, teachers would again have more formal education than most of the public with whom they deal, and the public might then be more willing to support competitive teachers' salaries. The proposal was intended to produce a cadre of talented teachers and was supported by the oversupply of teachers on the job market. Colleges of education could prolong a student's career without adversely affecting the supply of teachers needed by the public schools. It would now be a serious mistake to continue to give poor training to the nation's supply of teachers merely because the demand for teachers is growing. If the proposals of Stinnett and Henson, Gideonse, and The Holmes Group will create a more competent supply of teachers, then they should be attempted, even if they exacerbate the teacher shortage problem in the short run.

Changing the School System: Teacher Employment and Deployment

School districts should become as selective as colleges of education. Merely because there will be critical shortages in future years, districts ought not to grasp at any candidate regardless of that person's training. Districts should also recruit professionals whose academic training is not in education. Several districts, including the one studied in this book, have filled vacancies, especially in the sciences and mathematics, by recruiting individuals with advanced degrees and then permitting them to gradually meet some minimal certification requirements. This policy is especially important for the recruitment of teachers in junior and senior high school. A biology teacher with an M.S. in biology is likely to have a better command of his or her subject matter than is a graduate from a college of education with a major in biology education.

The National Commission on Excellence in Education (1983), The Holmes Group (1986), and Duke (1984) have all spoken about the establishment of career ladders for teachers. One incentive for teachers to remain in education, as well as to continue to be enthusiastic, would be if those teachers believed that their hard work and dedication led to a series of promotions that involved increased salary and increased autonomy and authority. Borrowing considerably from the proposals of The Holmes Group (1986; see especially Currence in *Education Week*, June 12, 1985:5), I propose a five-stage career ladder. The five stages would be as follows: (1) the teacher candidate, who would take up to five years of courses in a university, including four years in an arts and sciences major; (2) the postgraduate teacher intern, who would continue to take courses but would work in a school under the supervision of a master teacher; (3) the novice teacher, who would work on certification and be supervised, although less rigidly, by a master teacher; (4) the career teacher, who would excise full control over his or her classroom; and (5) the professional career teacher, who would supervise new teachers, help develop campus curriculum and academic policies, and perhaps even be involved as an adjunct faculty member in a college of education.

Since teachers seem to be most effective in promoting higher levels of student achievement if they have had five years of experience in the classroom, school districts should not be lured into seeking out less costly neophyte teachers when they recruit. They should be especially careful when seeking personnel for programs for gifted and talented children. Of course, it would be foolish to assume that only teachers in their fifth or sixth year are best qualified and that more experienced or less experienced teachers axiomatically are less effective with such children. Nevertheless, years of experience ought to be considered, without making the assumption that, because a teacher has been in a classroom for twenty years, he or she is therefore better qualified than one who has spent only one-fourth that amount of time instructing children.

What I have suggested is a policy for the future recruiting of academically trained teachers—not for those who go through diluted courses for teachers. The ponderous problem, however, is how to attain higher student achievement levels given the current group of public school teachers. What does a district do with individuals who are minimally competent and who prefer to pursue some career other than teaching but are not skilled enough to find work elsewhere? Aside from assigning these teachers to the average-scoring children, perhaps alternative career counseling and retraining programs are needed to make room for better-trained, more enthusiastic teachers. The problem is staggering, and the consequences of inaction or inappropriate action loom large.

If pushing out teachers is unpalatable to school districts, then one alternative is to upgrade the skills and rekindle the enthusiasm of the existing teaching staff. I have already spoken of the need to make principals better and more trusting colleagues of their teachers. It might also be advantageous for school districts to encourage their current teaching staffs to participate in short-courses offered by universities; to grant sabbaticals or other forms of release time for retraining; to upgrade skills which could be used to teach other subject areas; and to attend workshops sponsored by the National Science Foundation or the National Endowment for the Humanities. For teachers who have skills valued by industry and who would prefer to remain in teaching if economic considerations were not otherwise, the creation of work and teaching programs with industry might be a viable option. Here, teachers could spend summers working in corporate settings and sharpening their skills (in communication, management, or research) and then return to teaching in the fall. Perhaps exchange programs with industry could be developed where able professionals could take a sabbatical year to teach in a school setting. With such flexible arrangements, the likelihood of burnout would be reduced and bright students would be less likely to be burdened by a burned-out (and perhaps less than competent) teacher.

Changing the School System: The Principal as Manager

I have spent a considerable amount of time, both in chapter 3 and in this conclusion, on the crucial role that principals play in breaking the functional link between job stress and burnout. It cannot be emphasized too strongly that principals, much more than other teachers or unions, have the power to alter the level of teacher burnout in their schools. Perhaps they have too much power. If there were more career ladders for teachers and a greater division of labor within the campus of a school district, then the principal and the school district administration might be less willing to vest so much power in the hands of a single agent.

Mandating that principals become better managers seems like a plausible suggestion. Holding principals responsible for the morale of

their teachers likewise seems plausible. However, dividing responsibilities for staff morale among the principal and a group of master
teachers may make the job of principal ultimately less stressful. School
districts must recognize that mandating collegiality on the part of principals, or even rewarding collegial principals with more school resources
and better pay raises, may create problems for principals who must also
serve as teacher evaluators. The roles of colleague and of evaluator are
sometimes incompatible with one another. For some principals the fear
of not being liked by their teachers, and hence being punished by the
district for lack of collegiality, may lead them to default on their obliga-
tions to make thorough personnel decisions. By contrast, state and district
mandates for teacher competency evaluations and the enforcement of
district policies regarding teachers may necessitate a degree of aloofness
on the part of principals when interacting with teachers. At one time I
consulted with a school district whose staff development office had
recruited master teachers to work with new staff members in schools
which had previously experienced considerable teacher turnover. The
master teachers were to serve as mentors and ombudsmen to the new
teachers. Although the district was concerned with teacher turnover, it
was also concerned with removing incompetent teachers. Thus while the
master teachers had to become the confidants of the new teachers to help
them "learn the ropes" in the school, they also had to serve as infor-
mants to the principal and the district administrators. This role ambiguity became highly stressful. It is not inconceivable that principals who
want to be both colleagues and evaluators would also find balancing
those roles highly stressful.

A Final Note on Teacher Salaries

Survey data have shown that public school teachers value school
resources and better student discipline over matters of salary. The data in
this work have also shown that salaries and income independence exert
small effects on the various aspects of teacher burnout and commitment.
Teachers are attracted to their careers by a sense of calling (Lortie, 1975;
National Education Association, 1982); they do not choose teaching as a
route to wealth. Nevertheless, as long as teachers' salaries are not competitive, school districts will continue to have to select among the less in-
tellectually able in addition to that minority who, despite their ability to
find better-paying jobs, are called to teaching. As Duke observes,
"higher salaries alone . . . are no guarantee that bright, committed individuals will be attracted to teaching. . . . Higher salaries, though, can
serve as a powerful magnet to contemporary college students considering

various career options and a concrete symbol of the public's regard for education and teachers'' (1984:128).

Competitive salaries for better-trained teachers, coupled with professional autonomy and a colleagial administrative style among school principals, could reduce burnout, plans to quit, and actual quitting behavior among teachers and heighten the academic achievement of brighter students. If schools recruited highly competent teaching staffs, paid them well, and treated them with respect, teacher morale would remain high. With morale high, teachers with translatable skills would probably still remain in teaching (recall that satisfaction and solidarity accounts for commitment among high translatables). It is likely that only when so many of the best and the brightest elect never to consider a career in public school teaching or quit after a short tenure in teaching, that one could expect to find, as we have, that teacher commitment has such a tiny effect upon student learning.

The public and its elected representatives in the state legislatures (who control school budgets and teachers' salaries), as well as state education agencies (who regulate teacher certification), are ultimately those who can mandate the proposals offered here. It is unlikely that our society can significantly alter the magnitude of teacher burnout in American schools without putting forth a monumental effort.

Appendix A.
Operationalizations of Constructs

CONSTRUCT	VARIABLE	CODING INTERPRETATION
Actor Traits	Age	Actual age in years.
	Sex	Male = 0 Female = 1.
	Race: black white brown	Black = 1, nonblack = 0. White = 1, nonwhite = 0. Brown = 0,0.*
	Father's class	Entrepreneur, petit bourgeoisie = 1. Manager = 2. Worker = 3.
	Education	No formal education = 01, through doctorate = 11. College graduate = 08.
	Locus of control	Number of external responses (0–8).
	Stereotyping	Number of prejudiced responses (0–6).
Side-bets	Years teaching	Actual number of years.
	Tenure status	No contract = 1. Monthly contract = 2. Probationary contract = 3. Permanent contract = 4.
	Major duty code	Principal, vice-principal = 5.

CONSTRUCT	**VARIABLE**	**CODING INTERPRETATION**
	(occupational title)	Other administrator, coordinator = 4. Counselor = 3. Classroom teacher = 2. Other certified personnel = 1.
	Extra education	Education in specialty beyond B.A. or B.S. (Education code minus 08).
	Mobility experience	Upward move in major duty code = 1. No move in major duty code = 0. Downward move in major duty code = -1.
	Salary	Salary in dollars.
	Income independence	Difference between total family income and salary, expressed in dollars.
	Translatability	Ability to move to a private sector job with given skills and without substantial retraining. Translatable = 1. Not Translatable = 0.
Satisfaction and Solidarity	Administrative Style Difference	A discrepancy score is computed between the teacher's evaluation of 10 acivities in a principal's role and that teacher's own principal's evaluation of the activities. The scale is unidimensional. Absolute differences are used. The higher the difference score, the greater the discrepancy between the evaluation by the principal and the teacher.
	Discrimination	Perception of whether or not one's own racial group has experienced discrimination on the campus in terms of pay, promotions, tenure, benefits, or assignments. Discrimination = 1. No discrimination = 0.

CONSTRUCT	VARIABLE	CODING INTERPRETATION

	Racial norms	Perception of norms supportive or unsupportive of interracial collegiality among faculty. Scores from 1–6; the higher the score, the greater the support for interracial collegiality.
	Attitude toward Singleton Ratio	Attitude toward the district's faculty desegregation mandate. Items were factor analyzed, and a factor score was computed. Negative values represent disagreement, positive values represent agreement with the Singleton Ratio.
	Assignment attitude	Attitude toward the racial composition of the student body of the school to which the teacher is assigned. Assignment to a school whose student body composition is desirable = 1. Assignment to a school whose student body composition is neutral = 0. Assignment to a school whose student body composition is undesirable = -1.
	Transfer experience	Attitude toward the racial composition of the student body of a school to which the teacher is currently assigned as opposed to the previous school of assignment. Transferred from undesirable to desirable school = 1. No change in desirability or no transfer = 0. Transferred from desirable to undesirable school = -1.
Building characteristics	RAISOST	Racial Isolation from Students, expressed as 100 per cent minus the percentage of students of teacher's own race.

CONSTRUCT	VARIABLE	CODING INTERPRETATION
		The higher the score, the greater the isolation.
	RAISOTE	Racial Isolation from Teaching Staff, expressed as 100 percent minus the percentage of certified staff of teacher's own race.
	PERMINGR	Percentage of Minority-Group Members on the campus, expressed as the percentage of non-whites, regardless of student, faculty, or staff status, assigned to the campus. The higher the score, the higher the percentage of minorities on the campus.
	Peer turnover rate	Percentage of certified personnel leaving the campus in the previous two years.
	School size	Absolute numbers of students assigned to the campus as per the district's annual report to the Texas Education Agency.
	Grade level	Elementary school = 1. Junior high school/middle school = 2. Senior high school = 3.
	Race of school†	Black school = 1, nonblack school = 0. White school = 1, nonwhite school = 0. Brown school = 1, nonbrown school = 0. Balanced school = 0,0,0.*
	Magnet school†	Dummy variable for magnet schools. Magnet = 1, nonmagnet = 0.
	Busing†	Percentage of students bused to school.
Student characteristics	Age	Age in years.
	Sex	Boy = 1. Girl = 0.

CONSTRUCT	VARIABLE	CODING INTERPRETATION
	Race	Black student = 1, nonblack student = 0.
		Brown student = 1, nonbrown student = 0.
		White student = 0,0.
	Race of teacher and student	Teacher and student of the same race = 1.
		Teacher and student of different races = 0.
	Sex of teacher and student	Teacher and student of the same sex = 1.
		Teacher and student of different sexes = 0.
	Sex and race of teacher and student	Both of same sex and race = 1. Not of same sex and race = 0.
	Socioeconomic status of student (SES)	Index-score-computed income, occupation, education, and rental or housing value of neighborhood in which student lives. The higher the score, the higher the SES.
Absenteeism	Absence	Ratio of days absent from school to total number of days enrolled in school.
Achievement	Iowa Test (year 1)	Grade level equivalent achievement score for first year.
	Iowa Test (year 2)	Grade level equivalent achievement score for second year.
	Gain score	Grade level equivalent of Iowa Test in year 2 minus grade level equivalent of Iowa Test in year 1.
Burnout	Burnout (role-specific alienation)	Factor score of 8 Likert-type items assessing meaninglessness, powerlessness, isolation, and normlessness. The higher the score, the greater the burnout.
Plans to Quit	Plans to quit teaching	Two-item, Likert-type measure. Score is average of the two responses; the higher the score, the greater the plans to quit teaching.

CONSTRUCT VARIABLE   **CODING INTERPRETATION**
Quitting (Role Quitting behavior   Dummy variable. Quit teaching
   Exit)   = 1.
                                   Did not quit teaching = 0.

Variable	*Term in the equation*	*Omitted term*
Race of teacher	If black, 1; if not, 0	If brown, 0,0
	If white, 1; if not, 0	
Race of student	If black, 1; if not, 0	If white, 0,0
	If brown, 1; if not, 0	
Sex of teacher	If male, 1; if not, 0	
Sex of student	If male, 1; if not, 0	
Race of school	If black school, 1; if not, 0	If balanced
	If brown school, 1; if not, 0	school 0,0,0
	If white school, 1; if not, 0	
Race of student/		
Race of teacher	If same race, 1; if not, 0	
Sex of Student/		
Sex of teacher	If same sex, 1; if not, 0	
Sex and race of		
student and teacher	If same sex and race, 1; if not, 0	

*It should be noted that dummy variables are usually entered into a regression equation such that there is one less term in the equation than there are dummy categories. Thus, for sex, a dummy variable would take the form of 1 = male and 0 = female. However for race, where three groups are considered, two dummy variables are entered into the regression. The first would be 1 = white and 0 = nonwhite, while the second would be 1 = black and 0 = nonblack. With such equations, browns are represented by the 0,0 condition (nonwhite and nonblack). The following represent the dummy variables used in chapter 4:

†Used only in chapter 4.

Appendix B.
Percentages, means and standard deviations for measured variables from the teacher and student data sets

VARIABLE	TEACHER DATA (Chapter 2)			STUDENT DATA (Chapter 4)		
	Percent	Mean	s.d.	Percent	Mean	s.d
Age of teacher	—	38.40	11.32	—	39.44	11.60
Sex of teacher						
Male	18.0	—	—	13.0	—	—
Female	82.0	—	—	87.0	—	—
Race of teacher						
Black	28.9	—	—	40.1	—	—
Brown	3.0	—	—	1.5	—	—
White	67.5	—	—	57.5	—	—
Father's class	—	2.39	0.84	—	2.48	0.79
Education of teacher	—	9.16	0.86	—	9.10	0.88
Locus of control	—	3.17	2.13	—	3.47	2.21
Stereotyping	—	3.76	1.95	—	3.68	2.05
Years teaching	—	9.93	8.58	—	11.93	9.46
Tenure status	—	3.58	0.70	—	3.79	0.45
Major duty code	—	2.07	0.80	—	1.97	0.18
Extra education	—	1.16	0.84	—	1.07	0.87

179

VARIABLE	TEACHER DATA (Chapter 2)			STUDENT DATA (Chapter 4)		
	Percent	Mean	s.d.	Percent	Mean	s.d
Mobility experience	—	0.06	0.37	—	0.02	0.16
Salary	—	$12,345.41	$2,536.23	—	$12,339.25	$1,812.58
Income in-dependence	—	$13,547.92	$9,739.12	—	$13,537.46	$9,815.55
Translatability	—	0.25	0.43	—	0.02	0.14
Administrative style difference	—	0.68	0.86	—	0.71	0.80
Discrimination	—	0.23	0.42	—	0.23	0.42
Racial norms	—	3.18	1.57	—	3.89	1.53
Attitude toward Singleton Ratio	—	-0.11	0.90	—	-0.06	0.93
Assignment attitude	—	0.07	0.74	—	0.21	0.70
Transfer experience	—	0.00	0.29	—	0.01	0.26
RAISOST	—	63.03	35.62	—	57.37	37.66
RAISOTE	—	50.70	14.90	—	51.12	11.94
PERMINGR	—	40.26	37.80	—	31.36	36.58
Peer turnover rate	—	31.89	30.68	—	21.12	18.48
School size	—	1,136.51	619.90	—	853.15	336.31
Grade level	—	1.99	1.30	—	see text	see text
Race of school						
Black	—	—	—	35.7	—	—
White	—	—	—	19.4	—	—
Brown	—	—	—	33.2	—	—
Balanced	—	—	—	11.6	—	—
Magnet school	—	—	—	—	0.15	0.35
Busing	—	—	—	—	3.98	9.76
Age of student	—	—	—	—	11.47	1.05
Sex of student						
Boy	—	—	—	50.2	—	—
Girl	—	—	—	49.8	—	—
Race of student						
Black	—	—	—	40.4	—	—
Brown	—	—	—	22.1	—	—
White	—	—	—	36.9	—	—

VARIABLE	TEACHER DATA (Chapter 2)			STUDENT DATA (Chapter 4)		
	Percent	Mean	s.d.	Percent	Mean	s.d
Teacher and student of same race	—	—	—	—	0.20	0.40
Teacher and student of same sex	—	—	—	—	0.52	0.50
Teacher and student of same sex and race	—	—	—	—	0.10	0.30
Student SES	—	—	—	—	10.57	0.75
Absenteeism	—	—	—	—	0.08	0.09
IOWA Test (year 1)	—	—	—	—	see text	see text
IOWA Test (year 2)	—	—	—	—	See text	See text
Gain score	—	—	—	—	0.90	0.58
Burnout	—	0.01	0.91	—	0.08	0.90
Plans to quit	—	2.54	1.29	—	2.44	1.25
Quitting behavior	—	0.12	0.33	—	0.15	0.36

Appendix C.
Factor Analyses For
Scale Construction

Table C.1

Factor Analysis of Alienation Items in Creating the Burnout Scale

Item	Factor I
Powerlessness 1	.404
Powerlessness 2	.704
Normlessness 1	.479
Normlessness 2	.564
Meaninglessness 1	.694
Meaninglessness 2	.686
Isolation 1	.619
Isolation 2	.665
Variance explained	100.0
Eigenvalue	3.50

Table C.2

Final Factor Analysis of Stess Scale Items

Item	Factor loading
Classroom teaching	.612
Teaching preparation	.634
Nonteaching duties	.639
Teaching students off level	.602
Salary received	.560
Disciplining students in class	.599
Disciplining students in halls	.714
Interacting with parents	.555
Interacting with administrators	.525
Interacting with teachers	.376
Job security	.453
Job benefits	.512
Using inadequate teaching supplies	.596
Total hours of work load	.584
Physical condition of building	.513

Eigenvalue = 4.88

Minimum significant factor loading = 0.350

Table C.3

Factor Analysis of Principal Support Items

Correlation Matrix

	1	2	3	4	5	6
1 Grievance procedures fair	1.000	.348	.274	.219	.172	.231
2 Opportunity to plan instruction		1.000	.317	.336	.239	.239
3 Principal lacks initiative			1.000	.485	.467	.451
4 Work appraised fairly				1.000	.506	.314
5 Never told if doing well					1.000	.322
6 Principal active in setting rules for students						1.000

Factor loadings	Factor I
Grievance	.402
Opportunity	.487
Principal lacks	.738
Work appraised	.677
Never told	.620
Principal active	.535

Variance explained by first factor: 92.2

Appendix D.
Commonality Analysis

Traditional OLS modeling tends to attribute shared variance to the strongest predictor, thereby overestimating its influence on the dependent variable. The commonality technique avoids this problem and is most appropriate for policy research because of the minimal numbers of assumptions that have to be made about the ordering of variables, most of which were collected at the same time and thus are cross-sectional (note that only the actual quitting behavior measure was collected after the enumeration of the measures). The technique arose out of the criticisms of the work of Coleman and his associates (1966). Attributed to the work of Mood (1969, 1971), and applied by Mayeske et al. (1969), Kerlinger and Pedhazur (1973), Cooley and Lohnes (1976), and Pedhazur (1982), the technique resolves a central problem associated with least squares modeling: the tendency for the strongest predictors to be inflated by the assignment to them of shared variances. Thus, when Coleman entered home effects into his stepwise regression first, variance shared by home and school were erroneously attributed to home effects because of the order in which the variables were entered. Likewise, when Mayeske reanalyzed the Coleman data using OLS modeling but without hierarchical ordering, again home effects, because of their stronger influence, were awarded the shared variance. When the data were reexamined using commonality analysis, the effect of home was shown to have a smaller percentage of unique variance than of confounded and shared variance. Specifically, Mayeske reported that of the 87 percent of the variance in academic achievement that could be accounted for by home effects, only 11 percent was uniquely home effects, 5 percent was uniquely school effects, and 71 percent was confounded by the mixing of home and school (Cooley and Lohnes, 1976: 220–221).

I. Introduction to the Equations

Commonality analysis partitions variance explained into unique and common elements. The variance in any structural equation involves both the variance uniquely contributed by a predictor (or a block of predictors) and variance shared with other predictors (or other blocks of predictors). For example, in a 3-variable model involving the variance in Y explained by X_1, X_2, and X_3, the variance in Y explained by X_1 contains some variance uniquely explained by X_1 and some variance shared with X_2 and X_3. When the variance shared with X_2 and X_3 is removed, a squared semipartial correlation coefficient remains which specifies the unique contribution of X_1.

Many of the models presented in chapters 2 and 4 involve 5-block commonality models. There are 5 unique variances to be computed. In such instances, the uniqueness of each block is computed by subtracting the R^2 due to all blocks other than the one for which a unique contribution is desired from the total R^2 of all blocks. Thus, the unique contribution of block X_1 is determined by subtracting the value of $R^2 y_{.2345}$ from $R^2 y_{.12345}$. The unique contributions of the 5 blocks in the models used in this study would then be computed as follows:

$$U_1 = R^2 y_{.12345} - R^2 y_{.2345}$$
$$U_2 = R^2 y_{.12345} - R^2 y_{.1345}$$
$$U_3 = R^2 y_{.12345} - R^2 y_{.1245}$$
$$U_4 = R^2 y_{.12345} - R^2 y_{.1235}$$
$$U_5 = R^2 y_{.12345} - R^2 y_{.1234}$$

The number of communal variances to be computed is a function of the number of blocks. The formula for determining the number needed is $-k + 2^k - 1$, where k is equal to the number of blocks in the regressions. Thus, a 5-block model would have $-5 + 2^5 - 1$ commonality equations, or a total of 26. Counting the unique variances, the total values which would apper in a commonality analysis table for a 5-block model would be 31. Clearly, as the number of blocks to be entered into the model increases, the use of commonality analysis becomes increasingly unwieldy. Furthermore, commonality is not intended to test hypotheses, but rather to correct for overly enthusiastic policy suggestions based upon analyses relying upon b's and beta's. Commonality analysis prevents us from overestimating the influence of a single block of variables by noting how much independent variables are contaminated by other independent variables.

Presented below are the algebraic equations involved in computing the commonality of the blocks of predictors in the 5-block models presented in chapters 2 and 4. In each case, the X's represent R^2 values for the regression of the dependent variable (Y) upon the combinations of blocks of independent variables. Thus, X_1 represents the regression of Y on block X_1, while X_1X_2 represents the regression of Y on X_1 and X_2.

Commonality	Algebraic polynomial expansion
C_{12}	$- (1-X_1) (1-X_2) X_3 X_4 X_5$
C_{13}	$- (1-X_1) (1-X_3) X_2 X_4 X_5$
C_{14}	$- (1-X_1) (1-X_4) X_2 X_3 X_5$
C_{15}	$- (1-X_1) (1-X_5) X_2 X_3 X_4$
C_{23}	$- (1-X_2) (1-X_3) X_1 X_4 X_5$
C_{24}	$- (1-X_2) (1-X_4) X_1 X_3 X_5$
C_{25}	$- (1-X_2) (1-X_5) X_1 X_3 X_5$
C_{34}	$- (1-X_3) (1-X_4) X_1 X_2 X_5$
C_{35}	$- (1-X_3) (1-X_5) X_1 X_2 X_4$
C_{45}	$- (1-X_4) (1-X_5) X_1 X_2 X_3$
C_{123}	$- (1-X_1) (1-X_2) (1-X_3 \; X_4 X_5$
C_{124}	$- (1-X_1) (1-X_2) (1-X_4) X_3 X_5$
C_{125}	$- (1-X_1) (1-X_2) (1-X_5) X_3 X_4$
C_{134}	$- (1-X_1) (1-X_3) (1-X_4) X_2 X_5$
C_{135}	$- (1-X_1) (1-X_3) (1-X_5) X_2 X_4$
C_{145}	$- (1-X_1) (1-X_4) (1-X_5) X_2 X_3$
C_{234}	$- (1-X_2) (1-X_3) (1-X_4) X_1 X_5$
C_{235}	$- (1-X_2) (1-X_3) (1-X_5) X_1 X_4$
C_{245}	$- (1-X_2) (1-X_4) (1-X_5) X_1 X_3$
C_{345}	$- (1-X_3) (1-X_4) (1-X_5) X_1 X_2$
C_{1234}	$- (1-X_1) (1-X_2) (1-X_3) (1-X_4) X_5$
C_{1235}	$- (1-X_1) (1-X_2) (1-X_3) (1-X_5) X_4$
C_{1245}	$- (1-X_1) (1-X_2) (1-X_4) (1-X_5) X_3$
C_{1345}	$- (1-X_1) (1-X_3) (1-X_4) (1-X_5) X_2$
C_{2345}	$- (1-X_2) (1-X_3) (1-X_4) (1-X_5) X_1$
C_{12345}	$-1-(1-X_1) (1-X_2) (1-X_3) (1-X_4) (1-X_5)$

II. Commonality Analysis of Plans to Quit Teaching (4-Block Model) from Chapter 2

Squared multiple correlations for plans to quit

Y = plans to quit; 1 = actor traits; 2 = building characteristics; 3 = side–bets; 4 = satisfaction and solidarity (including burnout)

$U_1 = .00928$
$U_2 = .00583$
$U_3 = .00477$
$U_4 = .28065$

$R_{y.1} = .05973$	$R_{y.12} = .07798$	$R_{y.123} = .09160$
$R_{y.2} = .03438$	$R_{y.13} = .07498$	$R_{y.124} = .36748$
$R_{y.3} = .02445$	$R_{y.14} = .36075$	$R_{y.134} = .36642$
$R_{y.4} = .34973$	$R_{y.23} = .04931$	$R_{y.234} = .36297$
	$R_{y.24} = .35925$	$R_{y.1234} = .37225$
	$R_{y.34} = .35419$	

Commonality partitioning of variance

Source of variance	R_1^2 (actor) traits)	R_2^2 (building)	R_3^2 (side–bets)	R_4^2 (satisfaction solidarity)
U_1	.00928			
U_2		.00583		
U_3			.00477	
U_4				.28065
C_{12}	.00295	.00295		
C_{13}	-.00105*		-.00105*	
C_{14}	.03301			.03301
C_{23}		.00090	.00090	
C_{24}		.01079		.01079
C_{34}			.00885	.00885
C_{123}	-.00016*	-.00016*	-.00016*	
C_{124}	.00529	.00529		.00529
C_{134}	.00236		.00236	.00236
C_{234}		.00073	.00073	.00073
C_{1234}	.00805	.00805	.00805	.00805
Total R^2	.05973	.03438	.02445	.34973

*Mayeske et al. (1969) suggest that negative commonality coefficients be considered equivalent to zero.

III. Commonality Analysis of Plans to Quit Teaching (5-Block Model) from Chapter 2

Squared multiple correlations for plans to quit

Y = plans to quit; 1 = actor traits; 2 = building characteristics; 3 = side–bets; 4 = satisfaction and solidarity; 5 = burnout.

$U_1 = .00928$
$U_2 = .00583$
$U_3 = .00477$
$U_4 = .00219$
$U_5 = .22102$

$R_{y.1} = .05973$	$R_{y.12} = .07798$	$R_{y.123} = .09160$
$R_{y.2} = .03438$	$R_{y.13} = .07498$	$R_{y.124} = .14236$
$R_{y.3} = .02445$	$R_{y.14} = .13097$	$R_{y.125} = .36518$
$R_{y.4} = .10030$	$R_{y.15} = .35807$	$R_{y.134} = .14067$
$R_{y.5} = .34679$	$R_{y.23} = .04931$	$R_{y.135} = .36395$
	$R_{y.24} = .12040$	$R_{y.145} = .36075$
	$R_{y.25} = .35670$	$R_{y.234} = .13000$
	$R_{y.34} = .11450$	$R_{y.235} = .36044$
	$R_{y.35} = .35124$	$R_{y.245} = .35925$
	$R_{y.45} = .34973$	$R_{y.345} = .35419$

$R_{y.1234} = .15123$
$R_{y.1235} = .37006$
$R_{y.1245} = .36748$
$R_{y.1345} = .36642$
$R_{y.2345} = .36297$

Commonality partitioning of variance

Source of variance	R_1^2 (actor) traits)	R_2^2 (building)	R_3^2 (side–bets)	R_4^2 (satisfaction solidarity)	R_5^2 (burnout)
U_1	.00928				
U_2		.00583			
U_3			.00477		
U_4				.00219	
U_5					.22102
C_{12}	.00295	.00295			
C_{13}	-.00105*		-.00105*		
C_{14}	.00034			.00034	
C_{15}	.01195				. 01195
C_{23}		.00090	.00090		
C_{24}		.00028		.00028	
C_{25}		.00473			.00473
C_{34}			.00011	.00011	
C_{35}			.00410		.00410
C_{45}				.05744	.05744
C_{123}	-.00016	-.00016	-.00016		
C_{124}	.00014	.00014		.00014	
C_{125}	.00199	.00199			.00199
C_{134}	-.00009		-.00009	.00009	
C_{135}	.00178		.00178		.00178
C_{145}	.02072			.02072	.02072
C_{234}		.00010	.00010	.00010	
C_{235}		-.00007	-.00007		-.00007
C_{245}		.00578		.00578	.00578
C_{345}			.00464	.00464	.00464
C_{1234}	-.00013	-.00013	-.00013	-.00013	
C_{1235}	.00393	.00393	.00393		.00393
C_{1245}	.00316	.00316		.00316	.00316
C_{1345}	.00067		.00067	.00067	.00067
C_{2345}		.00070	.00070	.00070	.00070
C_{12345}	.00425	.00425	.00425	.00425	.00425
Total R^2	.05973	.03438	.02445	.10030	.34679

IV. Commonality Analysis of Burnout (4-Block Model)
from Chapter 2

Squared multiple correlations for burnout
Y = burnout; 1 = actor traits; 2 = building characteristics;
3 = side–bets; 4 = satisfaction and solidarity (less burnout)

$U_1 = .05514$
$U_2 = .01582$
$U_3 = .00868$
$U_4 = .09661$

$R_{y.1} = .15504$	$R_{y.12} = .20969$	$R_{y.123} = .22358$
$R_{y.2} = .11153$	$R_{y.13} = .17399$	$R_{y.124} = .31151$
$R_{y.3} = .05910$	$R_{y.14} = .29463$	$R_{y.134} = .30437$
$R_{y.4} = .20589$	$R_{y.23} = .13836$	$R_{y.234} = .26505$
	$R_{y.24} = .24596$	
	$R_{y.34} = .23881$	$R_{y.1234} = .32019$

Commonality partitioning of variance

Source of variance	R_1^2 (actor traits)	R_2^2 (building)	R_3^2 (side-bets)	R_4^2 (satisfaction solidarity)
U_1	.05514			
U_2		.01582		
U_3			.00868	
U_4				.09661
C_{12}	.01042	.01042		
C_{13}	.01041		.01041	
C_{14}	.03008			.03008
C_{23}		.00106	.00106	
C_{24}		.03377		.03377
C_{34}			.00521	.00521
C_{123}	.01277	.01277	-.01277	
C_{124}	.01925	.01925		.01925
C_{134}	.00253		.00253	.00253
C_{234}		.00400	.00400	.00400
C_{1234}	.01444	.01444	.01444	.01444
Total R^2	.15504	.11153	.05910	.20589

V. Commonality Analysis of Gain Scores (5-Block Model) from Chapter 4

Squared multiple correlations for plans to quit
Y = gain scores; 1 = actor traits; 2 = side–bets;
3 = satisfaction and solidarity; 4 = building characteristics
5 = student characteristics

$U_1 = .01506$
$U_2 = .01994$
$U_3 = .01593$
$U_4 = .01874$
$U_5 = .01237$

$R_{y.1} = .03023$	$R_{y.12} = .05451$	$R_{y.123} = .08503$	$R_{y.1234} = .10601$
$R_{y.2} = .03419$	$R_{y.13} = .06138$	$R_{y.124} = .08850$	$R_{y.1235} = .09964$
$R_{y.3} = .03420$	$R_{y.14} = .06683$	$R_{y.125} = .07382$	$R_{y.1245} = .10245$
$R_{y.4} = .04940$	$R_{y.15} = .05208$	$R_{y.134} = .08436$	$R_{y.1345} = .09844$
$R_{y.5} = .02363$	$R_{y.23} = .06828$	$R_{y.135} = .07811$	$R_{y.2345} = .10332$
	$R_{y.24} = .07397$	$R_{y.145} = .08287$	$R_{y.12345} = .11838$
	$R_{y.25} = .05395$	$R_{y.234} = .09178$	
	$R_{y.34} = .06486$	$R_{y.235} = .08282$	
	$R_{y.35} = .05184$	$R_{y.245} = .08749$	
	$R_{y.45} = .06533$	$R_{y.345} = .07875$	

Commonality partitioning of variance

Source of variance	R_1^2 (actor) traits)	R_2^2 (side–bets)	R_3^2 (satisfaction solidarity)	R_4^2 (building)	R_5^2 (student)
U_1	.01506				
U_2		.01994			
U_3			.01593		
U_4				.01874	
U_5					.01237
C_{12}	.00463	.00463			
C_{13}	-.00010		-.00010		
C_{14}	.00176			.00176	
C_{15}	-.00083				-.00083
C_{23}		-.00036	-.00036		
C_{24}		.00159		.00159	
C_{25}		.00171			.00171
C_{34}			.00989	.00989	
C_{35}			.00158		.00158
C_{45}				.00224	.00224
C_{123}	-.00205	-.00205	-.00205		
C_{124}	.00482	.00482		.00482	
C_{125}	.00064	.00064			.00064
C_{134}	.00315		.00315	.00315	
C_{135}	.00040		.00040		.00040
C_{145}	.00076			.00076	.00076
C_{234}		.00057	.00057	.00057	
C_{235}		.00038	.00038		.00038
C_{245}		.00041		.00041	.00041
C_{345}			.00312	.00312	.00312
C_{1234}	.00118	.00118	.00118	.00118	
C_{1235}	-.00032	-.00032	-.00032		-.00032
C_{1245}	.00034	.00034		.00034	.00034
C_{1345}	.00012		.00012	.00012	.00012
C_{2345}		.00004	.00004	.00004	.00004
C_{12345}	.00067	.00067	.00067	.00067	.00067
Total R^2	.03023	.03419	.03420	.04940	.02363

VI. Commonality Analysis of Total Achievement (5-Block Model)
from Chapter 4

Y = total achievement; 1 = actor traits; 2 = side–bets;
  3 = satisfaction and solidarity; 4 = building characteristics
    5 = student characteristics

$U_1 = .00245$
$U_2 = .00316$
$U_3 = .00251$
$U_4 = .00350$
$U_5 = .58695$

$R_{y.1} = .03734$
$R_{y.2} = .05224$
$R_{y.3} = .09212$
$R_{y.4} = .20265$
$R_{y.5} = .85189$

$R_{y.12} = .08383$
$R_{y.13} = .12076$
$R_{y.14} = .21521$
$R_{y.15} = .85620$
$R_{y.35} = .85619$
$R_{y.45} = .85880$
$R_{y.123} = .16833$
$R_{y.124} = .24587$
$R_{y.125} = .85955$
$R_{y.134} = .24711$
$R_{y.135} = .86026$
$R_{y.145} = .86152$
$R_{y.234} = .26530$
$R_{y.235} = .86098$
$R_{y.245} = .86224$
$R_{y.345} = .86089$

$R_{y.23} = .14345$
$R_{y.24} = .22961$
$R_{y.25} = .85648$
$R_{y.34} = .23375$

$R_{y.1234} = .28019$
$R_{y.1235} = .86364$
$R_{y.1245} = .86463$
$R_{y.1345} = .86398$
$R_{y.2345} = .86469$
$R_{y.12345} = .86714$

Commonality partitioning of variance

Source of variance	R_1^2 (actor traits)	R_2^2 (side–bets)	R_3^2 (satisfaction solidarity)	R_4^2 (building)	R_5^2 (student)
U_1	.00245				
U_2		.00316			
U_3			.00251		
U_4				.00350	
U_5					.58695
C_{12}	.00064	.00064			
C_{13}	-.00006		-.00006		
C_{14}	.00021			.00021	
C_{15}	.01244				. 01244
C_{23}		-.00005	-.00005		
C_{24}		.00022		.00022	
C_{25}		.02992			.02992
C_{34}			.00158	.00158	
C_{35}			.03181		.03181
C_{45}				.10836	.10836
C_{123}	-.00031	-.00031	-.00031		
C_{124}	.00077	.00077		.00077	
C_{125}	-.00217	-.00217			.00217
C_{134}	.00047		.00047	.00047	
C_{135}	.00143		.00143		.00143
C_{145}	.00978			.00978	.00978
C_{234}		.00002	.00002	.00002	
C_{235}		-.00237	-.00237		-.00237
C_{245}		.01427		.01427	.01427
C_{345}			.04860	.04860	.04860
C_{1234}	.00014	.00014	.00014	.00014	
C_{1235}	-.00186	-.00186	-.00186		-.00186
C_{1245}	.00452	.00452		.00452	.00452
C_{1345}	.00487		.00487	.00487	.00487
C_{2345}		.00132	.00132	.00132	.00132
C_{12345}	.00402	.00402	.00402	.00402	.00402
Total R^2	.03734	.05224	.09212	.20265	.85189

VII. Commonality Analysis of Attendance Behavior (5-Block Model)
from Chapter 4

Y = absenteeism; 1 = actor traits; 2 = side–bets;
   3 = satisfaction and solidarity; 4 = building characteristics
      5 = student characteristics

$U_1 = .00731$
$U_2 = .00824$
$U_3 = .00492$
$U_4 = .00410$
$U_5 = .03739$

$R_{y.1} = .00438$
$R_{y.2} = .01402$
$R_{y.3} = .00903$
$R_{y.4} = .01463$
$R_{y.5} = .05392$

$R_{y.12} = .02245$
$R_{y.13} = .01455$
$R_{y.14} = .01716$
$R_{y.15} = .05795$

$R_{y.123} = .03160$
$R_{y.124} = .03228$
$R_{y.125} = .06786$
$R_{y.134} = .02573$
$R_{y.135} = .06387$
$R_{y.145} = .06293$
$R_{y.234} = .03395$
$R_{y.235} = .06437$
$R_{y.245} = .06556$
$R_{y.345} = .06387$

$R_{y.23} = .02379$
$R_{y.24} = .02613$
$R_{y.25} = .06038$
$R_{y.34} = .02223$
$R_{y.35} = .05803$
$R_{y.45} = .05979$
$R_{y.1234} = .03950$
$R_{y.1235} = .07279$
$R_{y.1245} = .07197$
$R_{y.1345} = .06865$
$R_{y.2345} = .06958$
$R_{y.12345} = .07689$

Commonality partitioning of variance

Source of variance	R_1^2 (actor traits)	R_2^2 (side–bets)	R_3^2 (satisfaction solidarity)	R_4^2 (building)	R_5^2 (student)
U_1	.00731				
U_2		.00824			
U_3			.00492		
U_4				.00410	
U_5					.03739
C_{12}	-.00253	-.00253			
C_{13}	-.00090		-.00090		
C_{14}	.00111			.00111	
C_{15}	-.00176				.-00176
C_{23}		.00080	.00080		
C_{24}		.00068		.00068	
C_{25}		.00553			.00553
C_{34}			.00001	.00001	
C_{35}			.00230		.00230
C_{45}				.00380	.00380
C_{123}	-.00074	-.00074	-.00074		
C_{124}	-.00005	-.00005		.-00005	
C_{125}	.00048	.00048			.00048
C_{134}	-.00004		-.00004	-.00004	
C_{135}	.00150		.00150		.00150
C_{145}	.00115			.00115	.00115
C_{234}		.00019	.00019	.00019	
C_{235}		.00055	.00055		.00055
C_{245}		.00260		.00260	.00260
C_{345}			.00192	.00192	.00192
C_{1234}	-.00013	-.00013	-.00013	-.00013	
C_{1235}	-.00083	-.00083	-.00083		-.00083
C_{1245}	-.00019	-.00019		-.00019	-.00019
C_{1345}	.00006		.00006	.00006	.00006
C_{2345}		-.00052	-.00052	-.00052	-.00052
C_{12345}	-.00006	-.00006	-.00006	-.00006	-.00006
Total R^2	.00438	.01402	.00903	.01463	.05392

Appendix E. Decomposition of Path Models

Table E.1
Decomposition of the Path Models of Plans To Quit, Burnout, and Illness for Four Types of Principals

TYPE 1: PRINCIPAL UNINFLUENTIAL AND UNSUPPORTIVE

Independent Variables	Total Covariate r	Direct	Indirect	Total causal	Non-causal
Dependent variable: plans to quit teaching					
Burnout	.576	.507	—	.507	.069
Stress	.401	.226	.164	.390	.011
Victimization	.244	.156	.116	.272	-.028
Fear	.220	.037	.259	.296	-.076
White teacher	.272	.093	.180	.273	-.001
Grade level	-.073	-.124	-.028	-.152	-.079

$R = .649 \quad R^2 = .421 \quad F = 3.40$
Residual = .760

Dependent variable: burnout					
Stress	.380	.323	—	.323	.057
Victimization	.141	.229	-.055	.174	-.033
Fear	.387	.300	.089	.389	-.002
White teacher	.386	.356	.000	.356	.030
Grade level	-.204	-.105	-.055	-.160	-.044

$R = .643 \quad R^2 = .414 \quad F = 4.09$
Residual = .766

Dependent variable: stress					
Fear	.253	.274	—	.274	-.021

$R = .253 \quad R^2 = .064 \quad F = 2.43$
Residual = .967

Independent Variables	Total Covariate r	Direct	Indirect	Total causal	Non-causal
Dependent variable: victimization					
Grade level	-.242	-.242	—	-.242	.000
	R = .242	R² = .058	F = 2.05		
	Residual = .971				
Dependent variable: illness					
Victimization	.446	.439	—	.439	.007
Grade level	-.116	-.035	-.106	-.141	.025
	R = .447	R² = .200	F = 3.99		
	Residual = .894				
Dependent variable: victimization					
Grade level	-.242	-.242	—	-.242	.000
	R = .242	R² = .058	F = 2.05		
	Residual = .971				

TYPE II: PRINCIPAL UNINFLUENTIAL AND SUPPORTIVE

Independent Variables	Total Covariate r	Direct	Indirect	Total causal	Non-causal
Dependent variable: plans to quit teaching					
Burnout	.613	.602	—	.602	.011
Victimization	.256	.099	.195	.294	-.042
External	.449	.095	.340	.435	.014
	R = .625	R² = .390	F = 4.91		
	Residual = .781				
Dependent variable: burnout					
Victimization	.407	.342	—	.342	.065
External	.556	.565	.000	.565	.009
	R = .690	R² = .476	F = 6.29		
	Residual = .724				
Dependent variable: illness					
Victimization	.526	.501	—	.501	.025
White teacher	.172	.246	—	.246	-.074
Grade Level	.367	.370	—	.370	-.003
Black school	.327	.343	—	.343	-.016
	R = .744	R² = .553	F = 7.13		
	Residual = .668				

TYPE III: PRINCIPAL UNINFLUENTIAL AND UNSUPPORTIVE

Independent Variables	Total Covariate	Direct	Indirect	Total causal	Non-causal
Dependent variable: plans to quit teaching					
Burnout	.608	.649	—	.649	-.041
Stress	.238	.065	.132	.197	.041
Fear	.313	.139	.224	.363	-.050
Victimization	.131	.104	.056	.160	-.029
White teacher	.193	.189	.000	.189	.004

$R = .658$ $R^2 = .433$ $F = 6.42$
Residual = .753

Dependent variable: burnout					
Stress	.274	.204	—	.204	.070
Fear	.290	.345	.000	.345	-.055
Victimization	.202	.104	.086	.190	.012

$R = .451$ $R^2 = .203$ $F = 3.65$
Residual = .893

Dependent variable: fear					
Victimization	.250	.250	—	.250	.000

$R = .250$ $R^2 = .062$ $F = 3.13$
Residual = .968

Dependent variable: illness					
Male teacher	-.340	-.340	—	-.340	.000

$R = .340$ $R^2 = .116$ $F = 4.78$
Residual = .940

TYPE IV: PRINCIPAL INFLUENTIAL AND SUPPORTIVE

Dependent variable: plans to quit teaching					
Burnout	.525	.597	—	.597	-.072
External	.517	.322	.208	.530	-.013
Male teacher	.172	.252	.000	.252	-.080
White teacher	.204	.258	.000	.258	-.054
Grade level	-.184	-.046	-.178	-.214	.030

$R = .720$ $R^2 = .518$ $F = 6.32$
Residual = .694

Independent Variables	Total Covariate r	Direct	Indirect	Total causal	Non-causal
Dependent variable: burnout					
External	.366	.349	—	.349	.017
Grade level	-.199	-.299	.000	-.299	.100

$$R = .406 \qquad R^2 = .165 \qquad F = 3.46$$
$$\text{Residual} = .914$$

Independent Variables	Total Covariate r	Direct	Indirect	Total causal	Non-causal
Dependent variable: illness					
Victimization	.416	.379	—	.379	.037
White teacher	.184	.032	.125	.157	.027
Black school	.202	.091	.088	.179	.023

$$R = .426 \qquad R^2 = .182 \qquad F = 2.67$$
$$\text{Residual} = .904$$

Appendix F.
The Components of a Gain Score: Disaggregation of the Achievement Dependent Variable

Previously I had examined the impact of the blocks of variables on the composite, or summary, achievement score. The Iowa Test of Basic Skills is composed of five sub-sets of assessments. These sub-sets include vocabulary skills, reading comprehension, language skills, work study skills, and arithmetic skills. With the exceptions of the vocabulary and reading comprehension sub-tests, each of the parts of the Iowa Test of Basic Skills is further subdivided into sections. Thus, language skills contains separate sub-tests for spelling, capitalization, punctuation, and usage. Work-study skills are subdivided into tests of map reading, reading graphs and tables, and knowledge and use of reference materials. Finally, arithmetic skills tests contain sections or arithmetic concepts and arithmetic problem solving. (For a detailed analysis of each of these tests, see Thorndike and Hagen, 1977; or Grondlund, 1968).

Numerous investigators have contended that the impact of school, teacher, and home resources affect these sub-sets differently. It is therefore appropriate to inquire into the uniformity of impact of the various conceptual blocks of independent variables upon each of the sub-sets. Table F.1 presents the intercorrelations between the five dimensions of the Iowa test, as well as the composite test, each computed as a gain score. It is evident from the table that the association between each component of the Iowa test gain and the composite gain score is moderately high. However, the associations between individual sub-tests are much weaker. It is reasonable to expect that the blocks of independent variables will have somewhat different effects upon the sub-sets. To verify that, separate regression runs were conducted in which a sub-set score computed as a gain score was regressed upon the blocks of independent variables. What follows in this appendix is an analysis of those regression runs.

The individual regression runs are displayed in Tables F.2 through F.6. Inspection of these tables reveals that slightly different combinations of variables explain each aspect of achievement gain. There is, however, considerable overlap. Additionally, there are small differences in the total amount of variance in each sub-set of achievement gain explained by the blocks of independent variables. Thus, the model explains 6.1 percent of the variance in vocabulary gain scores, 4.7 percent of the variance in reading comprehension gain, 9.9 percent of the variance in language skill gain, 5.3 percent of the variance in the gain in work-study skills, and 7.5 percent of the variance in the gain in arithmetic skills. Rather than discuss the individual findings for each of the components of the Iowa Test, it is preferable to examine those findings which are consistent across tests and to explore the implications of significant findings which are present in only one subtest or one particular group of subtests.

Teacher's stereotyping remains a significant factor in elevating gain scores across all tests which emphasize vocabulary and the use of language skills. Stereotyping increases vocabulary gain by nearly one-half month, reading comprehension by one-half month, and language skill by over a week. Stereotyping plays no role in work-study skills or arithmetic skills.

As with the analysis of the composite gain scores, teachers who subsequently quit do elevate achievement scores for the students in their classes. However, the effect is significant only for work-study skills, while non-significant effects are observable for the other sub-sets. Teachers who subsequently quit elevate work-study skill gain scores by over one and one-half months. Teacher burnout and plans to quit play a negligible role. Burnout does reduce gain in vocabulary by a month, but has no effect elsewhere.

Except for reading comprehension, where there are no significant effects, the race of the student is associated with differences in subtest achievement gains. Black children are associated with more than a two and one-half month reduction in vocabulary gain, a two and one-third month reduction in language skill gain, nearly two months reduction in work skill gains, and a two and three-quarter month reduction in

Table F.1

*Intercorrelations Between Each Component of Achievement Gain Scores
and Composite Gain Scores*

Variable	Comp.	Vocab.	Read. Comp.	Lang. Skills	Work- Study	Arith. Skills
Composite	1.000	.612	.594	.714	.656	.653
Vocabulary		1.000	.094	.327	.239	.222
Reading Comprehension			1.000	.272	.203	.213
Language Skills				1.000	.395	.387
Work-Study Skills					1.000	.409
Arithmetic Skills						1.000

Table F.2

*Regression of Subset of Iowa Test Scores on Predictors:
Vocabulary Gain*

Variable	Covar.r	b	se	F	Beta
Stereotyping	.049	.040	.016	5.93	.077
Inexperience	.102	.081	.033	5.92	.112
Administrative Style Difference	-.114	-.138	.049	7.87	-.090
Discrimination	-.080	-.233	.085	7.57	-.090
Burnout	-.015	-.107	.045	5.57	-.088
Black Child	-.151	-.260	.090	8.46	-.121
Grade	.064	.096	.039	6.02	.074
White School	.143	.187	.085	4.84	.084
Intercept = .699	R = .248	R^2 = .061	F = 5.30		

arithmetic skill gain. Only on work-study skills is the brown child
variable associated with any effect. Thus, brown children are associated
with a reduction of nearly one and one-half months in work-study skills.
Since that is a skill in which the school plays a relatively monopolistic
role, it is intriguing that brown children are primarily disadvantaged
there, rather than in the sphere of language, where bilingualism is
prevalent. However, it should be noted that brown schools are im-

Table F.3

Regression of Subset of Iowa Test Scores on Predictors:
Reading Comprehension Gain

Variable	Covar.r	b	se	F	Beta
Stereotyping	.066	.052	.016	10.78	.102
Discrimination	-.069	-.206	.078	7.09	-.082
Grade	.111	.155	.040	15.05	.122
Student SES	.076	-.102	.043	5.60	.072
Absenteeism	-.079	-1.408	.464	9.21	-.091
Intercept = 1.20	R = .218	R² = .047	F = 5.85		

Table F.4

Regression of Subset of Iowa Test Scores on Predictors:
Language Skill Gain

Variable	Covar.r	b	se	F	Beta
Stereotyping	.030	.027	.013	4.31	.065
External	-.128	-.025	.012	3.54	-.061
Experience	.009	-.011	.003	7.34	-.095
Inexperience	.138	.063	.020	9.83	.112
Assignment					
Attitude	.086	.076	.038	3.31	.063
Norms	-.084	-.044	.018	6.02	-.088
Administrative					
Style Difference	-.097	-.073	.033	4.77	-.070
Teacher Turnover	-.141	-.595	.290	3.16	-060
Sex of Student	.088	.138	.050	7.63	.082
Black Child	-.169	-.237	.058	21.87	-.159
Absenteeism	-.077	-.731	.360	3.95	-.059
Brown School	-.063	-.222	.077	8.31	-.103
Intercept = .088	R = .315	R² = .099	F = 6.44		

plicated in learning disadvantages in language skill gain, with a reduction of two and one-quarter months, and with arithmetic gain scores, with a reduction of nearly two-months in achievement gain. Black schools are not implicated in any effect on the subtests, however; white schools are associated with almost a two-month gain in vocabulary and, similarly, a nearly two-month gain in arithmetic. In no setting and on no subtest does the race or sex of the teacher make a difference, despite the contentions to the contrary by Murnane (1975) and Gold and Reis (1982).

Table F.5
Regression of Subset of Iowa Test Scores on Predictors: Work-Study Gain

Variable	Covar.r	b	se	F	Beta
Singleton Ratio Attitudes	-.032	- .068	.028	5.78	-.082
Plans to Quit	-.061	-.050	.020	6.19	-.077
Quit	.039	.162	.076	4.60	.068
Teacher Turnover	-.158	-1.481	.316	21.91	-.162
Black Child	-.104	-.188	.052	12.43	-.113
Brown Child	-.029	-.144	.059	5.76	-.073
Absenteeism	-.064	-.563	.280	3.55	-.050
Intercept = -.931	R = .231	R² = .053	F = 5.42		

Table F.6
Regression of Subset of Iowa Test Scores on Predictors: Arithmetic Gain

Variable	Covar.r	b	se	F	Beta
Tenure	-.027	-.172	.076	5.19	-.097
Inexperience	.098	.056	.024	5.49	.102
Norms	-.076	-.058	.018	10.27	-.110
Peer Turnover	-.115	-1.120	.335	11.20	-.117
Student's Age	.042	-.111	.040	7.74	.142
Black Child	-.120	-.275	.071	15.14	-.167
Grade	.031	.142	.051	7.80	.144
Brown School	-.043	-.198	.080	6.11	-.096
White School	.078	.186	.073	6.49	.186
Intercept = .374	R = .274	R² = .075	F = 6.61		

Notes

Chapter 2. Burnout, Plans to Quit Teaching, and Quitting Behavior

1.   Three pieces of information are needed to construct the measure of assignment attitudes: (1) the kinds of schools in which the teacher would not like to teach (expressed in terms of the racial makeup of the student body), (2) the kinds of schools in which the teacher would prefer to teach, and (3) information on the actual ethnic distribution of students at the school to which the teacher has been assigned. An effect-coded dummy variable is constrcted in which a score of -1 is given to an actual assignment to a school which is disliked; a score of +1 to an actual assignment to a school which is preferred; and a score of 0 to an assignment to a school which is neither prefered nor disliked. It is hypothesized that assignment to a school which is disliked will lead to higher burnout, plans to quit, and actual quitting behavior than a school which is preferred, and that a neutral school would provide an intermediate response on the dependent variables. Dworkin (1980) found that assignment to a disliked school was associated with higher percentages of teachers wanting to quit teaching.

2.   Transfer experience operates similarly to, and was constructed in a like fashion to, the assignment attitude measure. An additional piece of information is used: the racial composition of the school from which one transferred voluntarily or involuntarily. Thus, assignment from a desired school to an undesired school yields a transfer experience score of -1; assignment from an undesired school to a desired school yields a score of +1; and any other kind of transfer or no transfer at all yields a score of 0. Again, it is hypothesized that a positive transfer experience will be negatively associated with burnout, plans to quit, and actual quitting behavior. Teachers assigned to desired settings after leaving undesired settings will display less burnout, plans to quit, and actual quitting behavior than teachers in neutral settings, who in turn will display less burnout, plans to quit, and actual quitting behavior than teachers assigned to undesired settings after being transferred from desired ones.

207

3. Previous work on the variable of administrative style differences had indicated that it yields three orthogonal factors (Caram, 1982; Caram, Dworkin, and Croft, 1983). The ten items were submitted to principal axis factor analysis. All items except management of the school's budget loaded on one of the three obtained factors. Using oblique rotation, it was found that the factors bore an interfactor correlation of less than .20, thereby suggesting that there were essentially three orthogonal measures. The first factor represented two items which focused upon the evaluation and surveillance role of the principal and was labeled "faculty evaluation." The second factor dealt with academic administration issues and was labeled "academic management," and the third factor focused upon the interpersonal and community relation roles of the principal and was labeled "social management." Factor score coefficients were computed for each subject. In turn, these coefficients, one for each of the three factors, represented the teacher's score on the factor. From this score was subtracted the factor score obtained from the responses by the principal for whom the individual teacher worked. In most cases, there was a score for a principal for each teacher. However, because there was almost no variance in the responses by principals (nearly all rated each of their activities as very important), a mean score for all principals could be subtracted from the score of any teacher for whom there was no scale score for his or her principal. The discrepancy between the evaluation made by the principal and that made by the teacher represented the assessment of disagreement on administrative style for each factor and for each teacher. The earlier work indicated that there was no significant association between any of the dependent variables and a difference score on either the academic management or the social management discrepancy scales. In fact, there was almost no discrepancy at all between the principals and the teachers on the social management discrepancy scale. However, there were significant differences between the teachers and their principals on the faculty evaluation scale. Likewise, that scale was significantly associated with the dependent variables. Thus, only the factor scores representing the faculty evaluation dimension will be used in computing the measure of administrative style difference in the present research.

4. Early work with the models involved the use of years teaching as a single variable. However, the correlations between years teaching and the dependent variables were negative, but the b's and beta's were positive. Graphing the associations revealed that they were not linear, but rather that plans to quit, burnout, and quitting increased very steeply during the first five years and then gradually declined after the fifth year. Under such a condition, it is appropriate to compute a spline (see Poirier, 1976; and Sanders, 1984). Two variables were constructed, thereby eliminating the problem of curvilinearity. The first variable, termed "inexperience," has a positive r, b, and beta with the dependent variables. The second variable, termed "experience," has a negative r, b, and beta with the dependent variables. Inexperience is computed by coding 0 through 5 years as 0,1,2,3,4,5 and 6 through 40 years (the highest value) also as 5. Experience is computed by coding 0 through 5 years as 0, and subtracting 5 from all successive years.

It is interesting to note that McNamara et al. (1977) and Murnane (1975) found a similar curvilinear pattern for the impact of teacher experience on student achievement. Student achievement gains increased rapidly for each additional year of teacher experience through year five, and then diminished slowly for each additional year.

5. Given the large sample size of the data sets, a criterion that a significant F value is necessary for the inclusion of a predictor is too liberal. Many independent variables will attain statistical significance and still not merit inclusion. To be included in a final regression, a predictor must also have a b value which is twice the size of its standard error.

6. Swafford (1980) has argued that it is inappropriate to compute OLS regression models with dichotomous dependent variables. Because such variables technically have no variance, alternative techniques ought to be used. In light of this argument, the model of quitting behavior was recomputed using a linear discriminant function analysis (one acceptable alternative). The standarized canonical coefficients in such instances represent the equivalent of beta's and the canonical correlation coefficient the equivalent of a Multiple R. Analysis of the vectors which bore significant discriminatory power in distinguishing quitters from nonquitters exactly replicated the effect of the predictors in the final model presented in table 2.3. As such, inclusion of the discrimination function analysis here would be unnecessary.

Chapter 3. Stress, Burnout, and Support Among Those Who Stay in Teaching

1. Stinnett and Henson (1982) and Duke (1984) have pointed to the supportive role that peers (other teachers) can play in reducing the stress associated with teaching. They have also suggested a supportive role for unions. However, Duke (1984) acknowledges that in the South unions are weak. Previous work, plus a brief analysis presented later in this chapter, has led to a decision to minimize the social support provided by all but the principal.

2. Factor analytic work done on these data for a previous analysis revealed that attacks upon the person were greater stressors than attacks on property. Consequently, the victimization items selected here are obscene gestures, swearing, subtle threats, physical threats, assaults not needing medical attention, and assaults needing medical attention.

3. An initial concern was that the items which comprised the support scale were too similar to those which comprised the burnout scale. If this were the case, then a hypothesis that principal's support ameliorates burnout would be tautological. To relieve the concern over the similarity between the two sets of items, the eight items from the burnout measure and the six items from the principal's support measure were combined and submitted to a factor analysis using oblique rotation. Should two factors emerge, with the burnout items on one factor and the support measures on another, and the two factors bear a near-zero

correlation, then our concerns regarding a tautology would be considerably relieved. This is in fact exactly what happened. Two factors emerged, with the eight burnout items loaded on the first factor between .41 and .84, and with all of the principal support items loaded on that factor between .09 and -.10. On the second factor, the burnout items were loaded between .07 and .22, while the principal support items were loaded on that factor between .40 and .78. The correlation between the two factors was .18. I therefore conclude that the two measures are distinct scales.

4. I tested a plausible rival hypothesis that the locus of control is not homogeneous across teachers assigned to the four types of principals. If teachers who are assigned to unsupportive principals are more internal while those assigned to supportive principals are more external, then the argument could be confounded. Since externals burn out more than internals, it might be that assignment rather than the action of principals accounts for the absence of locus of control as a predictor of burnout in supportive cases. A one-way analysis of variance permitted me to reject this rival hypothesis. The variance in locus control was homogeneous across all four types of principal assignments (F = 1.076, d.f. = 3/260, p = .37).

Chapter 4. The Impact of Teachers on Students

1. The obtained sample of 8,203 students provided a confidence interval of +/− .0083 at the .05 level for the entire population, and a confidence interval of +/− .0149 at the .05 level for each grade level. Thus, if a conclusion about the whole population is made, one can assume that 95 times out of 100, the percentage given will differ from the population as a whole by less than 1 percent and for each grade by less than 1.5 percent.

References

Adelson, Joseph
  1958 "A study of minority group authoritarianism." Pp. 475–492 in Marshall Sklare (ed.), *The Jews, Social Patterns of an American Group.* New York: The Free Press.

Aiken, M., and J. Hage
  1966 "Organizational alienation: A comparative analysis." *American Sociological Review* 31:497–507.

Alexander, K. E., and M. A. Cook
  1982 "Curricula and coursework: A surprise ending to a familiar story." *American Sociological Review* 47:626–640.

Alexander, K. E., M. A. Cook, and E. L. McDill
  1978 "Curriculum tracking and educational stratification: Some further evidence." *American Sociological Review*: 42:47–66.

Alexander, K. E., and E. L. McDill
  1976 "Selection and allocation within schools: Some consequences of curriculum placement." *American Sociological Review* 41:963–980.

Alexander, Karl E., Edward L. McDill, James Fennessey, and Ronald J. D'Amico
  1979 "School SES influences—composition or context?" *Sociology of Education* 52:222–237.

Alutto, J. A., L. G. Hrebiniak, and R. C. Alonzo
  1973 "On operationalizing the concept of commitment." *Social Forces* 51:448–454.

Anderson, Barry D., and Jonathan H. Mark
  1977 "Teacher mobility and productivity in a metropolitan area: a seven year case study." *Urban Education* 12:15–36.

Andrisani, Paul J
  1978 *Work Attitudes and Labor Market Experience: Evidence from the National Longitudinal Surveys.* New York: Praeger.

211

Angle, Harold L., and James L. Perry
    1983   "Organizational commitment." *Sociology of Work and Occupations*
            10:126–146.

Armor, David J.
    1980   "White flight and the future of school desegregation." Pp. 187–225 in
            Walter G. Stephan and Joe R. Feagin (eds.), *School Desegregation:
            Past, Present, and Future.* New York: Plenum Press.

Bartholomew, John
    1976   "Schooling teachers: the myth of the liberal college." Pp. 114–124 in G.
            Whitty and M. Young (eds.), *Explorations in the Politics of School
            Knowledge.* Nafferton, Driffield, England: Nefferton Books.

Becker, Gary S.
    1964   *Human Capital: A Theoretical and Empirical Analysis, with Special
            Reference to Education.* New York: Columbia University Press.

Becker, Howard S.
    1952   "The career of the Chicago public school teacher." *American Journal
            of Sociology* 57:470–477.

    1960   "Notes on the concept of commitment." *American Journal of
            Sociology* 66:32–40.

Becker, Howard S., and Blanche Geer
    1958   "The fate of idealism in medical school." *American Sociological
            Review* 23:50–56.

Becker, H. S., and A. Strauss
    1956   "Careers, personality, and adult socializaiton." *American Journal of
            Sociology* 62:253–263.

Betz, Michael, and James Garland
    1974   "Intergenerational mobility rates of urban school teachers." *Sociology
            of Education* 47:511–522.

Blau, Peter M., and W. Richard Scott
    1962   *Formal Organizations: A Comparative Approach.* San Francisco:
            Chandler Publishing Company.

Blau, Zena S.
    1981   *Black Children/White Children: Competence, Socialization, and Social
            Structure.* New York: The Free Press.

Blauner, Robert
    1964   *Alienation and Freedom.* Chicago: University of Chicago Press.

Blumer, Herbert
    1956   "Sociological analysis and the 'variable'." *American Sociological
            Review* 21:683–690.

Boggs, Sarah L.
    1971   "Formal and informal crime control: an exploratory study of urban,

suburban, and rural orientations." *The Sociological Quarterly* 12:319–327.

Bowles, Samuel, and Herbert Gintis
1976   *Schooling in Capitalist America.* New York: Basic Books.

Bowles, Samuel S., and Henry M. Levin
1968   "More on multicollinearity and the effectiveness of schools." *Journal of Human Resources* III:393–400.

Braun, Carl
1976   "Teacher expectation: Sociopsychological dynamics." *Review of Educational Research* 46:185–213.

Bridge, R. Gary
1974   *Nonresponse Bias in Mail Surveys: The Case of the Department of Defense Post-Service Survey.* Defense Advanced Research Project Agency, ARPA, R-1501.

Bridge, R. Gary, Charles Judd, and Peter R. Moock
1979   *The Determinants of Educational Outcomes: The Effects of Families, Peers, Teachers, and Schools.* New York: Teachers College Press.

Brookover, Wilber, and Edsel L. Erickson
1975   *Sociology of Education.* Homewood, Illinois: Dorsey Press.

Brophy, J. E., and T. L. Good
1970   "Teacher communication of differential expectations for children's performance: Some behavioral data." *Journal of Educational Psychology* 61:365–374.

1974   *Teacher-Student Relationships: Causes and Consequences.* New York: Holt, Rinehart, and Winston.

Brown Brothers v. Board of Education of Topeka, Kansas. 347 U.S. 483, at 494 May 17, 1954.

Brown Brothers v. Board of Education of Topeka, Kansas, et al. 349 U.S. 294. May 31, 1955.

Campbell, Richard T.
1983   "Status attainment research: End of the beginning or the beginning of the end?" *Sociology of Education* 56:47–62.

Camus, Albert
1946   *The Stranger.* New York: Alfred A. Knopf, Inc.

Cannon, W. B.
1929   *Bodily Changes in Pain, Hunger, Fear, and Rage.* New York: Appleton and Company.

Caplan, Robert
1971   "Organizational stress and individual strain: A social psychological study of risk factors in coronary heart disease among administrators,

engineers, and scientists.'' Unpublished Ph.D. dissertation, Ann Arbor:
University of Michigan.

Caplan, R., and J. R. P. French, Jr.
1968   "Final Report to NASA." Unpublished manuscript. Ann Arbor:
University of Michigan.

Caram, Dorothy Farrington
1982   "An analysis of factors associated with job dissatisfaction and quitting
behavior among urban public school teachers." Unpublished Ed.D.
dissertation, University of Houston.

Caram, Dorothy F., Anthony Gary Dworkin, and John C. Croft
1983   "Some relationships between administrator's opinions and teacher's
quitting behavior in an urban public school system." Paper presented at
the American Educational Research Association meetings, Montreal.

Carchedi, Guglielmo
1977   *On the Economic Identification of Social Classes.* Boston: Routledge
and Kegan Paul.

Carlson, Richard O.
1951   "Variations in the myth in the social status of teachers." *The Journal of
Educational Sociology* 35:104–118.

Carnegie Task Force on Teaching as a Profession
1986   *A Nation Prepared: Teachers for the 21st Century.* New York: Carnegie
Corporation.

Caroll, Jerome F. X., and William L. White
1982   "Theory building: Integrating individual and environmental factors
within an ecological framework." Pp. 41–60 in W. S. Paine (ed.), *Job
Stress and Burnout: Research, Theory, and Intervention Perspectives.*
Beverly Hills, California: Sage.

Cedoline, Anthony J.
1982   *Job Burnout in Public Education: Symptoms, Causes, and Survival
Skills.* New York: Teachers College Press, Columbia University.

Center for National Policy Review and National Institute of Education
1977a *Trends in Black School Segregation, 1970–1974.* Vol. 1. Washington
D.C.: U.S. Government Printing Office.

1977b *Trends in Hispanic Segregation, 1970–1974.* Vol. 2. Washington, D.C.:
U.S. Government Printing Office.

Chafetz, Janet Saltzman
1980   "Conflict resolution in marriage: Toward a theory of spousal strategies
and marital dissolution rates." *Journal of Family Issues* 1:397–421.

Chafetz, Janet Saltzman, and Anthony Gary Dworkin
1986 *Female Revolt: Women's Movements in World and Historical Perspective.* Totowa, New Jersey: Rowman and Allanheld.

Chapman, David W., and Sigrid M. Hutcheson
1982 "Attrition from teaching: A discriminant analysis." *American Educational Research Journal* 19:93–105.

Charters, W. W., Jr.
1963 The social background of teaching." Pp. 718–722 in N. L. Gage (ed.), *Handbook of Research on Teaching.* Chicago: Rand McNally.

1970 "Some factors affecting teacher survival in school district." *American Educational Research Journal* 7:1–27.

Cherniss, Cary
1980 *Professional Burnout in Human Service Organizations.* New York: Praeger.

1982 "Cultural trends: Political, economic, and historical roots of the problem." Pp. 83–94 in W. S. Paine (ed.), *Job Stress and Burnout: Research, Theory, and Intervention Perspectives.* Beverly Hills, California: Sage.

Cherniss, C., E. S. Egnatios, and S. Wacker
1976 "Job stress and career development in new public professionals." *Professional Psychology* 7:428–436.

Cisneros v. Corpus Christi Independent School District. 467 F.2d 142. August, 2, 1972.

Clark, Kenneth B.
1965 *Dark Ghetto: Dilemmas of Social Power.* New York: Harper and Row.

Clark, Todd
1970 "Integration, the first year: A role-playing simulation on school integration." ERIC:ED050215.

Clement, Dorothy C., Margaret Eisenhart, and John W. Wood
1976 "School desegregation and educational inequality: Trends in the literature, 1960–1975. Pp. 1–78 in National Institute of Education, *The Desegregation Literature: A Critical Approach.* Washington, D.C.: U.S. Government Printing Office.

Clifton, Rodney A.
1981 "Ethnicity, teachers' expectations, and the academic achievement process in Canada." *Sociology of Education* 54:291–301.

Clifton, Rodney, Raymond Perry, Karen Parsonson, and Stella Hryniuk
1986 "Effects of ethnicity and sex on teachers' expectations of junior high school students." *Sociology of Education* 59:58–67.

Coleman, James S., Ernest Q. Campbell, Carol J. Hobson, James McParland, Alexander M. Mood, Frederick D. Weinfeld, and Robert L. York
1966 *The Equality of Educational Opportunity.* Washington, D.C.: U.S. Department of Health, Education, and Welfare, U.S. Government Printing Office.

Collins, Thomas W.
1979 "From courtrooms to classrooms: Managing school desegregation in a deep South high school." Pp. 89–116 in Ry C. Rist (ed.), *Desegregated Schools: Appraisal of an American Experiment.* New York: Academic Press.

Collins, Thomas W., and George W. Noblit
1976 "The process of interracial schooling: An assessment of conceptual frameworks and methodological orientations." Pp. 79–110 in National Institute of Education, *The Desegregation Literature: A Critical Approach.* Washington, D.C.: U.S. Government Printing Office.

Conklyn, E. D.
1976 "Role definition by the principal: Effects and determinants." Presented at the American Educational Research Association meetings, San Francisco.

Cooley, W. W., and P. R. Lohnes
1976 *Evaluation Research in Education.* New York: John Wiley and Sons.

Cooper, Harris M.
1979 "Pygmalion grows up: A model for teacher expectation communication and performance influence." *Review of Educational Research* 49:389–410.

Corwin, Ronald G.
1970 *Militant Professionalism: A Study of Organizational Conflicts in a High School.* New York: Appleton-Century-Crofts.

Coughlan, Robert J.
1970 "Dimensions of teacher morale." *American Educational Research Journal* 7:221–234.

Crain, Robert L., and Rita E. Mahard
1981 "Minority achievement: Policy implications of research." Pp. 55–84 in Willis D. Hawley (ed.), *Effective School Desegregation: Equity, Quality, and Feasibility.* Beverly Hills, California: Sage.

Culbertson, Manie
1972 *May I Speak?: Diary of a Crossover Teacher.* Gretna, Louisiana: Pelican Publishing Company.

Currence, Cindy
1985 "Major universities adopt tougher teacher-training requirements." *Education Week,* June 12:5.

Darling-Hammond, Linda
  1984   *Beyond the Commission Reports: The Coming Crisis in Teaching.* Santa
          Monica, California: Rand Corporation.

Davis, James A.
  1965   *Undergraduate Career Decisions.* Chicago: Aldine Publishing Com-
          pany.

Dean, D. G.
  1961   "Alienation: Its meaning and measurement." *American Sociological
          Review* 26:753–758.

Deutscher, Irwin
  1973   *What We Say/What We Do: Sentiments and Acts.* Glenview, Illinois:
          Scott, Foresman.

Dohrenwend, B. S., and B. P. Dohrenwend (eds.)
  1974   *Stressful Life Events: Their Nature and Effects.* New York: John Wiley
          and Sons.

Donnenworth, G., and H. G. Cox
  1978   "Attitudinal militancy among teachers." *The Sociological Quarterly*
          19:459–468.

Drury, Darrel W.
  1980   "Black self-esteem and desegregated schools." *Sociology of Education*
          53:88–103.

Duke, Daniel Linden
  1984   *Teaching—The Imperiled Profession.* Albany, New York: State Univer-
          sity of New York Press.

Dusek, Jerome B.
  1975   "Do teachers bias children's learning?" *Review of Educational
          Research* 45:661–684.

Dusek, Jerome B. (ed.)
  1985   *Teacher Expectancies.* Hillsdale, New Jersey: Lawrence Erlbaum
          Associates, Publishers.

Dworkin, Anthony Gary
  1965   "Stereotypes and self-images held by native-born and foreign-born
          Mexican Americans." *Sociology and Social Research* 49:214–224.

  1968   "No siesta mañana: The Mexican-American in Los Angeles." Pp.
          387–439 in R. W. Mack (ed.), *Our Children's Burden: Studies of
          Desegregation in Nine American Communities.* New York: Random
          House.

  1974   "Balance on the Bayou: The impact of racial isolation and interaction
          on Stereotypy in the Houston Independent School District." Pp. 7–51

in A. G. Dworkin, R. G. Frankiewicz, and H. Copitka, *Intergroup Action Project Report*. Houston: Houston Council on Human Relations.

1980 "The changing demography of public school teachers: Some implications for faculty turnover in urban areas." *Sociology of Education* 53:65–73.

1982 "Work commitment and quitting behavior: A study of urban public school employees." Paper presented at the Southwestern Sociological Association meetings, San Antonio.

Dworkin, Anthony Gary, and Janet Saltzman Chafetz
1983 "Work commitment and mobility among male and female urban public school employees: An application of Kanter's approach to a semi-profession." Paper presented at the Southwestern Sociological Association meetings, Houston.

Dworkin, Anthony Gary, and Rosalind J. Dworkin
1976 *The Minority Report: Introduction to Race, Ethnic, and Gender Relations*. New York: Praeger.

1982 *The Minority Report: Introduction to Race, Ethnic, and Gender Relations*. 2nd ed. New York: Holt, Rinehart, and Winston.

Dworkin, A. G., R. G. Frankiewicz, and H. Copitka
1975 "Impact and assessment of stereotype reduction activities in the public schools." Paper presented at the Southwestern Scoiological Association meetings, San Antonio.

Dworkin, Anthony Gary, Virginia W. Joiner, and Paula Bruno
1980 "Locus of control and intention to remain in unpleasant situations: The case of the public school teacher." Paper presented at the Southwestern Social Science Association meetings, Houston. Also available through ERIC.

Dworkin, Anthony Gary, Frank S. Black, Jimy M. Sanders, James F. McNamara, Waymon Webster, and Virginia W. Joiner
1977 "Mrs. Jones doesn't teacher here anymore: The results of the mail-out survey of the attitudes of HISD personnel about the impact of the Singleton Ratio upon students and staff." Report to the Board of Education of the Houston Independent School District, December 12, 1977. Houston: Houston Independent School District.

Dworkin, Anthony Gary, Jimy M. Sanders, Virginia Joiner, James F. McNamara, and Frank Black
1978 "The Singleton Ratio: The impact of faculty desegregation upon faculty alienation and student achievement in an urban public school district." Paper presented at the Southwestern Sociological Association meetings, Houston.

Ebaugh, Helen Rose Fuchs
1977 *Out of the Cloister: A Study of Organizational Dilemmas.* Austin, Texas: University of Texas Press.

Eder, Donna
1981 "Ability grouping as a self-fulfilling prophecy: A microanalysis of teacher-student interaction." *Sociology of Education* 54:151–161.

Elam, Stanley (ed.)
1973 *The Gallup Polls of Attitudes Toward Education, 1969–1973.* Bloomington, Indiana: Phi Delta Kappa, Inc.

Elam, Stanley M., and Pauline B. Gough
1980 "Comparing lay and professional opinion on Gallup poll questions." *Phi Delta Kappan* 62:47–48.

Entwisle, Doris R., and Leslie Alec Hayduk
1981 "Academic expectations and the school attainment of young children." *Sociology of Education* 54:34–50.

Entwisle, D. R., and M. Webster
1974 "Expectations in mixed racial groups." *Sociology of Education* 47:301–318.

Entzioni, Amitai (ed.)
1969 *The Semi-Professions and Their Organization.* New York: The Free Press.

Evangelauf, Jean
1985 "Panel analyzes education graduate's college transcripts, finds weak grounding in liberal arts, urges 25 reforms." *The Chronicle of Higher Education*, June 26:11.

Falk, William W., Carolyn Falkowski, and Thomas A. Lyson
1981 " 'Some plan to become teachers': Further elaboration and specification." *Sociology of Education* 54:64–69.

Falk, William W., Michael D. Grimes, and George F. Lord III
1982 "Professionalism and conflict in a bureaucratic setting: The case of a teachers' strike." *Social Problems* 29:551–560.

Festinger, Leon
1964 *Conflict, Decision, and Dissonance.* Stanford, California: Stanford University Press.

Form, William H.
1973 "Auto workers and their machines: A study of work, factory and job satisfaction in four countries." *Social Forces* 52:1–15.

Fox, W. S., and M. H. Wince
  1976 "Structure and determinants of occupational militancy among public school teachers." *Industrial and Labor Relations Review* 30:47–58.

Frazier, Nancy, and Myra Sadker
  1973 *Sexism in School and Society.* New York: Harper and Row.
Freudenberger, H. J.
  1974 "Staff burn-out." *Journal of Social Issues* 30:159–165.

  1982 "Counseling and dynamics: Treating the end-stage person." Pp. 173–188 in W. S. Paine (ed.), *Job Stress and Burnout: Research, Theory, and Intervention Perspectives.* Beverly Hills, California: Sage.

Fruchter, Benjamin
  1954 *Introduction to Factor Analysis.* Princeton, New Jersey: Van Nostrand.

Fuchs, Estelle
  1969 *Teacher's Talk: Views from Inside City Schools.* New York: Doubleday.

Fulcher, J.
  1970 "The making of a radical teacher." *English Journal* 59:384–386.

Gallup, George H.
  1980 "The 12th annual Gallup poll of the public's attitudes toward the public schools." *Phi Delta Kappan* 62:33–46.

  1981 "The 13th annual Gallup poll of the public's attitudes toward the public schools." *Phi Delta Kappan* 63:33–47.

  1982 "The 14th annual Gallup poll of the public's attitudes toward the public schools." *Phi Delta Kappan* 64:37–50.

Geer, Blanche
  1966 "Occupational commitment and the teaching profession." *The School Review* 74:31–47.

Gerard, Harold B., and Norman Miller
  1975 *School Desegregation: A Long-Term Study.* New York: Plenum Press.

Gideonse, Hendrik D.
  1982 "The necessary revolution in teacher education." *Phi Delta Kappan* 64:15–18.

Ginsburg, Mark B.
  Forth- "Reproduction, contradictions, and conceptions of curriculum in
  coming preservice teacher education." *Curriculum Inquiry.*

Ginsburg, Mark B., and Katherine K. Newman
  1985 "Social inequalities, schooling, and teacher education." *Journal of Teacher Education* 36:49–54.

Gold, Dolores, and Myrna Reis
  1982 "Male teacher effects on young children: a theoretical and empirical consideration." *Sex Roles* 8:493–513.

Gottlieb, David
  1964 Teaching and students: The views of Negro and white teachers." *Sociology of Education* 37:345–353.

Greenblatt, Susan L., and Charles V. Willie
  1980 "The serendipitous effects of school desegregation." Pp. 51–66 in Walter G. Stephan and Joe R. Feagin (eds.), *School Desegregation: Present, Past, and Future*. New York: Plenum Press.

Gronlund, Norman E. (eds.)
  1968 *Readings in Measurement and Evaluation*. New York: Macmillan.

Haller, Emil J., and Sharon A. Davis
  1981 "Teacher perceptions, parental social status and grouping for reading instruction." *Sociology of Education* 54:162–173.

Hanushek, Eric A.
  1972 *Education and Race*. Lexington, Massachusetts: Lexington Books.

Harman, Harry H.
  1967 *Modern Factor Analysis*. 2nd ed., rev. Chicago: University of Chicago Press.

Haskins, Jim
  1969 *Diary of a Harlem Schoolteacher*. New York: Grove Press.

Hauser, Robert M.
  1971 *Socioeconomic Background and Educational Performance*. The Arnold M. and Caroline Rose Monograph Series. Washington, D.C.: American Sociological Association.

Havighurst, Robert J.
  1964 *The Public Schools of Chicago*. Chicago: The Board of Education of Chicago.

Hawley, Willis D.
  1981 *Effective School Desegregation: Equity, Quality and Feasibility*. Beverly Hills, California: Sage.

Hawley, Willis D., Robert L. Crain, Christine H. Rossell, Mark A. Smylie, Ricardo R. Fernandez, Janet W. Schofield, Rachel Tompkins, William T. Trent, and Marilyn S. Zlotnik
  1973 *Strategies for Effective Desegregation*. Lexington, Massachusetts: Lexington Books.

Hearn, J. J.
  1971 "Teachers' sense of alienation with respect to school system structure." *Phi Delta Kappan* 52:312.

1974   "Alienation: Another administrative agony." *Contemporary Educa-*
        tion 45:32–36.

Heath, Douglas
1981   *Faculty Burnout, Morale, and Vocational Adaptation.* Boston: Na-
        tional Association of Independent Schools.

Herzberg, Frederick
1966   *Work and the Nature of Man.* Cleveland: World Publishing Co.

Holian, John, Jr.
1972   "Alienation and social awareness among college students." *The*
        Sociological Quarterly 13:114–125.

Holmes Group, The
1986   *Tomorow's Teachers: A Report of The Holmes Group.* East Lansing,
        Michigan: The Holmes Group, Inc.

Holmes, T. H., and Rahe, R. H.
1967   "The social readjustment rating scale." *Journal of Psychosomatic*
        Research 11:213–218.

Hughes, Larry W., William M. Gordon, and Larry W. Hillman
1980   *Desegregating America's Schools.* New York: Longman.

Hurn, Christopher J.
1978   *The Limits and Possibilities of Schooling.* Boston: Allyn and Bacon.

Israel, J.
1971   *Alienation: From Marx to Modern Sociology.* Boston: Allyn and
        Bacon.

Iwanicki, E. F., and R. L. Schwab
1981   "A cross validation study of the Maslach Burnout Inventory." *Educa-*
        tional and Psychological Measurement 41:1167–1174.

Jackson, G., and C. Cosca
1974   "the inequality of educational opportunity in the Southwest: An obser-
        vational study of ethnically mixed classroom." *American Educational*
        Research Journal 11:219–229.

Jackson, Philip
1968   *Life in Classrooms.* New York: Holt, Rinehart, and Winston.

Janis, I. L., and L. Mann
1977   *Decision-Making: A Psychological Analysis of Conflict, Choice, and*
        Commitment. New York: The Free Press.

Jencks, Christopher S.
1972   "The Coleman Report and the conventional wisdom." Pp. 69–115 in
        Frederick Mosteller and Daniel P. Moynihan (eds.), *On Equality of*
        Educational Opportunity. New York: Vintage Books.

Jencks, Christopher, James Crouse, and Peter Mueser
  1983 "The Wisconsin model of status attainment: A national replication with improved measures of ability and aspiration." *Sociology of Education* 56:3–19.

Jencks, Christopher, Marshall Smith, Henry Acland, Mary Jo Bane, David Cohen, Herbert Gintis, Barbara Heyns, and Stephan Michelson
  1972 *Inequality: A Reassessment of the Effects of Family and Schooling in America.* New York: Basic Books.

Jenkins, C. David
  1971 "Psychologic and social precursors of coronary disease." *New England Journal of Medicine* 284:244–255, 307–317.

  1979 "Psychosocial modifiers of response to stress." Pp. 265–278 in J. E. Barrett (ed.), *Stress and Mental Disorder.* New York: Raven Press.

Johnson, Eugene B., Harold B. Gerard, and Norman Miller
  1975 "Teacher influences in the desegregated classroom." Pp. 243–259 in Harold B. Gerard and Norman Miller (eds.), *School Desegregation: A Long-Term Study.* New York: Plenum Press.

Jones, J. W.
  1980 *The Staff Burnout Scale for Health Professionals.* Park Ridge, Illinois: London House Press.

Jones, Landon Y.
  1980 *Great Expectations: America and the Baby Boom Generation.* New York: Ballantine Books.

Kahn, R. L., D. M. Wolfe, R. P. Quinn, J. D. Snoek, and R. A. Rosenthal
  1964 *Organizatonal Stress: Studies in Role Conflict and Ambiguity.* New York: John Wiley and Sons.

Kanter, Rosabeth Moss
  1968 "Commitment and social organization: A study of commitment mechanisms in utopian communities." *American Sociological Review* 33:499–517.

  1977 *Men and Women of the Corporation.* New York: Basic Books.

Kaplan, Howard B.
  1983 "Psychological distress in sociological context: Toward a general theory of psychosocial distress." Pp. 195–264 in H. B. Kaplan (ed.), *Psychosocial Stress: Trends in Theory and Research.* New York: Academic Press.

Katzell, R. A., A. K. Korman, and E. L. Levine
  1971 *Research Report #1: Overview of the Dynamics of Worker Mobility.* National Study of Social Welfare and Rehabilitation Workers, Work, and Organizational Contexts. Washington, D.C.: U.S. Department of

Health, Education, and Welfare, Social and Rehabilitation Services, U.S. Government Printing Office.

Katzman, Martin T.
1971 *The Political Economy of Urban Schools.* Cambridge, Massachusetts: Harvard University Press.

Kehle, T. J.
1974 "Teachers' expectations: Ratings of student performance as baised by student characteristics." *The Journal of Experimental Education* 43:54–60.

Kerlinger, Fred N., and Elazar J. Pedhazur
1973 *Multiple Regression in Behavioral Research.* New York: Holt, Rinehart, and Winston.

Knoblock, Peter, and Arnold P. Goldstein
1971 *The Lonely Teacher.* Boston: Allyn and Bacon.

Larkin, Ralph W.
1975 "Social exchange in the elementary school classroom: The problem of teacher legitimation of social power." *Sociology of Education* 48:400–410.

LaRocco, J. M., J. S. House, and J. R. P. French, Jr.
1980 "Social support, occupational stress, and health." *Journal of Health and Social Behavior* 21: 202–218.

Lazarus, Richard S.
1966 *Psychological Stress and the Coping Process.* New York: McGraw-Hill.

1971 "The concept of stress and disease." Pp. 53–58 in L. Leni (ed.), *Society, Stress, and Disease.* London: Oxford University Press.

LeCompte, Margaret D.
Forth- "Defining the differences: Cultural subgroups within the educational coming mainstream," *Urban Review.*

Lefcourt, Herbert M.
1976 *Locus of Control: Current Trends in Theory and Research.* Hilsdale, New Jersey: Lawrence Erlbaum Associates.

Leiter, Jeffrey
1983 "Classroom composition and achievement gains." *Sociology of Education* 56:126–132.

Levy, Gerald E.
1970 *Ghetto School.* New York: Pegasus Western Publishing Company.

Lewin, Kurt
1948 *Resolving Social Conflicts: Selected Papers on Group Dynamics.* New York: Holt, Rinehart, and Winston.

Libraries and the Learning Society
1984 *Alliance for Excellence: Librarians Respond to A Nation At Risk.* Washington, D.C.: U.S. Government Printing Office.

Lortie, Dan C.
1969 "The partial professionalization of elementary teaching." Pp. 15–30 in Amitai Etzioni (ed.), *The Semi-Professions and Their Organization.* New York: The Free Press.

1975 *Schoolteacher: A Sociological Study.* Chicago: University of Chicago Press.

Luce, Sally R., and Robert D. Hoge
1978 "Relations among teacher rankings, pupil-teacher interactions, and academic achievement: A test of the teacher expectancy hypothesis." *American Educational Research Journal* 15:489–500.

Lystad, Mary H.
1972 "Social alienation: A review of current literature." *The Sociological Quarterly* 13:90–113.

Mahard, Rita E., and Robert L. Crain
1980 "The influence of high school racial composition on the academic achievement and college attendance of Hispanics." Paper presented at the American Sociological Association meetings, Montreal.

Mark, Johathan H., and Barry D. Anderson
1978 "Teacher survival rates—a current look." *American Educational Research Journal* 15:379–383.

Marx, Karl
1906 *Capital: A Critique of Political Economy.* New York: Charles H. Kerr and Company (Modern Library).

1959 *Basic Writings on Politics and Philosophy* Edited by Lewis S. Feuer. Garden City, New York: Anchor Books.

Maslach, Christina
1976 "Burned-out. *Human Behavior* 5:16–22.

1978a "The client role in staff burn-out." *Journal of Social Issues* 34:111–124.

1978b "Job burnout: How people cope." *Public Welfare* 36:56–58.

1982 "Understanding burnout: Definitional issues in analyzing a complex phenomenon." Pp. 29–40 in W. S. Paine (ed.), *Job Stress and Burnout: Research, Theory, and Intervention Perspectives.* Beverly Hills, California: Sage.

Maslach, C., and S. E. Jackson
1979 "Burned-out cops and their families." *Psychology Today* 12:59–62.

1981 "The measurement of experience burnout." *Journal of Occupational Behavior* 2:99–113.

Maslach, C., and A. Pines
1979 "Burnout: The loss of human caring." Pp. 245–252 in A. Pines and C. Maslach (eds.), *Experiencing Social Psychology*. New York: Knopf.

Mason, Ward S.
1961 *The Beginning Teacher: Status and Career Orientations.* Washington, D.C.: U.S. Dept. of Health, Education and Welfare, U.S. Government Printing Office.

Mason, Ward S. and Robert K. Bain
1959 *Teacher Turnover in the Public Schools: 1957–1958.* Washington, D.C.: U.S. Government Printing Office.

Mattingly, M.A.
1977 "Sources of stress and burnout in professional child care work." *Child Care Quarterly* 6:127–137.

Mayeske, G. W., C. E. Wisler, A. E. Beaton, F. D. Weinfeld, W. M. Cohen, T. Okada, J. M. Proshek, and K. Tabler
1969 *A Study of Our Nation's Schools.* Washington, D.C.: U.S. Dept. of Health, Education, and Welfare, Department of Education, U.S. Government Printing Office.

Maykovich, Minako Kurokawa
1972 "Reciprocity in racial stereotypes: White, black, and yellow." *American Journal of Sociology* 77:876–897.

McCarthy, John D., and William L. Yancey
1971 "Uncle Tom and Mr. Charlie: Metaphysical pathos in the study of racism and personal disorganization." *American Journal of Sociology* 76:648–672.

McNamara, James F., Anthony Gary Dworkin, Frank Black, Wayman Webster, Majorie Hanson, and David Gardner
1977 "The impact of the Singleton Ratio Plan on teacher assignments and learning outcomes in the HISD elementary schools." Reports to the Board of Education of the Houston Independent School District, December 12, 1977. Houston: Houston Independent School District.

Merton, Robert K.
1964a "Social structure and anomie." Pp. 131–160 in Robert K. Merton, *Social Theory and Social Structure.* New York: The Free Press.

1964b "Continuities in the theory of social structure and anomie." Pp. 161–194 in Robert K. Merton, *Social Theory and Social Structure.* New York: The Free Press.

1968 "Bureaucratic structure and personality." Pp. 249–260 in Robert K. Merton, *Social Theory and Social Structure: Revised Edition.* New York: The Free Press.

Meyer, Adolf
1951 "The life chart and the obligation of specifying positive data in psychological diagnosis." Pp. 52–56 in E. E. Winters (ed.), *Medical Teaching. The Collected Papers of Adolf Meyer,* 3. Baltimore: The Johns Hopkins Press.

Michelson, Stephan
1970 "The association between teacher resourcefulness with children's characteristics." In U.S. Department of Health, Education, and Welfare, Office of Education, *Do Teachers Make a Difference?* Washington, D.C.: U.S. Government Printing Office.

Mobley, W. H., R. W. Griffeth, H. H. Hand, and B. M. Meglino
1979 "Review and conceptual analysis of the employee turnover process." *Psychological Bulletin* 86:493–522.

Moeller, Gerald H.
1964 "Bureaucracy and teachers' sense of power." *The School Review* 72:137–157.

Mood, Alexander M.
1969 "Macro-analysis of the American educational system." *Operations Research* 17:770–784.

1971 "Partitioning variance in multiple regression analysis as a tool for developing learning models." *American Educational Research Journal* 8:191–202.

Moore, Helen A., and David R. Johnson
1983 "A reexamination of elementary school teacher expectations: Evidence of sex and ethnic segmentation." *Social Science quarterly* 64:460–485.

Morrow, T.
1981 "The burnout of almost everybody." *Time* 118 (September 21):84.

Mosteller, Frederick, and Daniel P. Moynihan (eds.)
1972 *On Equality of Education Opportunity.* New York: Vintage Books.

Mottaz, Clifford J.
1981 "Some determinants of work alienation." *The Sociological Quarterly* 22:515–530.

Murname, Richard J.
1975 *The Impact of School Resources on the Learning of Inner City Children.* Cambridge, Massachusetts: Ballinger.

National Center for Educational Statistics, U.S. Department of Education
1982   *The Condition of Education: 1982 Edition.* Washington, D.C.: U.S. Government Printing Office.

National Commission on Excellence in Education
1983   *A Nation at Risk: The Imperative for Educational Reform.* Washington, D.C.: U.S. Government Printing Office.

National Education Association
1965   *Report of the Taskforce Appointed to Study the Problem of Displaced School Personnel Related to School Desegregation.* Washington, D.C.: National Education Association Publications.

1974   *Teacher Supply and Demand in Public Schools, 1973.* Washington, D.C.: National Education Association—Research.

1982   *Status of the American Public School Teacher, 1980-81.* Washington, D.C.: National Education Association—Research.

1983   *Teacher Supply and Demand in Public Schools, 1981-82.* Washington, D.C.: National Education Association—Research.

National Institute of Education
1976   *The Desegregation Literature: A Critical Approach.* Washington, D.C.: U.S. Government Printing Office.

1978   *Violent Schools—Safe Schools: The Safe School Study Report to Congress*, vol. 1. Washington, D.C.: Dept of Health, Education and Welfare, U.S. Government Printing Office.

National Science Foundation
1984   "Program announcement: Grants for research on the teaching and learning of science and mathematics." (Pamphlet). Washington, D.C.: National Science Foundation, 84-74, O.M.B. 3145-0058.

Nias, Jennifer
1981   " 'Commitment' and motivation in primary school teachers." *Educational Review* 33:181-190.

Noblit, George W.
1979   "Patience and prudence in a Southern high school: Managing the political economy of desegregated education." Pp. 65-88 in Ray C. Rist (ed.), *Desegregated Schools: Appraisals of an American Experiment.* New York: Academic Press.

Ogbu, John U.
1974   *The Next Generation.* New York: Academic Press.

Okada, T., W. M. Cohen, and G. W. Mayeske
1969   "Growth in achievement for different racial, regional, and socio-economic groupings of students." Unpublished mimeograph, U.S. Of-

fice of Education. Presented in F. Mosteller and D. P. Moynihan (eds.), *On Equality of Educational Opportunity.* New York: Vintage Books, 1972, Pp. 22-24.

Orfield, Gary
1975 "Examining the desegregation process." *Integrated Education* 13:127-130.

Ornstein, Allen C.
1980 "Teacher salaries: Past, present, future." *Phi Delta Kappan* 61:677-679.

1981 "The trend toward increased professionalism for teachers." *Phi Delta Kappan* 63:196-198.

Paine, Whiton Steward (Ed.)
1982a *Job Stress and Burnout: Research, Theory, and Intervention Perspectives.* Beverly Hills, California: Sage.

1982b "Overview: Burnout stress syndrome and the 1980's." Pp. 11-28 in W. S. Paine (ed.), *Job Stress and Burnout: Research, Theory, and Intervention Perspectives.* Beverly Hills, California: Sage.

Pavalko, Ronald
1965 "Aspirants to teaching: Some differences between high school girls and boys." *Sociology and Social Research* 50:47-62.

1970 "Recruitment to teaching: Patterns of selection and retention." *Sociology of Education* 43:340-353.

Pedhazur, Elazar J.
1982 *Multiple Regression in Behavioral Research.* 2nd ed. New York: Holt, Rinehart, and Winston.

Persell, Caroline Hodges
1977 *Education and Inequality: The Roots and Results of Stratification in America's Schools.* New York: The Free Press.

Pettigrew, Thomas F., Elizabeth L. Useem, Clarence V. Normand, and Marshall S. Smith
1973 "Busing: A review of 'the evidence'." *The Public Interest* 30:88-118.

Phillips, Burman N., and Matthew Lee
1980 "The changing role of the American teacher: Current and future sources of stress." Pp. 93-111 in C. L. Cooper and J. Marshall (eds.), *White Collar and Professional Stress.* New York: John Wiley and Sons.

Pines, Ayala M.
1982 "Changing organizations: Is a work environment without burnout an impossible goal?" Pp. 189-212 in W. S. Paine (ed.), *Job Stress and Burnout: Research, Theory, and Intervention Perspectives.* Beverly Hills, California: Sage.

Pines, Ayala M., Elliot Aronson, and Ditsa Kafry
  1981   *Burnout: From Tedium to Personal Growth.* New York: The Free Press.

Poirier, Dale J.
  1976   *The Econometrics of Social Change, with Special Emphasis on Spline Functions.* Amsterdam: North Holland Publishing Company.

Porter, L. R., R. Steers, R. Mowday, and P. Boulian
  1974   "Organizational commitment, job satisfaction, and turnover among psychiatric technicians." *Journal of Applied Psychology* 59:603–609.

Porter, Lyman W., and Edward E. Lawler III
  1965   "Properties of organization structure in relation to job attitudes and behavior." *Psychological Bulletin* 64:23–51.

Poulantzas, Nicos
  1975   *Class in Contemporary Capitalism.* London: New Left.

Price, James L.
  1977   *The Study of Turnover.* Ames, Iowa: Iowa State University Press.

Ramirez, M., III, and A. Castanada
  1974   *Cultural Democracy, Bicognitive Development, and Education.* New York: Academic Press.

Remsberg, Charles, and Bonnie Remsberg
  1968   "Chicago voices: Tales told out of school." Pp. 273–386 in Raymond W. Mack (ed.), *Our Children's Burden: Studies of Desegregation in Nine American Communities.* New York: Random House.

Rist, Ray C.
  1970   "Social class and teacher expectations: The self-fulfilling prophecy in ghetto education." *Harvard Educational Review* 40:411–451.

  1973   *The Urban School: A Factory for Failure.* Cambridge, Massachusetts: The M.I.T. Press.

  1979   *Desegregated Schools: Appraisals of an American Experiment.* New York: Academic Press.

Ritzer, George, and Harrison Trice
  1969   "An empirical study of Howard Becker's side-bet theory." *Social Forces* 47:475–478.

Robinson, John P., and Phillip R. Shaver
  1973   *Measures of Social Psychological Attitudes.* Ann Arbor: Institute for Social Research.

Rosenthal, Richard, and Lenore Jacobson
  1968   *Pygmalion in the Classroom.* New York: Holt, Rinehart, and Winston.

Ross v. Eckels (Civil Action No. 10444).
September 18, 1970.

Rotter, Julian B.
1966 "Generalized expectancies for internal versus external control of reinforcements." *Psychological Monographs* 80:1-28.

Ryan, William
1971 *Blaming the Victim*. New York: Pantheon.

St. John, Nancy H.
1975 *School Desegregation: Outcomes for Children*. New York: Wiley-Interscience.

Sales, S. M., and J. House
1971 "Job satisfaction as a possible risk factor in coronary heart disease." *Journal of Chronic Disease* 23:861-873.

Sanders, Jimy M.
1978 "An analysis of the effects of teacher assignment in the Houston Independent School District on student academic achievement." Unpublished M.A. thesis, University of Houston.

1984 "Faculty desegregation and student achievement." *American Educational Review* 21:605-616.

Sarason, Seymour B., Kenneth S. Davidson, and Burton Blatt
1962 *The Preparation of Teachers: An Unstudied Problem in Education*. New York: John Wiley and Sons.

Sarason, Seymour B.
1977 *Work, Aging, and Social Change*. New York: The Free Press.

Sarason, Seymour B.
1978/ "Again, the preparation of teachers: competency and job satisfaction."
1979 *Interchange* 10:1-11.

Schaffer, Albert, and Ruth C. Schaffer
1970 "The law, faculty desegregation, and social change." *Phylon* 31:38-47.

Schlechty, Phillip C., and Victor S. Vance
1981 "Do academically able teachers leave education?: the North Carolina case." *Phi Delta Kappan* 63:106-112.

Schelling, Thomas C.
1956 "An essay on bargaining." *American Economic Review* 46:281-306.

1960 *The Strategy of Conflict*. Cambridge, Massachusetts: Harvard University Press.

Schwab, R. L., and E. F. Iwanicki
1982 "Received role conflict, role ambiguity, and teacher burnout." *Educational Administration Quarterly* 18:60-74.

Seeman, Melvin
1959 "On the meaning of alienation." *American Sociological Review* 24:783–791.

1967 "On the personal consequences of alienation in work." American Sociological Review 32:273–285.

1975 "Alienation studies." *Annual Review of Sociology* 1:91–123.

Seyle, Hans
1936 *The Stress of Life.* New York: McGraw-Hill.

Shaw, Stan F., Jeffrey M. Bansky, and Benjamin Dixon
1981 *Stress and Burnout: A Primer for Special Education and Special Services Personnel.* Reston, Virginia: Council for Exceptional Children.

Shepard, Jon M.
1970 "Functional specialization, alienation, and work specialization." *Industrial Labor Relations Review* 23:207–219.

1977 "Technology, alienation, and job satisfaction." *Annual Review of Sociology* 3:1–21.

Shibutani, Tomotsu
1966 *Improvised News: A Sociological Study of Rumor.* Indianapolis, Indiana: Bobbs-Merrill.

Shinn, Marybeth
1982 "Methodological issues: Evaluating and using information." Pp. 61–82 in W. S. Paine (ed.), *Job Stress and Burnout: Research, Theory, and Intervention Perspectives.* Beverly Hills, California: Sage.

Shoemaker, D. J., W. E. Snizek, and C. D. Bryant
1977 "Toward a further clarification of Becker's side-bet hypothesis applied to organizational and occupational commitment." *Social Forces* 56:598–603.

Shoemaker, J., and H. W. Fraser
1981 "What principals can do—some implications from studies of effective schools." *Phi Delta Kappan* 63:178–182.

Silberman, Charles E.
1970 *Crisis in the Classroom.* New York: Basic Books.

Simpson, R. L., and I. H. Simpson
1969 "Women and bureaucracy in the semi-professions." Pp. 196–265 in A. Etzioni (ed.), *The Semi-Professions and Their Organization.*" New York: The Free Press.

Singleton v. Jackson Municipal Separate School Districts et al. 419 F.2d 1211. January 14, 1970.

Spaniol, L., and J. Caputo
1979 *Professional Burnout: A Personal Survival Kit.* Lexington, Massachusetts: Human Services Associates.

Sparks, Dennis, and Janice Hammond
1981 *Managing Teacher Stress and Burnout.* Washington, D.C.: ERIC Clearinghouse on Teacher Education.

Spector, Paul E.
1982 "Behavior in organizations as a function of employee's locus of control," *Psychological Bulletin* 91:483–497.

Srole, Leo
1956 "Social integration and certain corollaries: An exploratory study." *American Sociological Review* 21:709–716.

Stapleton, J., J. Croft, and R. Frankiewicz
1979 "The relationship between teacher brinkmanship and teacher job satisfaction." *Planning and Changing* 10:157–168.

Stephan, Walter G., and Joe R. Feagin (eds.)
1980 *School Desegregation: Past, Present, and Future.* New York: Plenum.

Stephen, John D.
1979 "Class formation and class consciousness: A theoretical and empirical analysis with reference to Britain and Sweden." *British Journal of Sociology* 30:389–414.

Stevens, J. H., J. M. Beyer, and H. M. Trice
1978 "Assessing personal, role, and organizational predictors of managerial commitment." *Academy of Management Journal* 21:380–396.

Stinnett, T. M., and Kenneth T. Henson
1982 *America's Public Schools in Transition: Future Trends and Issues.* New York: Teachers College.

Stub, Holger R.
1968 "The professional prestige of classroom teachers: A consequence of organizational and community status." Pp. 236–267 in R. Bell and H. Stub (eds.), *The Sociology of Education.* Homewood, Illinois: Dorsey Press.

Swann et al. v. Charlotte-Mecklinburg Board of Education. 402 U.S.1. April 20, 1971.

System Development Corporation
1977 *The Sustaining Effects Study.* Santa Monica, California: System Development Corporation.

Swafford, Michael
1980 "Parametric techniques for contingency table analysis." *American Sociological Review.* 45:664–690.

Task Force on Education for Economic Growth (Education Commission of the States)
1983   *Action for Excellence.* Denver, Colorado: Education Commission of the States.

Telschow, Ruth Rice
1982   "Technical report on the active state of stress among teachers in the Houston Independent School District." Unpublished M.A. thesis, University of Houston.

Thibaut, J., and H. H. Kelley
1959   *The Social Psychology of Groups.* New York: John Wiley and Sons.

Thorndike, Robert L., and Elizabeth Hagen
1977   *Measurement and Evaluation in Psychology and Education*, 4th Ed. New York: John Wiley and Sons.

Title IV, Civil Rights Act of 1964 (78 U.S. Stat. 241 [1964]).

United States v. Texas Education Agency. 467 F.2d 848.
August 2, 1972.

United States Commission on Civil Rights
1973   *Teachers and Students: Differences in Teacher Interaction with Mexican American and Anglo Students.* Report V: Mexican American Education Study. Washington, D.C.: U.S. Government Printing Office.

1979   *Twenty Years After Brown: A Report of the United States Commission on Civil Rights.* Wathington, D.C.: U.S. Government Printing Office.

Vance, Victor S., and Phillip C. Schelchty
1982   "The distribution of academic ability in the teaching force: policy implications." *Phi Delta Kappan* 64:22–27.

Waller, Willard
1932   *The Sociology of Teaching.* New York: John Wiley and Sons.

Wexler, Philip
1976   *Sociology of Education: Beyond Equality.* Indianapolis, Indiana: Bobbs-Merrill.

Wiles, David K.
1970   "The mosaic composition of urban school teachers." *Urban Education* 5:141–150.

Williams, Trevor
1976   "Teacher prophecies and the inheritance of inequality." *Sociology of Education* 49:107–133.

Winkler, Donald R.
  1972   "The production of human capital: A study of minority achievement."
         Ph.D. dissertation, University of California, Berkeley. Reported in
         Richard J. Murname, *The Impact of School Resources on the Learning
         of Inner City Children.* Cambridge, Massachusetts: Ballinger
         Publishing Company, 1975, Pp. 22–27.

Wright, Erik Olin
  1976   "Class boundaries in advanced capitalist societies." *New Left Review*
         98:3–41.

  1978   "Race, class, and income inequality." *American Journal of Sociology*
         83:1368–1397.

Wright, Erik O., and Luca Perrone
  1977   "Marxist class categories and income inequality." *American
         Sociological Review* 42:32–55.

Index